# Stanislavsky's Protégé: Eugene Vakhtangov

by *Ruben Simonov*

TRANSLATED AND ADAPTED BY
*Miriam Goldina*

TRANSLATION EDITOR:
*Helen Choat*

DBS PUBLICATIONS, INC.
DRAMA BOOK SPECIALISTS
NEW YORK, NEW YORK

68396

*Printed in U.S.A. by*
NOBLE OFFSET PRINTERS, INC.
NEW YORK 3, N. Y.

# Contents

In October of 1963, while touring Moscow, I had a long visit with Ruben Simonov at the Vakhtangov Theater, during which he handed me this book with the following inscription in it:

> Miriam Goldina:
> Let this book, again and again, remind you of our remarkable teacher, Eugene Vakhtangov, communion with whom made us a happy people in the theater.
> I wish you happiness and the best in your life.
>
> Respectfully,
> Ruben Simonov

While thanking Ruben for the book, I said, "Everybody gives me presents in Moscow ... and here I am a rich American. What can I give you?"

His answer was, "I am giving you this book as a present because I want you to translate it and publish it in America so that American people will know of a great Russian director, Eugene Vakhtangov, and his tremendous contribution to the growth of the Russian theater and the art of the theater in general. I feel strongly that you are the person to translate the book WITH VAKHTANGOV because of your knowledge of the Vakhtangov method in the theater as his former student and because of your excellent work on STANISLAVSKY DIRECTS."

# Preface

THE LAST two productions created by Eugene Vakhtangov before his death were *Princess Turandot,* a graceful production sparkling with joy and laughter, and composed of elements of the fantastic, the grotesque, and naturalism; and *The Dybbuk,* at once mystico-poetic and nightmarish. It would be a true tour de force for any man to rehearse and produce two such demanding productions at the same period of time—and this was a man who was suffering, a man who was dying. The première of *The Dybbuk* at the Habimah Theater took place on January 31, 1922, and the première of *Princess Turandot* at the Third Studio of the Moscow Art Theater on February 28, 1922.

Great joy of life as well as deep pain caused by the awareness of injustice and tragedy all around him lived in Vakhtangov's heart side by side. He loved nature passionately, and his love for people was limitless. "If I can't give of myself to people, I shouldn't live," I have often heard him say. He inherited selflessness from Stanislavsky, whose artistic principles were the foundation of Vakhtangov's life and work in the theater. Yet Vakhtangov never took blindly anything that Stanislavsky taught; he listened to his deeply loved and respected teacher with an open mind, tested whatever Stanislavsky said—on himself first, as he used to say—and only then accepted and applied it in his teachings. This is one of the reasons, I believe, that Vakhtangov absorbed Stanislavsky's System to a greater degree than anyone else I know. Stanislavsky used to say to Vakhtangov: "You, Eugene, teach my Method better than I." Stanislavsky's artistic principles were a runway for Vakhtangov's flight into the heights of creativity.

When I look back to the time when I was lucky enough to be present at some of his rehearsals of *The Dybbuk,* I see him as an eagle spreading his wings. I believe that the degree of an actor's or a regisseur's talent depends on the degree of his inner freedom. Vakhtangov had that inner freedom to the nth degree.

He could penetrate the innermost depths of an actor's heart and bring the most out of it. He used to inflame those he worked with, the young and inexperienced, and the great talents such as Michael Chekhov (whom he coached in most of his roles). Every hour of a rehearsal with Vakhtangov was an inspiration: always a new discovery, never anything routine. He guarded his students from all that was tasteless, conventional, pedantic, or pretentious.

The professional creative activities of Vakhtangov—regisseur, actor, and leader of theatrical Soviet youth—lasted a little more than ten years. But because he was a great teacher, and because he not only taught his students the art of acting and directing but also educated them as people—their sense of values, their outlook on life—his death did not paralyze the efforts of his theater. His young and talented students did not disperse like a herd after the disappearance of their shepherd.

Ruben Simonov was Vakhtangov's favorite student. I believe that Vakhtangov was to Simonov what Stanislavsky was to Vakhtangov. Ruben Simonov absorbed Vakhtangov's teaching and together with the other Vakhtangov students kept their theater always growing and developing, always searching for new forms, always experimenting. On my visit to Moscow in 1963, I saw twenty-six plays in different theaters, and I found the Vakhtangov Theater the most interesting and alive. That is why when Ruben Simonov, the head of the Vakhtangov Theater, asked me to translate his book *With Vakhtangov* (the original title of this book) I gladly agreed, as I was sure that Ruben Simonov, a true disciple, was the man to present Eugene Vakhtangov to America.

Miriam Goldina
New York, 1969

viii

# Introduction

THERE ARE ARTISTS who because of the nature of their talent, their creative aspirations, and their world outlook seem to be living today, talking to us in the language of today; although physically they left us a long time ago. Eugene Vakhtangov was such an artist of the theater.

While working on the book about Vakhtangov, I was moved not only by my love and gratitude to my teacher but also by a great desire to comprehend and delve into the innermost depths of the creative principles of that remarkable regisseur* for the sake of the development of the theater of our day.

Recalling all that is connected with the creative work of Vakhtangov—plays directed by him, his mode of treatment of the plays, his work with actors—and analyzing his outlook on the theater, I am deeply convinced that our heritage from Vakhtangov is one of an immense, creative richness that is not fully realized in our art of the theater of today. I am sure that Vakhtangov's experience can and must help us to create and develop the present theater greatly.

In his article "The Responsibility of an Artist," Vakhtangov says: "Only people create—only people carry the creative force and the seed of future creativity. The artist commits a sin if he is not drawing from that force and searching that seed."

Eugene Vakhtangov left this world too soon. He died in 1922, but his words still resound for us clearly today and are

---

* In Russia the word "director," as we understand it in America, is known in the Russian theater as "regisseur." The word "director" in Russia usually implies the business head of the theater, rather than the creative director.

revolutionary. They still teach us how we are to serve our people. It was characteristic of Vakhtangov to create plays that were deep in thought and brilliant in form, and to find for each play a complete artistic image. Vakhtangov never rested or felt satisfied with his accomplishments. He always searched untiringly, passionately, for the new in art. This search expressed his constant anxiety that art should be understood by the wide audience that would fill the theaters after the October 1917 revolution.

This is why my thoughts on the problems of the contemporary theater always involuntarily turn to Vakhtangov. While working on the book about Vakhtangov directing the three plays—*A Wedding*, by Chekhov, *The Miracle of St. Anthony*, by Maeterlinck, and *Princess Turandot*, by Gozzi, in which I participated as an actor—I was anxious to clarify Vakhtangov's basic qualities and creative particularities as an artist of the stage. I wanted also to tell in this book about the significance of the Vakhtangov tradition for the contemporary theater. If I have accomplished this task and my book helps workers in the theater in their creative search and in the creation of brilliant and exciting performances about our contemporaneity, I will consider that, at least in some degree, I have fulfilled my duty to the memory of my great teacher, my comrades in art, and what is most important, to our audience.

My sincere gratitude to Mrs. Vakhtangov and to Mr. Taziev, the director of the theater museum, who permitted me the use of the materials on Vakhtangov. I also express my profound gratitude to the old, the middle, and the young generation of Vakhtangov's students who in their best acting and regisseur's work hold high the Vakhtangov Theater banner.

Ruben Simonov

# Part I

## Vakhtangov Directs

## *A Wedding*
by Anton Chekhov

WHEN I read some of the articles and books dedicated to the history of Soviet Theater art I am often astounded, as well as puzzled, by the severe and emphatic criticism of certain productions, the significance and success of which I remember very well. At first I was filled with indignation because of the injustice of such condemnation by theater historians. But after trying to comprehend the point of view that brought these historians to such peremptory negation of those productions—which they called almost depraved, although in 1920 when those works were actually produced they seemed joyful and definitely progressive—I see clearly that their logic, which on the face of it may seem convincing, lacks the historical approach to the phenomenon of art.

Historians of the theater tend to forget that they are *historians,* and as such involved with past events. They judge and examine productions of days gone by from the standpoint of today. Appraising a production from today's standards is one thing, but writing a review about a play that was directed in 1920 as though it were produced yesterday is altogether another thing. Just imagine that someone today would come up with a political program like that of the Decembrists.* Such a program would naturally seem to us backward, out-of-date, and even reactionary compared to present-day political developments. However, history does not deny the Decembrists their revolutionary and progressive significance. Realizing the historical limitations of the Decembrists' movement, we remember under what conditions, when and how the Decembrists protested, and we admire their heroism. Lenin said that the Decembrists had awakened Hertzen, and his passionate propagation inspired a generation of Russian rev-

* The participants of the nobility-revolutionary-liberation movement that culminated in the uprising on December 14, 1825.

1 |

olutionaries to fight for freedom. As long as an affair concerns history in its "pure" meaning—history of society, history of government—all is well. But when history is concerned with the history of art, the confusion begins. The historians of the theater pronounce judgment on theater productions of a half century ago, and they do not want to recall either what preceded these performances or under what conditions these productions were created, what they meant to the audience, what social ideas and artistic aspirations they expressed. Nevertheless, only when the theater historian takes into consideration all the circumstances surrounding a production can he understand which creation of art was truly progressive, why, and to what degree.

I allow myself to say that if the great Motchalov* were to appear on our stage today he would probably seem to us old-fashioned and pompous, regardless of his extraordinary and natural tragic temperament. But, for his time, he was great. And historians of the theater understand that perfectly. Unfortunately, their evaluation of productions betrays them as soon as they enter the sphere of the history of the Soviet theater. Here they often give free rein to their imagination and judge the productions of the twenties and thirties with the eyes of an audience of today. But the audience of the fifties is not the audience of the twenties or even of the forties. Time moves on, and art moves on; the criteria of art inevitably change. That is why we must evaluate each work of art from the historical point of view. We are interested not only in a particular work of art, but also in the epoch in which it was created and born. Without taking into consideration the political, ideological, philosophical, and social problems of a specific period of time, we cannot do justice in our judgment either to the novel, the picture, or the symphony; and most

* Motchalov—November 16, 1800. A famous Russian tragedian of the early nineteenth century.

| 2

certainly not to the theatrical performance, because the art of the theater is born with the turning on of the footlights, and it dies the moment those footlights are turned off. The theatrical performance is intrinsically bound to its time. The classic novel written in the nineteenth century we read even now with enjoyment, but the play that was performed in the nineteenth century no one can ever see. That is why the evaluation and understanding of the singularities of the time when the work of art was brought to life are essential to historians of the theater, who are called upon to explain the concrete conditions that influence the artistic form and the interpretation of the characters.

Each epoch interpreted, let us say, the immortal image of Hamlet differently; the character of that interpretation was each time explained, not by the whim of one or another actor and even not by the qualities of his particular talent, but first of all by how the given epoch, the given generation, perceived Hamlet, what each saw in Hamlet. The social atmosphere, the theater conditions of the times, always influences the artist, directly or indirectly. We are acquainted with Motchalov's Hamlet, which has been splendidly described by V. G. Belinsky* and compared with the Hamlets of Karatigin, Lensky, Mamontov-Dalsky, and others. In each instance the Danish prince appeared before the audience in a new interpretation. Even in our day, many Hamlets have marched before our eyes. Katchalov, in the production of *Hamlet* directed by Stanislavsky and Gordon Craig, played the tragedy of an intelligent and honest man completely alone in the avid, cynical, and malicious atmosphere of the court. The Hamlet of Michael Chekhov in the production of the First Studio of the Moscow Art Theater was the knight Don Quixote, rather than Hamlet. Vatran Papasian** strove to reveal

---

* A great critic. A militant liberal throughout most of his career, he exerted a strong influence on young Russian writers (1811-1848).
** A great Armenian actor.

in his Hamlet the struggle of the hero with his own indomitable character. Papasian played Hamlet as a man incapable of controlling the elements of his own passion. The Hamlet of Sandro Moici was a man devoid of will power, a man afraid of life. We know the debatable, false interpretation of Hamlet that was presented on the stage of the Vakhtangov Theater in 1932—in which the basic tragic conflict was built on a struggle between Hamlet and King Claudius for the throne. Which of all these Hamlets was the correct one, truly Shakespeare's? It is a very difficult question to answer. All is changing with the times; even the same text sounds different in different times. Absolute truth, as it is known, is concrete. The Hamlets that were truly Shakespeare's were those that corresponded to the most advanced thinking of their time.

The directorial art of Vakhtangov in the first after-Revolutionary years was considered by the overwhelming majority of theatergoers and connoisseurs of the theater as a most advanced art, imbued with talent and keen perception; contemporary and innovative in spirit. Gorky, Stanislavsky, Nemirovitch-Dantchenko, Chaliapin, Lunacharsky, Katchalov, and many other masters of Russian culture were great admirers of Vakhtangov's work. Nevertheless, several of the theater historians have stubbornly attempted to accuse Vakhtangov of quarreling with his great teacher Stanislavsky and of breaking away completely from the realistic art of Stanislavsky. I am convinced that all that unfair criticism of Vakhtangov, which aroused astonishment and legitimate bitterness in those who had witnessed Vakhtangov's productions as well as in the participants, is explained by two facts. First, by the extremely primitive and limited conception of scenic realism in general and Stanislavsky's creativity specifically; and, second, by the strange and unforgivable forgetfulness of the period when Vakhtangov created his inspiring productions. Contemporaneity influences every artist: painter, writer, composer, or actor. The artist grasps the contemporaneity with that special sensitiveness for the creative perception of life, and we may decidedly assert that the ability to sense the present scene is indicative of true talent in the artist. An artist without that awareness of contemporaneity serves no one. So-called "unappreciated geniuses" are usually people deaf to the demands and needs of their time. The artist is always influenced by the contemporary scene, even when he does not completely understand it, or even when he understands it incorrectly.

What was the tenor of the times in July and August of 1920 when Vakhtangov was working on the Chekhov play *A Wedding*? Only two years and seven months separated people from that historical event of universal significance—the signing by Lenin of the Decree on Land in Smolni. But what was not quite three years in actual time was equivalent to ten years with respect to the tremendous impact of events: the direction of history was turned, the mountain pushed down, the world of brute force and hate was annihilated. Bourgeois-capitalism clung to every ledge to check its fall, but the people won. Such was the urge for freedom; such was the hatred for the old world. The genius of Lenin foresaw the victory of the Revolution.

Moscow in the summer of 1920. The same streets, the same houses, the same boulevards, the same churches on each corner and in each lane; cobblestone roads on which automobiles and cabmen moved rarely. The new kind of people on the streets radically changed the face of the city. The crowds in Moscow had taken on a new look. No more officers in full-dress coats, no more uniform coats or uniform caps of students and high school boys. Instead one saw soldiers in greatcoats without soldier straps, workers in leather and cloth jackets. Along the streets marched the new master—the working people, Soviet people.

The Soviet people were admitted to the theaters free of charge. The new theatergoer mingled in the auditorium with the theater habitués who came to see the old repertoire. The new theatergoers came to learn about life and how to comprehend it; the old came to recall times dear to their hearts, which alas might be gone forever—or perhaps might come back. Who knows? The audience was divided into sharply different camps, and each reacted differently to what it saw on the stage. What at times brought tears to one part of the audience, brought laughter and joy to the other. Such division took place on the other side of the footlights, too. There were actors and directors who listened attentively to the reaction of the new theatergoer and drew vital conclusions for themselves. There were also those, it must be admitted, who thought it useless and ludicrous to play in front of an "ignorant, uneducated audience." Many writers, artists, composers, directors, and actors emigrated to Europe; others sat doing nothing, awaiting better times. The bulk of the artistic intelligentsia remained neutral.

In that year of 1920, Vakhtangov wrote to his students, "I would like all of you members of my studio to remember that you are responsible to the Moscow Art Theater, to K. C. Stanislavsky, to the government, to the Revolution." It is clear from those words that Vakhtangov tied the future of the young growing theater to the realistic art of the Moscow Art Theater, to the proletarian government, to the Revolution, and to the people.

But what sort of repertoire must the young theater have? What was Vakhtangov to produce? Chekhov, the dramatist who had determined the direction and the style of the Moscow Art Theater, was presented often on the stage at that time. The young theater, which was born under the strong influence of the Moscow Art Theater, was very much interested in Chekhov. But actors and regisseurs were aware that the new audience reacted differently to Chekhov's plays. While in the olden days Chekhov's plays had been listened to with intense silence, and, in fact, both male and female in the audience had often used handkerchiefs to wipe away their tears, now during the performances the audiences laughed. Different backgrounds breed different reactions. To the people who had always had to struggle for the mere necessities of life, the problems of the intelligentsia who complained about their lot instead of taking some action were a subject for laughter not for tears.

I cannot help but recall one evening in Vakhtangov's studio. Aslanov, a talented actor from the First Studio of the Moscow Art Theater, had come to us to read some of the Chekhov stories. Our young actors enjoyed his reading very much and laughted uncontrollably. At the end, they applauded him wildly. But Aslanov was upset and hurt. He inquired of Vakhtangov, "Why did your students react so strangely to my serious reading? Whom did they laugh at? Me? Did I read so badly?" Vakhtangov assured Aslanov that he had read all the stories excellently and that our reaction was natural because those Chekhov stories are full of hidden humor and irony. Aslanov was consoled, but he was still confused. Only after his repeated appearances in a number of other places elicited the same response did he accept it as a correct reaction. The reaction of his audiences taught the artist the new conception of Chekhov.

The art of the theater is built on the contact between the actors and the audience: the audience contributes to the work of the actors and directors. Not to heed its reaction is decidedly wrong. It was only natural that the interpretation given Chekhov's work twenty or thirty years earlier could not be repeated in those exciting after-the-Revolution years.

Vakhtangov wrote in his diary on March 26, 1921: "Let naturalism in the theater die. Oh, how can one direct Ostrovsky, Gogol, Chekhov? I have an impulse to get up"—he was ill in a sanitarium—"and run to tell them about my new ideas. I would like to direct *The Sea Gull* theatrically, as Chekhov wrote it. I want to present Pushkin's *Feast in Time of Plague* and Chekhov's *A Wedding* in one evening. In *A Wedding* there is a 'feast in time of plague.' Those infected with plague are even unaware that there is no more plague, that humanity is liberated, and that people do not need 'generals' at their weddings. There is no lyricism in Chekhov; there is tragedy. When a man shoots himself, it is not lyricism; it is either banality or a heroic act. Neither the Banal, nor the Heroic, ever possesses lyricism. The Banal, as the Heroic, has its tragic mask. Lyricism sometimes is banal."

When Vakhtangov wrote those lines, his production of Chekhov's *A Wedding* had already been performed in our Studio. Do they mean that Vakhtangov did not realize his new conception of Chekhov's play in that production? To the contrary. All Vakhantgov says about *Feast in Time of Plague* had entered into the direction of *A Wedding*. Every actor knows only too well that when the rehearsal period on the role has ended and he is approaching the dress rehearsal, he is filled with disturbing questions: Did I create that image? Is my interpretation correct? Did I grasp the seed of my role? The actor is still full of doubts, but the character is created; it lives. A director who is very demanding of himself lives through the same experience. In my opinion, in his regisseur's work Vakhtangov did create the image of the play; but he himself was not as yet aware of all its novelty, all its significance, its actuality.

During the work on *A Wedding,* Vakhtangov often interrupted the rehearsals to share with us his thinking on art. Those of us present at the rehearsals remember how interesting those discussions were: filled with creative fire, energy, and searching, daring thoughts. He was excited about various themes: Chekhov in the Moscow Art Theater; *A Wedding* as a play—tragic, comic, satirical; how to realize a satirical play; the skill of the actor; about form and content; and finally, most of all, about what kind of a theater it could be whose aim would be lofty and would serve the Revolutionary people.

Chekhov in the Moscow Art Theater was a significant epoch. "Chekhov was the Art Theater's first love. And like a first love the heart will not forget him."* A new theater direction was formed; the art of psychological realism sprang up. Chekhov was interpreted magnificently in those years by the Moscow Art Theater when the Russian intelligentsia with shame and pain recognized the hopelessness of its existence; when the Russian intelligentsia revolted against the stagnation of social life and dreamed of reforming it. The progressive part of the intelligentsia was weighing the possibility of going to the people. The other part of the intelligentsia ascertained the complexity of the important problems of life, and that ascertainment led it to an absorption in personal feelings, to "searching in the innermost part of their souls for an answer to the important problems of life." From that came the path to the intimate theater, the theater of mood, to excessive psychologizing. The art of symbolism follows the art of psychological realism. New decadent movements sprang up, one after another: stylization, restoration of the old theatrical forms, the art of escapism, and so on. All those so-called high-flown approaches to art absolved the artist from the necessity of facing the problems of the epoch, the approaching Revolution. The bourgeois intelligentsia was afraid that the Revolution would destroy the heart of that refined "art for art's sake." That is exactly what happened. The people of the arts during the October Revolution retained that which soared from the realistic basis of great Russian art, all that was essential, eternal, truly valuable; but all the rubble, the cheapness of the everyday vogue was wiped away. How pretentious, how affected, modernistic and sym-

* N. Efros. He was a well-known critic of the times, and a close friend of the Moscow Art Theater.

bolic plays, novels, and poetry now seemed.

The young people of the years 1919 and 1920 used to choose for their entrance examinations the poems of the modernistic, decadent, symbolic poets; those in vogue at that time. The youth became acquainted with that poetry in the first years of the imperialistic war from the concerts in which their favorite artists used to recite those poems. One had therefore first to start to fight the lack of taste in the young. Vakhtangov wrote at the time, March 21, 1921: "Modern style is banality." Could anyone ever call the Halls of Versailles or the antique terraces of Greek and Roman theaters commonplace, banal? The auditorium of the big opera theater, rich and ornate, adorned by velvet and gold, could never seem garish to future generations. But the estate of Morosov on Vozdigenka, and other residences of merchants who were without taste, are gaudy and pretentious.

Several theater connoisseurs writing about Vakhtangov tried to tie his after-the-Revolution creations to modernistic and decadent trends, completely ignoring those words of his that I have just quoted. While attending all of Vakhtangov's rehearsals—hardly any of Vakhtangov's students ever missed his rehearsals during those three years—I never heard one word of approval from him of either the modernistic or expressionistic movements. Instead, he often spoke ardently about the significance of Stanislavsky's teaching and the realistic school of the Moscow Art Theater in the development of Russian dramatic art. Nevertheless, his profound respect for Stanislavsky and his adoration of him did not deprive Vakhtangov of his inner freedom, his creative independence, his clear understanding of the historic conditionality of one or another play directed by Stanislavsky. The search for new roads, the assertion of the need for theatricality, and the vivid scenic forms in the brilliant directorial works of Vakhtangov were all accomplished by him on the basis of the school of psychological realism, based on Stanislavsky's teaching. With all his admiration for Stanislavsky, Vakhtangov nevertheless did not find it necessary to treat Chekhov's work in 1920 as the Moscow Art Theater had treated it in 1898.

March 22, 1919, Vakhtangov, in his article *"To Those Who Write about the Stanislavsky System"* said: "None of the books by Stanislavsky were as yet published when a number of articles appeared in magazines and theater periodicals criticizing and analyzing the so-called 'Stanislavsky System.' Even a book appeared, dealing with criticism of Stanislavsky's teaching, and the author of that book postulated Stanislavsky's teachings as best suited his purpose.

"What would those brash, premature critics of Stanislavsky's teachings say once they read his works and realized that their daring, heated writings were dictated by nothing but their own imaginations and were complete fabrications. What for example will F.F. Komissargevsky—who states in his book *The Creativity of an Actor and the Stanislavsky Method* that Stanislavsky relinquishes the creative fantasy, does not recognize it—say when he learns that Stanislavsky considers fantasy 'the actor's second nature,' and that his whole system of actors' training is built precisely for the triumph of the creative fantasy? What will F. F. Komissargevsky say when he reads in the Stanislavsky book that Stanislavsky does not center a play on two, three, or four certain feelings—as Komissargevsky asserts—but on only one; and that not 'a feeling' but action for the purpose of which an author writes a play, and for the fulfillment of which the actors unite and work creatively under the regisseur's guidance. What will F. F. Komissargevsky say when he reads that according to Stanislavsky terminology the 'through action' of a play is not the basic feeling or the basic tone—as F. F. Komissargevsky supposes— but the 'through action' is what the two simple words imply, an action that passes through a play.

"How is it possible to subject to criticism the vast part of the Stanislavsky theory on feelings when one has heard only one isolated term of that vast theory, 'the affective memory'? How is it possible to resort first to a guess of the meaning of that term, and then to attempt to prove the absurdity of its essence? Isn't it simpler to wait until Stanislavsky's book is published and from it learn what Stanislavsky wants to say and how he says it?

"In the second and third part of the book *Hearth*, published by Proletcult, is an article on the Stanislavsky System. I know the author of that article intimately. I know that he feels and understands the Stanislavsky teachings. I trust the good intention that prompted the writing of that article, but I cannot, I must not, stop myself from reprimanding him for writing that article. I reprimand the author not for the form of his article, not because he failed to report fully on the System—anyway all of this is impossible to accomplish in a short article—but for reporting in fragments torn from the total postulation of the System, for pointing out only the details of the practical part of the Stanislavsky teachings when the overall aim, the overall plan, the overall foundation of the System is completely disregarded.

"If one wants to introduce the Stanislavsky System before Stanislavsky himself does so, the introduction ought to be in the form of a general survey of the System. The reporting on the merely practical part of it, its application, which is based on the undeviating methodical absorption of the System, will only harm those who accept that introduction as guidance for practical scenic work.

"The author of the above-mentioned article, Michael Chekhov, prefaces his article with a promise to explain two things: first, what the Stanislavsky System consists of—how it was formed and how an actor must use it; second, how the opponents of the System understand it and what they object to in it.

"This sounds marvelous—but Michael Chekhov did not keep his promise. He did not explain either what the System consists of, nor did he mention the process of its creation. One can write about it with much love and admiration and discuss in detail its brilliancy. Instead, Michael Chekhov elaborated on how one must work with a student and what a student must do. If he meant this to be a practical guide for a student, it does not accomplish its purpose because it is impossible to cover the practical part, the application of the Stanislavsky Method in three or four pages of a magazine article."

I recall my first meeting with Vakhtangov in the Chaliapin Studio in 1919, where Vakhtangov had been invited to direct Arthur Schnitzler's *The Green Parrot*. We—the students of that Studio—had requested our teacher to issue the invitation to Vakhtangov because he was a connoisseur of the Stanislavsky Method. Vakhtangov did not complete the direction of this play, however; he conducted only a number of the rehearsals, during which he introduced to us the method of work on a role that was advocated by the Stanislavsky Method. Comparing those lessons with the ones directly under Stanislavsky himself a year later—Stanislavsky gave a year's lessons at the Habimah, for which Vakhtangov's group, the Armenian group, and Chekhov's group joined together—I was convinced that Vakhtangov understood Stanislavsky's teachings thoroughly and passed them on to his students as a true follower of his great teacher.

Vakhtangov used to say that one must not merely teach but must also educate the young actor. He persisted in nurturing all the "qualities-abilities" of the future actor. One of the most important qualities for a young actor to develop is the ability to function on the stage in the improvisational state. That is, to behave in every performance of the play as though playing his role for the first time; to react to the scenic situations and to his partners as though he were relating to them for the first time. Vakhtangov considered as vitally important not only the first part of the Stanislavsky System—the work of an actor on himself during the creative process of living the role—but also the second part of the System—the work of an actor on himself in the creative process of the embodiment of the role.

Vakhtangov meant to train actors to develop their "qualities-abilities" and thereby cultivate such masters that their technique of speech, rhythm, gesture, and plasticity would reach a degree where they would be capable of arousing in themselves the most complex and exalted feelings in the plane of tragedy with lightning speed and expressing them on the stage. The actor should also be capable of arousing in himself, with the same lightning speed, the gay emotions.

In the question of scenic rendition, Stanislavsky and Vakhtangov also took a common position. This we recognized during the lessons that had been organized by Nahum Zemach for Stanislavsky to give in the winter of 1921 at the Habimah Theater to the four leading studios, all of whom were working on Shakespeare's *Merchant of Venice*. All of those who studied with Stanislavsky that year will forever feel a very deep gratitude to that remarkable teacher and educator for what we learned from him in the various provinces of the actor's complex technique, and for our attainment of greater proficiency. In line with the lectures on his Method, Stanislavsky taught us stage movement—cultivating in us the ability to move freely and naturally on the stage—the historic bows, and showed us the various styles of behavior in different epochs, starting with ancient times and continuing on down to the nineteenth century. He worked with us on rhythm: first dividing musical compositions up into a number of bars, then making the design of movement more complicated and gradually bringing us to a free improvisational behavior in musical scenes which required the highest degree of rhythmicality, where it was absolutely essential for the right rhythm to be operating within the actor.

Once Stanislavsky devoted an entire lesson to the handling

| 14

of the theatrical cloak. He brought an ancient Roman cloak from his home and showed us approximately forty ways of using it, demonstrating how it could take on completely different shapes—different lines and folds—depending on the need and on the inner state of the character who was being portrayed. Concluding the lesson, Stanislavsky gathered up the cloak in the form of a turban, placed it on his head, and explained to us that on rainy days the Greeks and Romans had used their cloaks as a peculiar kind of hat-umbrella.

Stanislavsky devoted much time to the use of a word and a phrase: to voice, to diction, and to the reading of poetry. His work was made all the more difficult by the fact that the four groups with whom he was working included Jewish, Armenian, and Russian speaking students; but this difficulty merely stimulated his creative fantasy. He was deeply concerned that actors possess a perfect technique of speech, without which, he told us again and again, Shakespeare could never be played. When I asserted that Stanislavsky's and Vakhtangov's thoughts and creative means were close and kindred at that period, I do not want my reader to think that Vakhtangov as an artist never made a mistake. Vakhtangov's life was a passionate, spirited fight for the new in art, consonant with his time. But this fight took place in the first years of the October Revolution, and those were difficult years for any artist who worked in the Soviet theater during that crucial period. Clashes between the old and the new, struggles between different trends, were often quite complicated during that turbulent and interesting period. And it is only natural that Vakhtangov, a searching artist with a questioning mind, an experimentalist, committed errors during his search for new paths for the Soviet theater. Nevertheless, I want to protest the unjust accusations made against Vakhtangov by some theater historians. There are those who accused him of being a formalist. Those who took this line of criticism completely overlooked when and under what circumstances Vakhtangov created his inspiring productions and ignored everything that took place in the arts in the Soviet Union in 1920, 1921, and 1922. This is precisely what I refer to as the "anti-historical" approach to art. The most aggravating part of such false accusation is that it serves as a basis for the history of the Soviet Theater as taught in our schools and for the training of young actors and young regisseurs for the theater. Such a conception of the theater evinces disrespect for the remarkable history of the Soviet theater and reveals the peculiar nihilism of those writers who voice it. It was damaging to the further development of the Soviet theater. It limited the scope of creative research and denied the artist the right to experiment—which is absolutely necessary in every art if any progress is to be made. By offering a ready-made prescription for "correct" direction, and thus incorrectly orienting the youth of the theater, those pseudo-followers of realism trained actors to be afraid of any experiment or creative risk. Young regisseurs, intimidated by such severe, strict masters, could not assert themselves on the professional stage for a long period of time; especially those who had to work outside of Moscow, where work on a play is done in a much shorter time. How many directors nurtured on the stages of our theaters in recent years could we name as important artists who have brought to their productions new ideas, new thinking, and have developed the art of the stage as Vakhtangov did?

Innovation in the theater was always a characteristic in the development of Russian theater art: the spirit of innovation was inherent in Motchalov, the forefather of the romantic direction of the Russian actor's art; in Schepkin, the first great realist of the Russian stage; in the long galaxy of the Russian actors of the last century, all those who possessed enormous, creative range—from tragedy to vaudeville; in Lensky, who created the brilliant company of the Maly Theater, on the border of the nineteenth and twentieth centuries;

and in the founders of the Moscow Art Theater, those remarkable reformers of the Russian stage, Stanislavsky and
Nemirovitch-Dantchenko. The proletarian revolution demanded of the artist new feelings and enormous artistic
range, and the creation of new forms of scenic expressiveness
that would project the new ideas of the times. Vakhtangov
was generously endowed with that feeling for the new. In
1918 and 1919, he headed a gigantic pedagogical work in his
own Studio and also in a number of other studios. He was so
much in demand. That period of his creativity should be
called a pedagogical-directorial period. He worked steadily
with young students and actors, continually examined and
tested what he had learned from Stanislavsky and Nemirovitch-Dantchenko. In one of his letters to Nemirovitch-Dantchenko, written January 17, 1919, after a serious operation,
Vakhtangov wrote: "I feel saved. I live through so much these
days, and I feel most grateful; I feel so much love toward my
people. When I think back, I see how much wrong I did and
that my life on this earth would have been empty if I had not
entered the Moscow Art Theater. Here I learned all I know.
Here I am being purified; here I am aware of the meaning
of my days. You, Nemirovitch-Dantchenko, accepted me into
the theater. You are the first one I owe for all I have, and I
cannot keep silent any longer. I must tell you that my heart
is filled with a deep gratitude toward you. I have never told
you how avidly I devoured your every word—especially about
the art of the actor. You have never guessed how keenly I
looked to you for an answer to many questions about the
theater, and I always found it."

I will quote two more excerpts from Vakhtangov's diary to
show that Stanislavsky and Nemirovitch-Dantchenko saw in
Vakhtangov an extraordinary teacher and a brilliant regisseur, to be called upon to solve the problems presented to the
theater at that particular time. "Today, February 16, 1919,
Nemirovitch-Dantchenko invited me to his home and offered

me the organization of the Musical Comedy Studio." "Today, February 17, 1919, Stanislavsky invited me to the Bolshoi Theater and suggested that I, along with Gsovskaya, organize lessons for the artists of that theater." Enumerating many more invitations to teach at that period, Vakhtangov exclaims: "Oh God! How did I deserve all that?" But he did deserve "all that," and much more.

Chekhov's *A Wedding* was given first as a part of *Chekhov's Evening*, which included *The Thieves, Jubilee,* and *A Wedding. Chekhov's Evening* was a very important step in the formation of Vakhtangov's directorial skill. Working on that program, Vakhtangov began to search out new possibilities for broadening the realistic trend of the Moscow Art Theater school. He was excited by the discovery of graphic styles in the theater and by scenic forms that expressed the ideological essence of a play; by the author's world outlook, the stylistic singularity of his creativity, and the penetration into the spirit of an epoch, when the play was embodied on the stage. That work unified the fundamental group of the future artists of the Vakhtangov Theater. Later on *A Wedding* was presented with *The Miracle of St. Anthony,* a one-act play by Maeterlinck, in one evening. The latter play was shown to the Moscow Art Theater Company, headed by Stanislavsky and Nemirovitch-Dantchenko, in 1921, and as a result of that showing the Vakhtangov Studio was accepted into the family of the Moscow Art Theater. The opening night of the Studio on Arbt 26 took place on November 13, 1921. *The Miracle of St. Anthony* was played, and after that opening performance a concert took place in which Stanislavsky, A. Yugin-Sumbotov, Vakhtangov, Michael Chekhov, and others appeared.

Completely carried away by Vakhtangov's work, we students looked upon it first of all as an excellent school for craftsmanship, although the full purport of Vakhtangov's intention was not quite clear to us at the time. Only much later, recalling the process of the formation of *Chekhov's Evening*, did we begin gradually to penetrate into the innermost depths of the new scenic solutions discovered by Vakhtangov. It was a true discovery. Vakhtangov gave to Chekhov's work a contemporary scenic interpretation which was considerably different from the Moscow Art Theater interpretation of pre-Revolutionary productions of Chekhov. Recalling the first five years of the stormy days after the October Revolution, one sees clearly how surprisingly exact and complete was Vakhtangov's conception of Chekhov's work, how characteristic of that particular time.

Chekhov's dramatic work, his novels, and his short stories sprang from a deep and intense observation of life, from his heartfelt comprehension of the "innermost secrets of the human soul." We actors and directors must develop in ourselves that precious gift of observation, must strive to acquire all-round knowledge of life, and to preserve that Chekhovian excitement about life, in order to keep in step with Chekhov's tradition. Hatred of Philistinism was the reverse side of Chekhov's love for man, a characteristic with which his sensitive creativity abounded. Look at his *Notebooks*. They are not merely a collection of anecdotes, of gay and entertaining events, of facts observed, or even of overheard dialogues. They embody universal truths. You may call it an author's confession; one that reveals his most profound interests, his innermost anxieties. "One should not live like that!" you can almost hear him say. Describing Russia, which he loved deeply, describing the Russian people in the clutches of the Tzarist autocracy, living under inhuman conditions, he does not tell us how to change such a life, but the desperate need for reconstruction of such a society is apparent on every page of his writing. The writer is pained by what he sees that debases man's life, and his writing convinces one of the necessity of living differently. From his *Notebooks* we learn of his concern with the year's harvests on the peasants' soil, of his concern with whether or not the peasant has a horse. He is upset by the rise in the price of flour, by the fact that a husband with his wife and five children had to eat soup made from goose foot for five days. We also read in his *Notebooks*: "In the spring, with the beginning of field work, the peasants would not have enough strength to work. They would go to bed tired and hungry." This is not just literature; this is eloquent testimony taken from real life, which aroused in the writer the realization that such life is intolerable.

When one tries to understand the reason for Chekhov's creation of the characters in *A Wedding*—Aplombov, Gigalov, Yat, Dimba—one must recall the conditions of life in Tzarist Russia, the social order that begot such ridiculous yet pitiful characters. What would be the genesis, let us say, of a character such as Aplombov? Chekhov knows his hero thoroughly, and using the mouth of Neunin he tells us about Aplombov: "The bridegroom, I say, is a splendid, open-hearted fellow. He is an evaluer in a pawnshop. You know, the best of men work in pawnshops these days, also the best of women." The very name Aplombov reveals to us the man's inner self. Chekhov, like other classical Russian writers—Gogol, Ostrovsky—often derives names for his characters from the predominating quality of their natures, as though prompting an actor as to what characteristic he should start with in portraying his character. Aplomb is a characteristic that is unavoidably developed in an evaluer in a pawnshop. In a pawnshop when talking to a customer, it was essential to use a categorical tone; one had to intimidate the person who wished to pawn something. The pawnbroker had to impress the caller with his authority, his confidence, the decisiveness of his word, by his aplomb. From that word, which conveyed the outstanding element in the character of the man, the name Aplombov was derived. The name Gigalov comes probably from the word "vidgiga," which means a cunning rogue. The character calls this to our attention himself. "Don't ever think that I am a cunning rogue of some kind, or a swindler; I act from my heart. It is my feelings that control my behavior." The name of the general, Revunov-Karaulov ("revunov" in Russian means to howl and "karaul" means to shout for help) may be suggesting the general's cry for help, as Karaulov's last line is "Man, show me out. Man, help me."

It is understood that all of Chekhov's characters in *A Wedding* are viewed through the prism of humor. "Comic" is represented here in all its many gradations: now caustic sarcasm, now quiet humor, now pointed satire or clever irony. Now let us recall, for example, Gigalov's speech on electricity: "Electricity, well, to my estimation electric lights are nothing but a swindle. Roguery, to my opinion. They insert a small piece of coal, while you are not looking, and think they are fooling you. Now, brother, if you want to give us light, give us something natural, substantial, that I can get a hold of. Give light, natural—not some invention." This seemingly funny speech has a tragic implication: the smallness of Gigalov's mind is frightening, his obvious unwillingness to recognize anything new. Gigalov's psychology is the psychology of the typical Philistine, who dreads any innovation in life, any change. He would rather endure the worst, just as long as that "worst" is the one he is used to. He wants nothing that changes life—"status quo" is his slogan. The significance of Chekhov's comedies goes beyond pure comedy and assumes a tragicomical character.

After the October Revolution, regisseurs could not interpret Chekhov as they had before, could not view his work in the light of a sentimental, compassionate relation to man. It was necessary to express a forthright repudiation, an active denunciation of Philistinism, of narrow-mindedness, of all the devouring banality of the old petty bourgeois class. Vakhtangov not only understood the new-to-us Chekhov, but found a new and contemporary interpretation of Chekhov's plays. By penetrating into the essence of Chekhov's work,

Chekhov's pain and anxiety about his country and his people, Vakhtangov achieved only the first part of what was needed to realize the author's purpose. It was also necessary to find the expressive means to embody correctly and brilliantly that new understanding of Chekhov's work. According to Vakhtangov, sturdy and striking means were needed to present scenes portraying a passing way of life. The seething passion of a clever satirist was required, but Vakhtangov did not follow the path of the caricaturist. He chose the path of a broader realism, condensing the inner and enlarging the outer design of the performance and thereby achieving the grotesque. Is that parting from the road of realism? Was the critics' accusation of Vakhtangov—that he supposedly opposed realism—correct? I will try to answer that question, and to illustrate my answer I will turn to painting.

No one will deny that Leonardo da Vinci, Velasquez, and Rembrandt were realists in their work. But each of those geniuses expressed realism in a different way. Each great master realist had his own school, his own manner of expression. Vakhtangov's realism was more colorful, more theatrical, more exciting—as befitted the times with their stirring events—compared with the realism of the Moscow Art Theater, which was appropriate in pre-Revolutionary days. But without question *The Cherry Orchard, Uncle Vanya*—and especially *The Brothers Karamazov*—undoubtedly exerted a decided influence on Vakhtangov. Those productions aroused and stimulated his imagination and helped him to mount *A Wedding* in his own way.

Vakhtangov, the regisseur, had at his disposal mainly young and inexperienced actors, so he had to concentrate on the psychological content of the roles. Psychological analysis of a role requires an actor to search within himself and draw on the elements of his personal character. The actor becomes a kind of doctor who observes a patient carefully, studies him from head to foot. Then comes a period when the doctor takes on the symptoms of his patient. This happens when the "professional" in the doctor dies, and the human being is awakened. Imagine that a doctor is taking care of a person who is very dear to him. Imagine that the life of this person is of enormous importance to him and his concern for his recovery causes him great anxiety. He would give his life to save his friend. In like manner the desire to help awakens the real man in an actor when he plays a positive character, when he loves the character he is creating. On the other hand, when an actor portrays a negative role, when he condemns his "hero," he becomes a district attorney in his relationship to him. Then his actions serve society, protect the ethical standards created by that society, call for correction of that society's vices.

Now, in what way was it necessary to portray Chekhov's characters, defending them or accusing them? That was the foremost, the decisive question for the regisseur. On the answer to that question depended the new interpretation given Chekhov's plays. In the pre-Revolutionary interpretation of those days, the prevailing tendency had been to justify all the heroes—*"tout comprendre c'est tout pardonner"* (to understand all is to forgive all). That approach to Chekhov was based on the premise that there is no real happiness on earth for man. That historical pessimism gives rise to compassion, pity, sentimentality, moodiness, inertia. But Chekhov repeated again and again that he did not write lyric dramas, but comedies; that his outlook on life was much more optimistic than the outlook of many of the producers and many of the actors of his plays. The swords of laughter are drawn for the fight against social evil, and in that fight Chekhov recognized the true mission of the comedy writer. To break with the past means to forge ahead to a better future. The more conclusively a man breaks with the past, the more strongly it must be brought out in art. That is the reason for the emphasis, the enlargement, the hyperbole that

is characteristic of comedy. That is the reason why Khlestakov's "thirty-five thousand couriers only" in Gogol's *Inspector General* is gross exaggeration, moreover an obvious lie.
But in Khlestakov's lie is contained the truth of Khlestakov's
character. An inveterate liar, he reveals to us an indisputable
truth regarding himself and, at the same time, the truth
about his listeners who believe him. Not without reason that
arch rogue the Inspector General says, "What if even a part
of what he is telling us is true?" The supreme realist Gogol
again and again proves the possibility of exaggeration in art,
and his grotesque novels *The Nose* and *The Portrait* could
not be called realism if measured by the usual primitive standards of realism. But that only means that the conception of
realism is much broader than it is understood to be by many
people. It means also that the grotesque and the fantastic undoubtedly could be the means of realistic art. It all depends
on the power of conviction, on the means and style by which
the creator-artist communicates with his reader and spectator.
Vakhtangov discovered the right degree of exaggeration permissible in Chekhov's *A Wedding*. A performance will influence the conscience and feelings of the audience if the director will show with poetic excitement the happiness and the
misery of human beings. In the theater one cannot create the
impression of truth by lectures, or talks, or treatises. The
power of the stage to influence an audience depends on the
scenic persuasiveness of the events of the play. Scenic persuasiveness may be limitlessly diverse. Let us take the art of
eccentrics. Gorky quotes Lenin's remark on eccentrics:
"There is a kind of satirical or sceptical relation to the generally accepted. There is an attempt to turn it inside out, to
distort it a little, to show a paralogism. Intricate but interesting." At the basis of apparent eccentricity lies the truth of
life. But whereas an actor in dramatic presentation has three
or four hours in which to reveal the character and psychology
of his hero, the actor-eccentric has at his disposal only five or

six minutes. In these he must live through a rich scenic life, filled with brilliant events, and create an impressive living image. An actor-eccentric must go through all the psychological transitions thoroughly in order to be convincing. Where the dramatic actor has a number of pages of text, an actor-eccentric (in vaudeville, for example) has just a few words— and sometimes no words—with which to communicate to his audience a complex psychological state of mind. How does a talented actor-eccentric accomplish his peculiar scenic truth? He does it by selecting the most typical and expressive details of that which he wants to convey to the audience and building them up to the fullest scenic expressiveness.

The works of the French painters Gavarni and Daumier are the art of the grotesque. Our contemporary artists Kukrinikci and Boris Efimov achieved by laconic means an extraordinary degree of influence on the onlooker, as the onlooker completed the artists' paintings—which are executed in the art of satirical design—with his own fantasy. Proportion and correlation between a canvas painted in oil and a laconic, graphic design is similar to that between the dramatic actor and the eccentric actor or clown. The exceptionally difficult art of an eccentric demands extraordinary skill and certainly could not be considered a second-rate art. To the contrary, at times it expresses most deeply and powerfully the phenomena of life.

Chekhov's *A Wedding* was written as many of his stories were, in a terse, laconic style; "a scene in one act," the author calls it. Because of their pithiness Chekhov's short stories, covering only a few pages, surpass in impact many voluminous novels. His one-act comedies exhibit the same merit of compactness: *A Wedding, The Celebration, The Boor, A Marriage Proposal,* and even a play in three pages, *The Harmfulness of Tobacco,* which is a "scene monologue in one act."

One must dwell on the last play in order to understand the

nature of Chekhov's one-act plays, in order to know the manner in which they should be depicted on the stage. Let us go through the author's remarks in the "lecture." First Neukhin —with long side whiskers, but no moustache—dressed in a threadbare frock coat, makes a majestic entrance, bows to his audience, and adjusts his waistcoat. As he lectures he combs his whiskers, straightens his vest, looks at his watch twice—all this he does solidly—and then suddenly breaks into song. Further on, he takes several brochures out of his pocket, looks around twice, approaches the footlights and flicks at his neck while telling the audience that he was married in this tail coat thirty years before. Then he tears the tail coat off and tramples on it. As he sees his wife in the wings, he looks around embarrassed, then he quickly puts on the tail coat, looks at his watch again, raises his voice in a song, and at the end bows and stalks majestically out. Do all those remarks of Chekhov keep within the usual conception of authenticity, of truth in life? Of course not. During his very short time on the stage the actor must show the difficult, miserable life Neukhin leads, show how low his dignity has been brought, what his life at home is like—where there is an insect even in the piano. He is at the same time a pitiful man and a ridiculous one. The character is grotesque, tragicomical. An actor playing the role of Neukhin must have extraordinary talent for expressiveness.

Grotesque, tragicomical traits characterized the interpretation that Vakhtangov gave to *A Wedding*. In that spectacle, produced in the first years after the Revolution, Vakhtangov spoke about the life which had existed not so long ago, and which had not so long ago been done away with. Yet echoes of that life were still heard and felt in the young Soviet Russia. Vakhtangov in his new interpretation of Chekhov was ridiculing the Philistine mode of life as though in an effort to banish it from the revolutionary present-day reality. The method of exaggeration, of the grotesque, chosen by Vakhtangov, corresponded ideally to the dramatic material and to its perception by the contemporary audience.

That method was organic to Vakhtangov himself as an actor. Portraying his roles, Vakhtangov consistently used the maximum of expressiveness. One has only to recall his portrayal of Tackleton in the play *Cricket on the Hearth,* his left eye screwed up, a frozen, angry, ironic smile on his face, and a hollow, rattled voice; or his portrayal of Frazier in *Deluge* —agile, full of temperament, never at a loss for a word. The imagination of the regisseur Vakhtangov in his work on *A Wedding* was fed by riches accumulated in the sphere of exaggeration and grotesque in Russian classic literature—Gogol, Pushkin, Dostoevsky. To embody on the stage the works of writers such as these by means of common realism was inconceivable. We know that the material in each given case demands a consonant form. The great Russian actors of the old days—as well as those of today—had the skill for such special keenness and the ability to combine the tragic and comic in their performances. One has only to recall the great actor Martinov, whose tradition has extended down into our own times. This tradition lived again in the performance of Stepanov-Kuznetzov, whom I saw in the same role of Lodijkin (the vaudeville *The Bridegroom*) in which Martinov had excelled in his days. Kuznetzov, in his personification of Lodijkin, after the succession of many funny moments in his performance, which kept the audiences hilarious, suddenly cried out, "Where to now?" That outcry stunned the audience, and from that moment there was a deathlike silence in the theater, as happens in tense moments of high tragedy. The suffering of that poor old man, who had lost his last hope to get out of prison, reduced the audience to tears. And when Lodijkin bowed low to the audience, after ending his monologue, and said, "And, now, goodbye," a complete and exciting fusion of the actor and audience took place.

Stanislavsky displayed an extraordinary skill for tragicomical grotesque in his roles of the Cavalier Di Ripafratta (*The Mistress of the Inn,* by Goldoni), Argon (Molière's *Imaginary Invalid*), and Krutitzky (*For Each Wise Man Enough Simplicity,* by Ostrovsky). I think I am not wrong in saying that Stanislavsky's vast experience in the school of vaudeville and operatic roles in his youth helped him to master the nature of the grotesque. Vaudeville, musical comedy, and operetta demand of an actor skill in singing and dancing; that he be a trained master of synthetic theater, a master who is musical, plastic, and has an excellent sense of rhythm. Without such all-round skill one cannot achieve the grotesque style.

Among the actors who came to the stage after the October Revolution, in my opinion Schukin and Khmelev most fully expressed Vakhtangov's understanding of the actor's mastery. They were the kind of actor Vakhtangov dreamed about. They possessed that mastery for which Vakhtangov trained his students. Schukin had studied directly with Vakhtangov and was his best student; Khmelev studied directly with Stanislavsky and Nemirovitch-Dantchenko and was their best student. Khmelev had met Vakhtangov in the Second Studio of the Moscow Art Theater; he saw all Vakhtangov's productions—*A Wedding, Miracle of St. Anthony, The Dybbuk, Princess Turandot*—and undoubtedly in his creative formation absorbed Vakhtangov's teaching. Khmelev in his portrayal of Tuzenbakh in *The Three Sisters,* of the duke in *Uncle's Dream,* Karenin in *Anna Karenina,* Peklevanov in *The Armored Train 14-69,* Alex Turbin in *The Days of the Turbins* certainly met Vakhtangov's lofty demands. Khmelev combined in his acting the depths of interpretation of the inner conflict with the brilliancy and exactness of its physical embodiment.

At times Vakhtangov used to tell us that he was dreaming of putting on Chekhov's *Seagull* "theatrically." What does that mean, "theatrically"? The word "theatrical," as the word "grotesque," for some reason frightens many theater workers and critics, even now. While the true theatricality aims at creating the most convincing and impressive scenic images, it also strives to excite, to captivate, to shake the audience. An actor can attain true theatricality only if his temperament is dynamic and he possesses deep, profound emotions which can express the crux of the character, its very essence. The artist's great accomplishment is when the theatergoer is so engrossed by the actor's personification of the character—for example, let us say, Hamlet—that he is too involved to evaluate the creativity of the actor who is playing Hamlet until after the performance is over. Then he begins to analyze the sensations that the actor aroused in him; he calls to mind certain *mise en scènes,* certain gestures, facial expressions, and intonations of the actor. At the end, after separating his sensations into their component parts, he gathers them again into a single whole and that whole stands before his eyes as the image created by the actor, and he retains that throughout his life.

The art of the regisseur is often unseen: it dies in action. And that phenomenon is the most remarkable, the most valuable in dramatic art. It is significant to note that in Molière's time the expression *"maître en scène"* was born: that means "teacher of stage." The highest manifestation of the regisseur's art is the strength of the scenic images of the play —of their power to arouse and influence the onlooker. The essence of theatricality is to create a deep, complete, poetically exciting scenic image. Only thus can we understand Vakhtangov's thought about the theatrical embodiment of Chekhov.

How then did Vakhtangov, together with his young actors, interpret the personages of Chekhov's *A Wedding?* Evdokim Zakharovitch Gigalov, civil servant retired, as played by V. B. Schukin was a man who on first sight is kind and generous, but in fact is cruel and rapacious. The steady trickle of amiable, tender words, the tendency to feign a simpleton, a man who is not practical—all that was a mask behind which was hidden a functionary, an unquestionable grafter, a boring Philistine, one who was indifferent to everything except easy gain and position. Look who surrounds the Gigalov family. Have they any true friends? No. All the guests at the wedding —the midwife, the telegraphist, the sailor from the Voluntary Fleet—are strangers who just happened to be at the wedding. The Philistine's complacency leads to loneliness, and that is the frightening aspect of Chekhov's *A Wedding*. The image created by Schukin, in compliance with Vakhtangov's demands, was a stark theme in relief, the theme of the spiritual bankruptcy and utter aloneness of the Philistine, Evdokim Zakharovitch Gigalov.

His better half, Nastasia Timofeevna Gigalova, portrayed by Schukina, looked a worthy companion of her husband— narrow-minded, quarrelsome, lachrymose. She managed even at her daughter's wedding to quarrel with Yat, the telegraphist. I remember the uneasy, anxious look of Mrs. Gigalova, always fearful lest she be taken advantage of. In the relationship of that married couple one could see immediately that it was the wife who had the upper hand. Schukina addressed her husband in angry, severe tones: "Don't poke your fork into the lobster. That is for the General. I still think he might appear." The words rang out so sharply that one could easily suspect that if no one had been around she might have hit him. The image of Gigalov's daughter, Dashenka—the bride-to-be—was magnificently delineated plastically by Nekrasova. Little, plump, red-cheeked, awkward, lazy, she was not even quite aware of the significance of the day—her wedding day. Her indifference to everything extended even to her young husband. The food on the table interested her much more than the guests. The role of the bridegroom, Apiminond Maximovich Aplombov, was played vividly and expressively by a young talented actor named Kudryavtzev. His monotonous, hollow voice, always on the same note, always with one intonation, bored into the audience as a drop of water wears away a stone. At times, in his most temperamental moments, his voice sounded like a dentist's drill. Not even such an exhausted-by-her-cares, nervous woman as Mrs. Gigalova could stand him.

"There was also an agreement, we had an understanding that a General will be here for supper tonight. Where is he, I ask you?" the discontented bridegroom demanded, swinging his hands up in front of his future mother-in-law's nose.

When the mother-in-law could stand that torture no more and retreated from the room, he followed her with a caustic remark, "I want you to have a sense of honor. That is all I want from you. Be honest. Be noble!"

Undoubtedly those claims, the nagging, the eternal carpings, will continue all through his married life. Aplombov probably carries a notebook in which he marks down all the things he expects to get from the Gigalov family; he writes them down, no doubt, in careful handwriting and with an accurate calculation to the kopeck.

In appearance Aplombov was not prepossessing. He had a big nose, angry eyes, and a tuft of hair that fell carelessly on his forehead. A thin, long figure arrayed in a dresscoat—quite obviously purchased in a secondhand store—he wandered onto the stage with a dissatisfied look and manner that could not help but depress his guests. It would be impossible ever to get close to the heart of this man. He will end his life a grumbler, a bigot, a malcontent; he will fulfill his earthly occupation, that of an appraiser in a pawnshop, and on his deathbed he will still be recalling some unkept promises made by Gigalov. The role of Andrey Andreevich Neunin—an agent in an insurance office, but a crook and a rascal—was played by Toltchanov. That profession requires the ability to talk a person into something, to force him to buy insurance, no matter how much he is against it. Neunin was pert, bald, with a husky voice, and saucily free in speech and actions.

When he started to talk, he gave no one a chance to utter a word. From his point of view people existed for only one reason: so that he might extract money from them by hook or crook. Neunin undoubtedly gambles in cards and billiards, and most likely is physically beaten very often by his partners for cheating in games. Neunin, like Gigalov, caters to and flatters people who are well off and has no use for the rest of the world. Anna Martinovna Zmeyukina, the thirty-year-old midwife, arrayed in a bright crimson dress, was played by Lyaudanskaya. The actress strongly emphasized in this role the traits of the Philistine. The narrow-mindedness was most sharply etched when the ridiculous bent for "loftiness" possessed Zmeyukina. The midwife felt like the queen of the ball—a charming, irresistible woman surrounded by a coterie of admirers. In truth, there was only one admirer—the telegraphist Yat. But for Zmeyukina even that was satisfactory. She desired to give the impression of an unusual, outstanding woman and Yat made an entirely suitable audience for her. Vakhtangov suggested to Lyaudanskaya and Lobashkov (he played the telegraphist) that they keep their dialogue in a serious tone with a dramatic verve:

> ZMEYUKINA: I cannot breathe among you—give me air! I am suffocating!
> YAT: (*in ecstasy*) Beautiful! Oh, beautiful creature!

The role of the master of ceremonies occupied a special place in this spectacle. H. M. Gorchakov, who played the role, carried the responsibility of the rhythmic and dancing part of the spectacle. The master of ceremonies at a wedding had to be a connoisseur of all kinds of quadrilles; he had to be experienced at arranging the dancing at Philistine balls and parties. During the rehearsals, Vakhtangov asked again and again for new improvisations of the dancers' episodes. He suggested to Gorchakov that he think up unusual figures for the quadrilles and give the dancing crowd new suggestions constantly. Vakhtangov strove to get an organic feeling from the guests at the wedding—an improvisational state of being. Anyone who has danced at weddings, or other such events, knows how much depends on the master of ceremonies keeping up the mood and the high spirits and never permitting the pulse of merriment to slacken. But there was almost no merriment, no gaiety, at the Gigalov wedding. Cheerless quadrilles were danced without any feeling of festivity, but the shouting of the master of ceremonies, Gorchakov, made a lot of noise, thus substituting bustle and commotion for gaiety. In this way a cheerless, doleful scene was created. The figure of the master of ceremonies who conducted the dancing with such ardor reminded one of an inadequate commander who is trying to incite his detachment into an attack, but to no avail. One felt that the art of conducting quadrilles had become the sole calling of that little man, more satisfying to him than his profession. The desire to be the center of attention is innate in every human being. Gorchakov, conducting the dancing with ardor and self-abandon, conveyed that desire excellently—the desire to be singled out among the guests in some degree. Lobashkov, in the role of the telegraphist, Yat, created a comic figure of an unlucky Don Juan, a romantic wooer from a very small station in life. Not very tall, with short legs and a very long back, and with a pince-nez dancing on his nose, he was ridiculous and rather pitiful.

The sailor from the Voluntary Fleet, as played by Zakhava, gave the impression of a cheerful person: an optimist, openhearted and unassuming. The important "positive hero" of Vakhtangov's production of *A Wedding* was the "General"— Captain Revunov-Karoulov—who was played by Basov with warmth, simplicity, and much charm. Vakhtangov insisted on simplicity in portraying this role, intentionally working toward a sharp contrast between the quiet naturalness of the old captain and the overstrung rhythm that marked the inner life of the majority of the guests. A foreigner of Greek origin, a confectioner by occupation, Kharlampy Spiridonitch Dimba, looked in that surrounding like an exotic plant in a Russian pine forest. Sociable, trusting, childishly hearty, he saw in every person at the wedding a bosom friend. Warmed by wine, he felt as though he were in a blissful dream: the holiday, the music, the dancing, the festive table made an enchanting impression on him. As soon as he found himself near the banquet table, he reached a state of enthusiasm. Touched to tears, he pronounced his quite incoherent speech: "I understand well. We are Greeks, you are Russians, and I need nothing. I can say the following: Which is Greece and which is Russia?"

I played the role of Dimba. That was my first role at the Vakhtangov Studio, and I had the greatest difficulty with it. Vakhtangov tried patiently and persistently to get from me the result he needed, the correct interpretation of the role. But it seemed to me that the excessive demands he made on me deprived me of freedom in working on the role, robbed me of my spontaneity. Every word pronounced by me was born in pain, with enormous effort. From rehearsal to rehearsal I felt more and more inadequate. I even thought of giving up the role altogether. We began to have dress rehearsals; then, next, there was to be the showing of the production to Stanislavsky, Nemirovitch-Dantchenko, and the company of the Moscow Art Theater. I went to the theater that particular night as though I were going to face a horrible ordeal, a sure failure. But, suddenly, the moment I walked onto the stage, from the very first word of my role, I felt free, relaxed, in a wonderfully creative state, with a desire to play the role, to communicate to my audience all my teacher had taught me during the rehearsals. The audience's cheerful reaction warmed me, and I became sure that there was nothing in my role I could not feel with all my being. After the performance, Vakhtangov came to our dressing room and for the first time praised me in my role of Dimba. I was rewarded for everything, for all the torture I had gone through during the rehearsals. Vakhtangov's pedagogical method became clear to me after that performance, and I have adopted that method throughout my life in teaching and also in my acting.

The rehearsal period must be used to master all the necessary elements of the role and of the spectacle. Calculation that inspiration will pull us through the performance is a poor and unreliable calculation. Inspiration comes to an actor only after the technical side of his role is mastered to perfection. No musical genius will ever allow himself to appear before the audience until he has studied every passage, perfected the technical part of the composition precisely, and polished every detail. Alas! For some reason a great number of actors think that dramatic art does not require preparation. Such dilettantism is born of a wrong understanding of the Stanislavsky Method and the school of "feeling the role." Such a tendency existed also in the time of Vakhtangov; it lives today, that tendency to think that all you have to do is to "feel the role" and the character will somehow be formed by itself. How often I have witnessed an actor feeling his role sincerely, crying real tears; yet all that sincerity did not reach his audience. The audience was left cold. An actor comes backstage expecting enthusiastic praise from his comrades, but instead he meets cold perplexity. What is wrong? We know from the biography of that remarkable Russian actor Stanislavsky of the great trauma that he lived through while playing the role of Saliery in Pushkin's play *Mozart and Saliery*. Stanislavsky "felt" Saliery, felt the envy and the unfortunate fate of the hard-working artist on that fateful day of his meeting Mozart. Yet Stanislavsky failed in his performance simply because, notwithstanding the sincerity of his emotions, Pushkin's verse was not heard. The rhythm and meter of the poetry was broken; the basis on which Pushkin's creation was built was lost; the poetry of a genius was mangled, distorted.

Vakhtangov understood perfectly the complexity of the actor's art, and from the very first steps in our theater work strove to inject in us the love for mastery, for perfection in technique. Working with young actors, Vakhtangov asserted the correct understanding of his teacher's method—a harmonious blending of the process of feeling the role with the process of embodying it. Also Vakhtangov used to adjust his method of work to each of his students, taking into consideration the psychology of the individual actor. Schukin, for example, had to be helped imperceptibly. Schukin used to come to rehearsal thoroughly prepared, bringing the materials that he had worked out carefully at home. Vakhtangov would further guide Schukin's fantasy with subtle and well-thought-out comments. He would raise new problems, one after another, for the talented young actor, each one more complicated than the other. Kudryavtzev had a special gift for absorbing Vakhtangov's regisseur's illustrations and incorporating them into his role easily and organically. When young actors would lose the continuity of the play, Vakhtangov would then have discussions with them, giving them exciting, stimulating problems, inspiring them to strive to penetrate into the essence of the play and their roles. Vakhtangov knew the character, habits, and psychology of each one of his students; he was not only teaching but educating us.

The question of ethics was just as important in our school as the work on a play. Each student was a member of the collective, a participator in the building of the young theater. Those who were most active, who had proven their dedication to that pursuit and their right to guide the theater, were included by Vakhtangov in the Central Organ. To be included in that highest organ one needed the consent of all the members of the Central Organ. These members had to serve as an example of discipline, of undeviating dedication to the goal of their work. The obligations and functions of the Central Organ were in keeping with the aims of the Art Council of our times. At that particular period when professional organization was quite weak, such a structure for our studio was expedient. And though that system of the studio self-government organized by Vakhtangov rested on his unshakable—to us—authority, still it proved its viability and effectiveness after Vakhtangov's death, when the theater named after him was able to preserve its independence and its "handwriting" and continue its path to the height of great art. The organization of the creative process was the aim of all the work in the Studio.

Working with each one of us on our roles, Vakhtangov simultaneously was molding an original form of Chekhov's spectacle, a form that corresponded to the spirit of the times. Without the form, the right form, scenic art is not complete, does not have its full value, just as no art of any kind can be of real importance without the right form for its content.

When naturalism reached its peak in French literature, Zola developed a special form that had an inherent naturalistic tenor—he began to paint life with maximum authenticity as he saw it in all its details, with all the aspects of human existence, savoring at times all the dirt and loathsomeness of it. With what enthusiasm in *The Trap* he describes streams of water flowing into a canal from the laundry, where the heroine Gervesa does her washing. Maupassant also frequently resorted to naturalistic details in his stories, enriching his reader by that means. The representatives of the naturalistic trend often pursued lofty and progressive endeavors, striving to give humanity a true document, to unfold human life as though it were reflected in a mirror. Leo Tolstoy, a realist, resorted to the naturalistic method in his *Kreutzer Sonata,* but created nevertheless a deeply impressive work of art. Hence, if today we deny naturalism as art, not suitable to large gen-

eralizations, as photographic copying of life, it does not mean
that naturalism could not be used by an artist-realist in certain circumstances with a certain purpose. The realistic
school reveals a human being from the high level of psychological art. The realist is interested in the first place in the
inner world of man, in his spiritual substance; the naturalist,
in the physical, physiological side of man. It would be unfair
though to think of Zola as a writer who did not know man
well; he knew people just as thoroughly as Stendhal, Balzac,
Maupassant, or Flaubert. But as an exponent of naturalism
he often intentionally used means for the sake of means; then
his naturalism was dogmatic, and the form killed the creation. As a whole his creativity had a progressive significance.
The naturalism of Zola was an antidote to false romanticism,
it was directed against aestheticism, against the deliberate
pettiness that misrepresents reality. The naturalism of Zola
at that time had played a pioneering role in bringing art
nearer to life, opening art to that stratum of society which,
from the point of view of romanticists and aestheticians, was
below the artist's attention. In the Russian art of painting, mobile painters* played an extremely progressive role,
though at times their canvases had elements of naturalism,
thus lessening the reality. Their canvases were photographs,
without insight into the innermost meaning of the depicted
events. Naturalism by stretching details often takes the position of formalism, because it emphasizes things of minor importance, savors minute descriptions. That departure from
the basic idea kills the content in the name of the form. The
question of the interrelationship of form and content is a
very complex one, and its concrete solution comes at times
spontaneously.

I do not claim here to analyze aesthetics. I only want to

* Progressive, democratically inclined artists-realists of the second
half of the nineteenth century; participants of the so-called Mobile Art
Exhibits.

stress one circumstance, which our aesthetes consistently leave out: One should not judge the interrelationship of content and form in works of art without analyzing the concrete circumstances of the epoch, the time when that particular work of art was created.

Did the form used by Vakhtangov for Chekhov's *A Wedding* correspond to Chekhov's realism? Not in the general sense of Chekhov's realism, but in a specific sense in the years when Vakhtangov produced the play. We saw that Vakhtangov's intention first of all was to reveal in each role its social and psychological basis, to dig into that which was latent, hidden, in the character of the human being. Vakhtangov's understanding of dramatic art—its laws, the Stanislavsky Method—was changing with the years; just as with the years Stanislavsky himself was changing his Method. While working with actors in his first period of work, Vakhtangov followed the Stanislavsky System religiously, step by step. The result of such work was seen in his direction of *The Deluge,* written by Berger, in the First Studio of the Moscow Art Theater in 1915. In the second period of his regisseur's work, after the October Revolution, Vakhtangov came to a new understanding of the laws of dramatic art, although, as before, he was resting on the principles of psychological realism, thoroughly studying and passionately propagandizing the Stanislavsky Method. Vakhtangov brought essential additions and specifications to the interpretation of this system, reorganizing the method of the actors' training and searching for new scenic forms. Refuting the conception of theater as a "trade," as did Stanislavsky, and asserting the theater of "living the role," Vakhtangov nevertheless gave serious consideration to the "art of representation." Vakhtangov was discovering those creative methods of the "school of representation" which are necessary to an actor's method of working on roles, which strengthen the realistic and true basis of the technique of "living the role."

The principles of the art of the "representation school" are expressed vividly and consistently by Didro in his book *Paradox of Acting*. Coquelin, in his book *The Art of an Actor*, uses such of Didro's formulas as: "An actor should not imitate nature, even beautiful nature." Formulists and aestheticians asserted that the further the creative fantasy of the artist moves away from reality, the more brilliantly the truth of art is revealed—and that truth is contrary to the truth of life. But Didro also said this about the art of an actor, which could be used as armament by the adherents of the school of "living the role," and I quote: "A great actor is created by the temperament of common sense and emotional ardor."

Now this formula of Didro's deserves our most serious attention. I will never forget the last meeting that we students of Vakhtangov had with Stanislavsky. The day was Stanislavsky's birthday, his seventy-fifth. We had gone to congratulate him and to wish him good health. The majestic, handsome man was sitting up in bed, leaning on the pillows. He was ill. A bottle of champagne and glasses were brought in. Stanislavsky suggested we drink a toast to the art of the theater. "What are you occupied with?" he asked us. "With art," one of us answered. "With art—or trade?" asked Stanislavsky, smiling. "We are trying to be occupied with art," we answered all together, and everyone burst out laughing. Stanislavsky, having learned about our work on Shakespeare's comedy *Measure for Measure*, expressed a thought which has remained with me throughout my life. "I am becoming more and more convinced," he said, "that while there may be five or ten minutes in a Shakespearean play in which an actor can depend exclusively on his emotions, the rest of the time an actor needs all the technique he can bring to his performance." These words were spoken in 1937. In my opinion, they show a definite evolution in the views of the creator of the System himself; he who originally had demanded of an actor that he depend only on the true feeling of his role throughout the entire play.

Vakhtangov in the beginning of the twenties understood the necessity for broadening the concept of the school of "feeling the role" by the addition of new aspects of the actor's mastery. In those days, the demand for the "true feeling" in some of the productions of the First Studio of the Moscow Art Theater called for negation of the expressive form. The belief in "feeling the role," as the beginning and the end of the actor's work, was impoverishing the art of the new revolutionary Soviet theater and limiting its scope. With the means of art founded exclusively on concentration of feelings, one could play the intimate psychological chamber productions; however, tragedy and the people's heroic Revolutionary repertoire were demanding different methods of inner technique —the "know-how" to arouse in oneself the great feelings and heroic passions and express them in a completely plastico-precise and, at times, even exaggerated form. It is understood when I speak of broadening the creative scope of the actor's art and of utilizing the technique of the "school of representation" that I do not mean to propagandize "trade" acting, or over-acting, use of clichés—all of which Stanislavsky and Vakhtangov fought fiercely.

Vakhtangov had dreams of an experimental production with the actors of our Studio. In those years, 1920-1921, Vakhtangov used to invite guests to our studio for discussions on art: Stanislavsky, Eugine-Sumbatov, Michael Chekhov, and also Mayakovsky's champion fighter, poet Vasilly Kamensky. Meeting with all those wonderful people gave us an opportunity to expose ourselves to people whose outlook and direction in the arts were most diverse. After these gatherings, Vakhtangov would summarize the discussions that took place, pointing out what was the most important thing for us to remember, what we had to learn from each one of the great masters. Stanislavsky, as far as Vakhtangov was concerned, understood the art of the actor better than anyone else, especially the inner technique of the actor's art. From Eugine-Sumbatov, Vakhtangov advised us to learn the art of scenic speech, to catch those subtle peculiarities of the Russian language and its pronunciation. From Michael Chekhov, Vakhtangov suggested we acquire his amazing spontaneity and naïveté. Vakhtangov also pointed out to us Chekhov's talent for the use of spontaneity of means, adjustments, and sharpness of scenic design in the portrayal of his roles—a sample of which we saw in his characterization of Khlestokov in *Inspector General.* By the way, Vakhtangov helped Chekhov with that role. Chekhov's portrayal of Khlestokov was an event in the theater life of that period. Chekhov did not play Khlestokov as a vaudeville rascal; instead he created a most convincing figure of a small functionary without, as we say, "Tzar in his head." In that production, where young and old generations of the Moscow Art Theater took part, Chekhov excelled as Khlestokov, excelled with a brilliant, grotesque style. Stanislavsky was the regisseur of that play and he valued Chekhov's work highly.

Now Vakhtangov's repeated attempts to analyze the experiences of the old generation—Stanislavsky, Eugine-Sumbatov —also the young generation—Michael Chekhov, the poet Kamensky—become to me so much clearer. Vakhtangov felt the necessity of combining all the experiences of the realistic school of the Moscow Art Theater and the Maly Theater with the new movements in the sphere of theater art, not limiting himself by adhering to only one particular direction. Sensing the birth of a new dramaturgy in content and form, Vakhtangov was trying to equip the actor for the new repertoire. The actors of the school of "feeling the role" could learn much from the adherents of the school of the "art of representation." The actors of the school of the "art of representation" had better speech, diction, and vocal technique than the actors of the "school of feeling."

*A Wedding*

My reader might well ask: What about Katchalov? He was an actor of the Moscow Art Theater who excelled in his vocal technique. Katchalov only proves my point, as he came to the Moscow Art Theater from a school which combined two directions, feeling and representation. In fact, Vakhtangov often brought Katchalov's name to our attention, using him as an example. The actors of the school of the "art of representation" move excellently; they are rhythmical, musical. The mastery of gesture, mimicry, and sculptural expressions is worked out thoroughly by them. The master who combined inner technique with faultless outward technique was the Russian genius Feodor Chaliapin. The tragic depths of Boris Godunov, the hero of Pushkin's play, found the ideal embodiment in this artist, not only because of his perfect understanding of the character, with its emotional excitement, and his passionate execution of it, but also because of the whole make-up of Chaliapin, which helped him to reveal the monumental tragic personage.

The acting for an opera singer is especially difficult. A singer depends on the orchestra, on the tempo established by a conductor. Actor-singers must control themselves in many aspects: follow the tempo given by the conductor; maintain the proper balance between the sound of their voice and the sound of the orchestra—which requires perfect control of their vocal instrument; keep harmonious musical contact with their partner in duets and in ensemble. The opera actor-singer, while fulfilling the conductor's demands, must in addition remember the demands of the regisseur: follow the established *mise en scène*; carry out the planned acting communion with his partners; stay in the character. With all those demands on you, just try to depend only on feeling the role! The actor-singer in opera is a central instrument soloist in a large and complicated musical aggregation named opera art. To stay in character, fulfill all the musical demands, and complete the scenic movements, he must be constantly in

43

control of himself. In opera especially an actor cannot take chances; he cannot depend on the right feeling being born at that precise moment on stage where it will help him harmonize all the elements required of him. He must be thoroughly prepared. It is not important whether the actor will cry over his role at home, or during rehearsals, on the street, or when he is working in his role on stage. The important thing is that he cannot count on the feeling coming to him spontaneously when he is on the stage.

The good sportsmen, track and field athletes, for example, come to a meet thoroughly prepared. They plan beforehand the diagram of the race, and they follow it precisely. But a very good runner always has a "reserve" which can be utilized by him in case his competitor turns out to be a better runner than he expected him to be. Nothing is left to chance, as far as the technical side of preparation is concerned; but in planning the tactics and strategy of the race, the athlete must be left free, because it is difficult, even impossible, to figure out beforehand what his competitor might decide to do at the last moment. In regard to his technique, on the other hand, the runner has no right to improvise. Salvini's formula —"I treat my role like a horseman treats a fiery horse"—must be understood by us in this way. There should be faultless preparation for a role, then the creative, improvisational state while actually playing the role. One may ask me: Doesn't the school of "feeling the role" require preparatory work? Yes, of course. But often the adherents of that school limit their regisseur's function to that of working exclusively on the inner line of the role: the analysis, the talking over the past of the role, the recollection of the actor's personal past of the same nature—in relation to the situation of the character being portrayed—the definition of scenic problems, the definition of the red thread and the overall problem of the role. In other words, all the preparation is done along the inner line of the character, but its physical expressiveness is completely left out. Vakhtangov, working on a role with his students, worked over all the elements of the System, then when necessary added a number of stirring scenic problems that helped the actor to master the form—which was different in every new play Vakhtangov presented.

While rehearsing *A Wedding*, Vakhtangov was searching for a tragicomical means of expression. With that in mind, the richness of an actor's adjustments played an important part. Adjustments—means by which the aim can be accomplished—depend on the actor's ability to be stimulated, incited, by scenic problems. The more talented an actor is, the more spontaneous, the more vivid, these adjustments will be. Here much depends on the actor's creative intuition, the degree of his susceptibility, and the range of his imagination. The actors who have experienced the feeling of that sudden illumination, the moment the necessary adjustment came spontaneously, know that happy, creative state that is so wonderful in our difficult art. Analyzing that state after the rehearsal or performance, an actor finds in his memory thoughts and sensations that served as a sudden jolt and made him spontaneously react under the scenic situation. Stanislavsky considered that that moment of subconscious illumination really depends completely on the actor, although a regisseur can help prepare the way for it to some degree and assist the feeling to be born. Vakhtangov worked toward getting the necessary result from an actor by analyzing the scenic problem action—"I want"—and thereby leading an actor to find the adjustment through the psychological process. Thus he brought the actor organically to the process of creating those brilliant, more expressive adjustments by dissecting the action into its component elements, developing that action logically, finding the right weapon, and placing the actor in the most comfortable scenic *mise en scène*.

In those years it was accepted that scenic problems were divided into the psychological and the physical. Many adherents of the Stanislavsky System were interested only in psychological problems, considering the physical ones to be inferior scenic problems not requiring special probing, either on the part of the actor or on the part of the regisseur. The supporters of the psychological problems considered the physical problems the "prose" of the theater, taking for granted that any drama student must know how to fulfill them. Vakhtangov, on the other hand, considered the physical problems the result of human imagination, of fantasy; he felt that the right adjustment prompts the actor to the necessary reaction. In life, our feelings are the reaction to what happens to us; on stage, our feeling must be born from the author's invention, which offers us an opportunity to become participants of events that did not really occur. How does one arouse in himself the necessary feelings? Only through the scenic problem. As the System teaches us, one should not "play" feelings. The feelings come as a result of scenic purpose—"I want"— and especially from the physical action taken to accomplish the "I want." With the help of our five senses, we experience taste, smell, touch, color, sound. We also remember our sensations in moments of anger, compassion, sorrow, and joy. We repeatedly experience these feelings in life. With the repetition they call for the same reaction. But repeated feelings on the stage, according to Vakhtangov, have nothing in common with the repeated feelings in life. There are only two "alive" feelings on the stage: I feel good if I live creatively, sincerely, well, those repeated feelings; or, I feel bad if I live them insincerely and badly. Vakhtangov used to say that those actors who after performing on the stage are tired and have heavy perspiration on their brows are either pretending or else acting on the stage under terrible muscle strain; their tiredness is purely physical. And we know only too well that muscular tension is not kindred to the creative state of being. Stanislavsky used to say that the correct scenic state constantly vibrates or oscillates and is similar to a plane balancing in the air, in that it must always be directed, adjusted. Now, a very experienced pilot could perform that work almost automatically. Summing up his thinking in the chapter "The Inner Scenic State," which is of great significance for the understanding of the actor's creativity, Stanislavsky quotes Salvini: "An actor lives on the stage; he cries and laughs, but while crying and ·laughing he observes his tears and his laughter. And in this duel life, in that equilibrium between life and stage, consists art."

Comparing that quotation with what Stanislavsky told us about playing Shakespeare, "While there may be five or ten minutes in a Shakespearean play in which an actor can depend exclusively on his emotions, the rest of the time an actor needs all the technique he can bring to his performance," we are becoming convinced that Stanislavsky, in 1936 and 1937, when he was completing his formulas for the laws of scenic art, was mainly occupied with the problems of the brilliancy of the scenic image and the perfection of its embodiment.

In 1920, Vakhtangov was looking for new forms and new interpretations of Chekhov's plays. The organic fusion of the school of "feeling the role" with the school of "the representation" gave very interesting results in the production of *A Wedding* in the tragicomic genre. In general, the actor's transformation necessarily combines in itself the inner mastery of the character with the illustration of it to the audience —living the role and presenting it. One has to have the correct proportion in the combination of the two systems. The more deeply I see and feel the image, the character of my role, the more vividly and strongly I strive to communicate it to the audience. The depth of the feeling is directly proportionate to the degree of its outward expressiveness. The elevated and involved genre of tragedy does not tolerate a formless art. Tragic passions demand a very definite, delineated form. The more passionate are the feelings of the hero, the more sculpturally and monumentally they must be embodied by an actor. The earlier example of Boris Godunov, in Chaliapin's delivery of that role, proves most convincingly the organic combination of feeling the role and representing it in the tragic genre. In the tragicomic genre the difficulty consists in knowing how to combine the comic and the tragic, how to support vividly expressive outward characteristics with inwardly filled comic and dramatic feelings. An actor of tragicomedy must be equally as susceptible to the dramatic or tragic as to comic or gay situations. He must be able to make the audience laugh at one moment, and in the next make it listen to him attentively and sympathetically, and a minute later reduce it to tears. When an actor frees himself from his own personality, when his "I" becomes different, when his behavior stems from the character, then his boldness, his freedom of scenic resourcefulness, is inexhaustible. The character's temperament prompts in the actor the most unexpected reactions and adjustments. The outward characteristic molds the feeling with lightning speed, no matter how unexpected it is, and directs it into the correct channel. It takes so much more courage for an actor to live in a strikingly characteristic image then to play the role "from himself," revealing his personal feelings. An actor puts himself into the situation when he is compelled to tell from the stage his personal biography, identifying the fate of the character he is playing with his own person—that is a dangerous occupation, and not always interesting for the audience.

The genre of tragicomedy is interesting also because it always verges between the tragic and the comic; that genre demands of an actor exceptional tact, taste, and a sense of proportion. The tragedian must beware of the feeling of pity for the character he is portraying: pity leads to sentimentality and tearfulness. The formula of the Greeks defines high tragedy wisely: "Tragedy with a smile on your face." How often we see a person in life behaving in some tragic situation completely differently from the way we would imagine him to behave. For example, great grief often shows no tears; then the tragedy seems so much deeper. But the definition "tragedy with a smile on your face" has also a second theatrical meaning. The state of an actor in the moment of the highest tragic expression was defined by Vakhtangov as "pleasant if I live the repeated feelings creatively, ably, well, and sincerely." Tragic moments arouse in the actor a joyous sensation of exaltation, the sensation of enthusiasm based on inspiration and causing the actor not sorrow but a creative joy. Reaction from the audience at that moment, which we define as a solemn moment, is a hearty compassion for the character, his fate, and his sorrow. On the other side of the tragicomic art is a joyous art, which gives rise to laughter. The reaction of laughter gives us a chance to test the communicativeness of our mastery of comedy. We are talking of course of the mastery of an actor who has fine taste, a sense of proportion and artistry in his adjustments. The comic temperament during the rehearsals and performances demands a high degree of fantasy and imagination, which help to bring out repeated comedy feelings. Observations of the humorous, cheerful, and gay sides of life, the capacity to see not only the obvious but also the innermost thoughts of a person are necessary, and such accumulated observations prompt an actor to the necessary adjustments, at times even born spontaneously and unexpectedly on stage. Some of the most exciting, marvelous scenes which stir an audience to peals of laughter have been born quite unexpectedly during performances.

The improvisational state of an actor is a necessary condition for comedy, since an actor must treat everything that happens to him on the stage as though totally unforeseen by him, as if it is happening for the first time—even when he is playing the role for the three-hundredth time. Naïveté, spontaneity, sincerity, and complete belief in the given circumstances of the role are the best allies of a comedian. In a comedy role, while remaining perfectly serious and believing in the given circumstances an actor wants the onlooker to see, together with him, that comic quality that he discovered in his character and in the behavior of the character. We are united with the audience by the same point of view on the comedy image. An actor by his mastery and interpretation must convince the audience that his understanding of the role is correct; this is the very essence of the art of an actor.

The depth of the comprehension of the tragic and comic in the role depends on the regisseur correctly defining the overall problem and the idea of the play, and on the actor's interpretation of the role. The overall problem of the play must be the same for the whole collective: regisseur, actors, set and costume designers, the composer, and—the audience. If the idea of the play was defined correctly by the regisseur the audience will accept it; on the contrary, the idea incorrectly conceived by the regisseur leaves the audience confused. But the overall idea of the play must not be presented nakedly or obviously, must not be labored or tendentious. With tendentiousness the artistic and ideological meaning of the play is lost. We know, I am sorry to say, a number of contemporary productions guilty of just that. Those guilty of that vice do not realize that the most important aspect of theatrical art is its emotional impact on the audience. And that impact is brought about by the action, through the precise scenic problems, through a complete image—sincere and fiery—through the emotions that are the result of action that touches the heart and awakens the thought of the audience. The overall problem is defined by the following words: "For the sake of what? For what purpose?" The author writes, the regisseur directs, the actors play their roles, and the audience watches the play which is the work of the author, the director, and the actors. After the performance the workers of the theater, the critics, and the audience sum up the result. How did Vakhtangov arrive at the overall problem of *A Wedding?*

*A Wedding*

I have already mentioned that Vakhtangov approached work on *A Wedding* feeling that there was a new way of interpreting Chekhov's play. The new audience, the post-Revolutionary audience, reacted differently to Chekhov's plays, perceived Chekhov's characters in a new way, and the awareness of the new audience decided Vakhtangov's interpretation of *A Wedding*.

Vakhtangov, not only in art but also in his personal life, proved his love for the way of life that is worthy of a human being. The son of a wealthy tobacco manufacturer, Vakhtangov gave up the tempting prospect of a rich life, left his home, and began to make a living for himself. Father and son broke off their relationship.

How many young men in pre-Revolutionary years would have relinquished the prospect of a wealthy, secure life? But for Vakhtangov, who in his student days was a member of social democratic organizations, the decision to devote himself to the life of a working man—to the arts—was only natural. The question of the social reconstruction of society excited him, although he did not have the necessary qualifications for an active revolutionary. His love for the stage, which he manifested in his school days when he appeared with amateur and semi-professional groups, finally, in spite of all the difficulties, brought him to his cherished aim: work as an actor and a regisseur. The theater gave Vakhtangov a splendid opportunity to serve society through the stage. In pre-Revolutionary years, Vakhtangov vacillated between social democratic ideas and the ideas of Leo Tolstoy; the October Revolution helped him to choose his path, that of serving the Revolutionary people. The artist who is truly searching for something cannot avoid anxiety and aggravations, and he will have his emotional ups and downs. These are unavoidable in our work. That inextinguishable fire, which reduces complacency to ashes, must burn eternally in our hearts. Throughout life Vakhtangov was impregnated with that creative restlessness. He never spared himself, dedicating himself whole-heartedly to the magnificent art of the theater; and through this art he served society and man. He was convinced that the theater that has the potential of organic growth, the theater that will leave an imperishable footprint in art, is the one that will adopt a common denominator—in direction, style, and taste—and subjugate all the components of the production to one important idea. The play of a dramatist whose ideas comprise the creative direction of the theater, a regisseur whose objective is based on the best traditions of the given theatrical collective, the scenic realization of that objective—which has a common denominator for the actors, the scenic designer, and the composer—are the main components that create the overall harmony of the performance and establish its aesthetic value. And finally—which is most important—there must be unity in the style of acting. The purpose for which this given work of theatrical art has been created must unite the whole collective.

Vakhtangov intended to present in one evening Pushkin's *Feast in Time of Plague* and Chekhov's *A Wedding*. Why? What do those two works have in common? I understood it when Vakhtangov told us about his plan of production for *Feast in Time of Plague*. We were still at the Mansurovsky Studio at that period.

A very large table at which the participants of the morbid feast are sitting during the time of the plague. They face the audience. Torches are burning, but the lights fall only on the faces of those celebrating. The actors are dressed in black costumes, which blend with the black velvet drapes. The sets—one table, some goblets, wine bottles, and torches. Those are all that is needed to mount the scene. That economy in the set allows the audience to concentrate on Pushkin's verse, which must be the first concern of the artist who presents Pushkin's work. *Feast in Time of Plague* is a dramatic poem. One should not complicate its presentation with too many

movements or use too complicated *mise en scène*. Those
would be unsuited to the style of a dramatic poem, where the
word is the cardinal component of the unfolding action. The
scenic action is expressed by the sculptural groupings of the
guests around the table. The audience's attention must be
concentrated on the verse and the faces of the people who
are feasting on the brink of death. The tragic fate of the personages of Pushkin's poem arouses in us neither terror nor
fear. The heroic behavior of those who feast is buttressed by
the chairman of the banquet in his remarkable monologue—
a challenge to the plague, Black Death.

> "Hence, praise to you, Black Death!
> We are not afraid of the darkness of the grave,
> And your summoning does not intimidate us.
> In concord, together, we fill our goblets
> And we are drinking maiden rose breath,
> Maybe . . . filled with Black Death."

The chairman of the banquet enters into the struggle with
inexorable danger. Pushkin's powerful, poetic verse is lofty
and monumental. There is also in this poem a magnificent
lyrical contrasting relief in the song of Mary:

> "There was a time
> Our country bloomed in peace,
> On Sundays our churches
> Were filled with people,
> The voices of our children
> Were heard in a noisy school
> And in our flowered fields
> Shined quick scythe and sickle."

The poet throws us into a different world here, a world of
happiness, of yesteryears; he thus underlines the tragic character of this moment.

What induced Vakhtangov to combine the production of Chekhov's *A Wedding* with Pushkin's poem? It was the contrast between the tragedy of the commonplace round of daily events and the tragedy that is heroic. He discovered the high theatricality in both genres; theatricality in which the form and content are equally important. Contrasting the daily round with the heroic would have called for a special reaction from the audience. As in paintings, the dark tones are often set off by the light colors; as in symphonies, the tragic part gains prominence because of the following scherzo, which is light and joyous. Thus the varying adjustments in one evening would have brought out its idea more in relief. The idea of it is a triumph of the free human spirit over Black Death, over the infection of the daily round. Vakhtangov was influenced in this idea by the post-Revolutionary spirit, and though the production of *Feast in Time of Plague* never materialized, he expressed that idea in *A Wedding* with immense passion. That idea permeated his whole regisseur's score of *A Wedding*.

Two rooms in the private building of the Mansurovsky Studio served as a stage; there was also a small auditorium with a capacity of fifty people. These adjoining rooms were located on the floor level with the auditorium. They proved a natural set-up for Chekhov's play. This set-up was used as the two rooms for the wedding of Aplombov and Gigalov's daughter. The tiled stove, placed obliquely in the first room, provided a suitable, decorative appearance for Andronov's second-rate restaurant. As there was not enough space for the two wedding tables in the first room, they extended, in an intricate curved line, into the next room. On the tables were placed authentic bottles of Madeira, vodka, and other beverages that bore the labels of such famous old firms as Shustova, Smirnova, and others. Table setting and candelabra were authentic. Bentwood chairs around the table were old and shabby. The light on the stage was arranged in such a way as to give the impression of being shed by kerosene lamps. Chekhov's one-act plays afford the possibility of creating the characters on the basis of rather short text material. Those are actually sketches by a virtuoso writer, in the form of a dramatic work. Plays with a number of acts portray the development of the characters in a much slower tempo. The central characters in a three- or four-act play show the beginning, growth, and conclusion of action; in this way the characters are revealed gradually. The characters in a one-act play must be immediately revealed by the actor and the regisseur; all exposition must be omitted and the characters shown fully defined in both their inner and outer design. Plays with several acts can be compared to a large river; plays in one act, to a rushing torrent. Vakhtangov started *A Wedding* with a brisk tempo. A noisy quadrille opened the play. A group of people, almost strangers to each other, danced to the shouted commands of the master of ceremonies, accompanied by the doleful, rattling sound of an out-of-tune piano. The dancers were noisy and jolly; bumping into each other, then taking off in a different direction. Yet in their noise and seeming merriment one felt an emptiness, the heartlessness of this marital feast. Vakhtangov showed in the beginning of the play a parade of the characters, and thus introduced them to the audience.

The master of ceremonies (Gorchakov), in hired tails, dances showily, his pompadour bouncing on his forehead. A sailor, Mozgovoi (Zakhava), runs at top speed, squatting rather than dancing the quadrille. A foreigner of Greek descent, a confectioner, Kharlampy Spiridonitch Dimba (Simonov), the possessor of an immense moustache, with his shock of black hair standing on end, is also dancing, but God knows what. He has much difficulty keeping in rhythm with the music. The telegraphist, Yat (Lobashkov), tears about recklessly, struggling with his feet in his endeavor to make the figure of a "pretzel." A young high school boy, who just happens to be at the party by accident, hops about gaily. The midwife, Zmeyukina (Lyaudanskaya), in a bright red dress, floats along gracefully.

That quadrille parade, which Vakhtangov introduced, brought the audience into the atmosphere of a wedding—noisy, but not really gay, as it always is at gatherings of people who have just met. Especially when they are expecting an important guest—in this case, the General.

The sound of the music stops abruptly. The master of ceremonies announces loudly: "Promenade." With the dancing stopped, the forced merriment abates. Couples disperse in all directions. Ladies in tasteless, very ordinary clothes fan themselves with cheap fans. Men fix their hair and tug at their neckties, which are all to one side. The musical "entre'-act" begins, or as it was called then, "music for the ear"; it is a fashionable waltz with the alluring name "The Young Zephyr Dancing." The waltz, in contrast to the wild quadrille, is filled with languor and anguish; it tears at one's heart.

Vakhtangov staged the first scene—the "having it out" dialogue between the bridegroom and the mother of his fiancée —with the same languor.

In an effort to avoid that conversation, the mother is pretending to be engrossed in household cares. She crosses to the wedding table, checking on the food and the drinks. But the bridegroom follows her—the unhappy victim—like a shadow. The mother, Gigalova (Schukina-Shukhmina), is dressed in a dark green silk dress and has a lace neckerchief over her hair, fastened with a pin. The bridegroom is in full dress— purchased in a secondhand store—that does not quite fit his skinny figure. Aplombov (Kudryavtzev) has a face à la Gogol, but minus the long falling hair that we are accustomed to see in portraits of that great writer. Aplombov's hair, parted in the middle, is sleeked over his forehead in the manner of a salesman who is out to conquer the fair sex.

In our century a man's hairdo does not play an important

part in his appearance, but in the period when *A Wedding* was written, the art of the barber was an extremely important one, practically a science. There was a hairdo with a part either on the side or in the center, one with a "butterfly" on the forehead, or simply short brushed-up hair. Beards *à la* King Henry, with variations; Russian beards, pointed, long, or short and semicircled; also whiskers and side-whiskers. All were popular. The moustache might be pushed up or combed down, and there was also the so-called "cockroach" moustache —a thin line on either side of the mouth. The art of the barber demanded a lot of imagination. Russian barbers, to enhance their prestige, called their enterprises "salons," and usually gave them French names, such as Salon Jean Basile, or Salon Paul.

Of course much more art was demanded of hairdressers. Ladies' long hair was set in various fashions: false hair was used—long braids, switches, and so on. The make-ups of the characters in *A Wedding* were kept strictly according to the fashion of the time. Gigalova combed her hair modestly with a part in the middle; the midwife, Zmeyukina, had a switch placed right in the center of her head; the bride-to-be, Dashenka, had her hair combed down in a cylindrical form on forehead, which gave her round and rosy face a moon-like appearance. Gigalov wore a poorly arranged small beard and a moustache which hung down dejectedly. The telegraphist, Yat, parted his very thin hair in the middle and boasted a small moustache with its ends pushed up dashingly. Dimba the Greek was the possessor of a large, luxuriant moustache and the same chevelure. Neunin had a tousled mop of hair and a moustache that thrust forward. The make-ups in *A Wedding* were exaggerated but strikingly characteristic; the costumes were most varied. Gigalov was dressed in an old-fashioned, double-breasted frock coat. Such coats were usually kept in a trunk under flake camphor and pulled out for gala occasions. Dimba the Greek was dressed in an obviously borrowed frock coat, and around his neck he had an immense red scarf tied in a bow. The telegraphist, Yat, wore a uniform. Revunov-Karaulov was in a sea officer's white tunic. The master of ceremonies was in tails, and wore a high starched collar. All this ill-assorted group of men mingled with ladies who were arrayed in dresses of striking colors, made by the cheapest dressmakers. Together they filled Andronov's cheap restaurant.

In the beginning of the play, during the quadrille, a lackey is arranging lay-outs, wine bottles, and hors d'oeuvres to the rhythm of the quadrille. The first scene, the "having it out" scene between Aplombov and Gigalova takes place around the table. In the middle of the scene Gigalova, in desperation, sinks into a chair. Aplombov stands by the chair, pounding on the back of it with the palm of his hand, as though playing an accompaniment to his words and trying to instill every word into Gigalova's consciousness. The dialogue between Zmeyukina and Yat takes place in front of the table and is accompanied by the rattling piano on which the pianist plays the waltz "The Young Zephyr." Now Zmeyukina, to keep in line with the etiquette of a woman of the world, fans herself at a rather quick nervous tempo. Lyaudanskaya, who played the role of Zmeyukina, sings the romance "I Love You" completely out of tune, and concludes her song with a piercing coloratura. On the high note, her voice breaks. Yat, seizing the fan, fans her majestically. The stylish pince-nez on his shiny nose vibrates in time with his movements. On Gigalov's cue, "Supper! Sit down," the guests move to the table and take their places.

Vakhtangov was trying to get from us the commotion characteristic of such a scene; he suggested to each one of us that we either move a chair noisily, push a plate on the table, rearrange the wine glasses, straighten our knives and forks, or reach for a napkin. All those small actions created an exceptionally realistic scene from the visual as well as the auditory aspect. As the guests are taking their places at the table the bride and groom take their seats at the center of the table, leaving a vacant seat next to the groom. This was reserved for the General who had not yet arrived. The mother takes the seat next to the bride, and the father of the bride sits next to Dimba the Greek. Zmeyukina and Yat, as guests of honor, take their seats also at the main table. At the side table, attached to the central one, were seated all those whom Neunin called, as he presented them to the General: "And others—the rest is rubbish." The master of ceremonies and the sailor Mozgovoi sat at the main table. The process of getting seated took place to the accompaniment of a bravura march. At last came the much anticipated hour for the guests: hors d'oeuvres are on the table and the glasses are filled with vodka, but to the annoyance of the guests they must postpone the joy of drinking it until after the speeches. Luckily the first speech is short and laconic because the speaker, the sailor Mozgovoi, is also most impatient to drink that first glass of vodka and to follow it with caviar and fillet of sturgeon. The sailor, rising, says: "Let us not wait, and begin right away. Ladies and Gentlemen: I propose a toast to the bride and groom!" The band played a short flourish. There was a clinking of glasses; then shouts of *"Bitter!"* caused an unimaginable din. *"Bitter! Bitter!"** Exclamations come from all sides of the table. The bride, as becomes a well-brought-up maiden, blushes with embarrassment. The groom, who is unhappy about the manner in which the wedding is arranged, and particularly because of the absence of the General, kisses the bride resentfully. He does it condescendingly, as if lowering himself to the level of a society unworthy of him. But the kiss is reacted to with laughter and applause and exclamations of "Bravo! Bravo!" Zmeyukina even screams

---

* The cry *"Bitter!"* at a Russian wedding is a signal for the bride and groom to kiss.

from pleasure. The general enthusiasm is followed by an exciting word from the telegraphist, Yat. After praising "a splendid party in a splendid setting" he touches upon the burning, topical question of electricity: "But you know what is missing to complete the celebration? Electric lights, excuse my expression." That phrase occasions an inconceivable uproar.

Vakhtangov spaced the gradation and strict succession of steps in the oncoming squabble with amazing exactness. On Yat's cue about electricity, Gigalov venemously retorts: "In my opinion, electric light is nothing but a swindle." At that moment, Aplombov, who is very unhappy with Yat's presence and only looking for an excuse to vex the telegraphist, says that he is in complete agreement with "Papa"; scientific discussions are out of place at a wedding. "One should choose a different time for them." Madame Gigalova, who does not quite grasp what the argument is about, assumes that Yat's remarks are addressed to her and she takes them as a personal insult, as a reproach to her lack of education. "Why do you have to come here," she says in anger, "if you think we are uneducated? Better to go to your educated friends." Yat tries to justify himself, but he gets more and more involved. Anxious to prove his respect for Gigalov's family, he reminds them that he always wished for a good groom for their daughter and that it is very difficult nowadays to find a good man. "It isn't easy these days when everyone aims to enter matrimony for strictly practical reasons—for money," he says. This remark stirs unexpected reactions. Aplombov retorts: "That is an insinuation!" The misunderstanding flares and grows to a point where it threatens the peace of the whole group. Everyone at the party attempts to calm the opponents and reconcile them. Several guests rush to the side of the groom and others rush to the side of the telegraphist. Over-shouting them all and attempting to prove his objectivity as far as Aplombov is concerned, Yat finally pronounces a decisive statement: "For goodness' sake, everyone knows you are marrying for love; the dowry is so small." That last remark transforms Madame Gigalova into a quarrelsome, vengeful old shrew. "No! Not small by any means!" she shouts. "And if you knew that Aplombov was marrying our Dashenka for her money, why didn't you say so before?" At that point, she bursts out sobbing; leaning over her daughter she cries, "Oh, my emerald! My diamond!" Aplombov reproaches Gigalova: "You believe him?!" he demands. He throws a menacing order to Yat: "If you should please me, get out!" With an affective gesture, he shows him the doors. A dozing pianist, taking Aplombov's exclamation for a command, hits the keys with a powerful flourish. The squabble reaches the culmination point. Aplombov and Yat rush at each other: the ladies, terror-stricken, shriek; the men endeavor to hold the combatants apart. Music thunders. Everyone is moving about. Vakhtangov leaves only one figure motionless, as a contrast to the general commotion: the phlegmatic bride. She remains at the table, eating imperturbably and watching the quarrel impassively. Finally, with enormous effort, the master of ceremonies restores order. A toast to the parents of the bride is picked up enthusiastically by all the guests, and the piano plays a flourish.

I entered the Vakhtangov Theater at the time when the rehearsals of *A Wedding* were in full swing. A novice, sitting in the auditorium, I watched with excitement Vakhtangov's remarkable staging of this scene and the others. Group scenes are the test of a director's skill. Great ability is required to organize the ensemble; to unite every member of a group scene in a common scenic problem without depriving an actor of his individuality; to fix the right *mise en scène*; set the rhythm, tempo, and climaxes. All these tasks are very complicated and demand outstanding directorial talent. Temperament is needed, also a sense of proportion; and, above all, superlative taste. Vakhtangov possessed all those qualities.

Over thirty years have passed since those rehearsals took place, but I can see Vakhtangov in front of me, rehearsing, as if it all occurred just a short while ago; my youthful memory was so deeply impressed with the high art that filled the rehearsal hours in the small hall of the Mansurovsky Studio. The rehearsals lasted for four or five hours without interruption. They were usually held in the evening, and the hours flew by because our remarkable teacher handled those rehearsals with so much inspiration and such high creative enthusiasm, and with no trace of fatigue. For some reason, in connection with the scene described above, there comes to my memory the quarrel scene between Onegin and Lensky, in Tchaikovsky's opera *Eugene Onegin*. The dramatic development of the quarrel between the two friends is given amazing cumulative growth: the dialogue against a musical background; the transition from the dialogue to Lensky's aria, with the gradual joining in of an ensemble and then the chorus; the orchestral colors getting more and more intense with the brass instruments and the rhythm becoming more and more rapid.

Vakhtangov was exceptionally musical; he loved both opera and ballet. He frequented the Bolshoi Theater. He loved romance and song. He played a number of instruments. I believe that the musicality of *A Wedding, The Miracle of St. Anthony,* and especially *Turandot,* was due to Vakhtangov's organic sense of rhythm, his delicate appreciation of music. He had an excellent ear for music and could not only pick up a tune quickly but also thoroughly understood the complicated orchestration of the musical composition. That understanding of the orchestration is as important for a regisseur of drama as for a conductor of opera or symphony. Thanks to that gift, Vakhtangov's productions excelled in a special musical formation, in theatricality, in true realism as opposed to a naturalistic, common, everyday style. The scenic truth is not a precise duplication of life truth.

The scenic truth is a truth which while prompted by life is reborn anew in the thoughts and feelings of an artist; theatrical truth. Isn't that remarkable phrase of Chekhov's (one has to ponder every word of it) : "If you should please me, get out!" a theatrical truth? Let us see what Chekhov suggests to the regisseur and the actors: "Gigalov cries; Gigalova cries." Vakhtangov directed an old woman, a hanger-on, a character with no lines, to cry too at that moment. And that scene is concluded with Yat's phrase: "Just think what human tears are! A faint-hearted psychasthenia and nothing more." The storm is over.

There comes a moment after the uproar and tears when the guests, to gloss over the unpleasant effect, suggest that Dimba the Greek deliver a speech. What does the Greek talk about? His speech is incoherent; the words are disconnected. But with those disconnected words he attempts to confide both his homesickness and his sincere love for Russia and the Russian man. He sees good in everything; he doesn't even notice the bad—and because of that he is loved by everyone. At first, he refuses to talk. He is embarrassed and holds onto his seat, but those next to him force him to get up. He doesn't know how to begin: He pours himself a glass of vodka, takes a piece of salami and puts it on a fork, he gulps some water, then he forgets about the salami altogether and, finally, completely embarrassed, begins his speech. He talks most enthusiastically. All the guests give him their complete attention, expecting something unusually funny from him. They react to his every phrase with laughter. He ends his speech with the same phrase with which he started: "I can say such . . . which is Russia and which is Greece. . . ." The generous applause grows into an ovation.

Vakhtangov suggested to Schukin, who played Gigalov, that he rush over to the Greek and kiss him. Schukin embraces the Greek and kisses him three times, adhering to Russian tradition. Vakhtangov developed the *mise en scène* further by directing the telegraphist Yat to give Dimba a large glass of wine. Zmeyukina blew kisses to Dimba, accompanying them with exclamations of "Bravo! Encore!" Her coquetry and laughter fill Dimba with much pleasure. Dimba's appearance was turned by the regisseur into the central event of *A Wedding*.

This seemed to all of us so right. We know only too well that the kind of people who gather at a wedding have a weakness for anything that is foreign. Dimba the Greek represented an exotic phenomenon to this Philistine gathering. Who knows how long the ovation would have lasted if Neunin did not rush in, tremendously excited, and announce: "Wait, people! Stop eating! Stop everything."

This new event moved the spectacle in another and even more elated rhythm. The climax of the play is beginning. Neunin is bringing information about the arrival of the long-awaited General. Informing the mother with an excited whisper that at last he had found a genuine general, Neunin begins to relate the exciting story of his conversation with the General. He addresses everyone present. Being an agent with an insurance company, Neunin was an expert at this kind of talk—his profession had trained him well for it. The guests listened to the glorious news of the arrival of the General: Such luck! Such honor! The wedding was acquiring tremendous significance. Each of the guests was beginning to feel as though he were climbing several steps higher on the social ladder, becoming a different person. Neunin sees Revunov-Karaulov entering the door. As the commander of a parade, Neunin shouts in a long-drawn-out manner: "Musicians—a march!" Bravura music thunders forth. The guests, stepping on one another's toes, rush forward toward the General. Each one is trying to get close to him, to be in the "field of vision" of this person of high rank. Vakhtangov directed that scene in a satirical, grotesque manner. The yearning to be close to a person of importance, to make the acquaintance of a general, or a celebrity, is not unknown, alas, in our days also. A general at the wedding, I regret to say, is still not an old-fashioned idea for a satirical work.

An old sailor, half-blind, Revunov stops in the center of the stage in front of the wedding table. Next to him, as it becomes an aide-de-camp, stands Neunin erect. On the General's left stand the bride and groom. The faces of all the guests are wreathed in artificial smiles. Some of the guests assume a servile pose, bowing down—as do Gigalov, Neunin, and the master of ceremonies. Some of the others—the sailor Mozgovoi and the telegraphist Yat—tighten up in a military manner like soldiers during a parade standing at attention in front of a chief. The General holds out his hand and in his senile voice says softly: "Delighted, much delighted." In contrast to the pomposity that Neunin tried to create, Basov—who played the role of Revunov—was simple, bashful, the picture of a humble man who lives alone and goes out into society very seldom.

Neunin—who is a cunning rogue—is introducing guests to the General, pointing at some with an imperious gesture, and pulling others negligently by the hand out of the group. Those who were honored by being thus introduced, such as Aplombov, the bride, Yat, and Dimba the Greek move back to their seats radiant, thrilled by the honor bestowed on them. The rest of the guests, whom Neunin called "nothings," just creep away. The General is very confused by the magnificent reception. He takes Neunin aside and whispers to him: "I, Brother, am a little embarrassed. Why do you all address me as 'Your Honor'? I am not a general; I am a captain of the second rank. You know, that is even beneath a colonel." Neunin whispers back—God forbid anyone might overhear their conversation—"I know, but Feodor Yakovlevitch, please, allow us to continue to address you as 'Your Honor.' This family, you know, is patriarchal and respects elders. They also love and honor rank." Once more thanking all those present, Revunov, bowing right and left, is led to the center of the table by Neunin, where he takes his honored seat. A reverential silence falls. The long-awaited happiness is here—the General is at the wedding, surrounded by Gigalov, Aplombov, and Yat. These little people are growing in their own eyes.

Vakhtangov defined the genre of the play *A Wedding* as tragicomic, and found in his interpretation of the play not only comic and satiric but also dramatic colors. All the frightening narrow-mindedness of this group of people at times aroused pity. In his production of *Deluge,* in the First Studio of the Moscow Art Theater, Vakhtangov brought out the idea that when people face a deadly danger they change, become more sensitive, more attentive, and more considerate of each other. Undoubtedly, this same theme continued to excite him when he was working on *A Wedding.*

The arrival of the General is in some degree the fulfillment of a dream about a more beautiful life. The General's presence at the wedding gives Chekhov's characters the opportunity to re-evaluate themselves. Aplombov's question to the General: "How long since you retired?" sounded as though it came from a different Aplombov, a much more dignified one. On the other hand, Vakhtangov was developing a servile attitude on the part of some of the other personages. A simple question that Revunov put to Mozgovoy: "You must be a sailor?" made Mozgovoi jump from his seat and stand at attention and report with his hackneyed soldiery: "Just so." The servility of these people manifests itself when Neunin raises a toast "to the health of the Honorable Feodor Yakovlevitch Revunov." A flourish thunders: "Hurrah!" The cheer rolls all along the table. The guests leave their seats, crowding around the General, anxious to clink glasses with him, their hands stretched out over each other's shoulders and heads in an effort to do so. The excitement lasts for a long time. But then, the resourceful Yat attracts everyone's attention with his tale about the difficulties of a telegrapher's job.

All those elements made a very entertaining scene. Yat, excited by his story about his profession, begins to tap out a telegraphic message on a plate with his fingers. He keeps tapping for quite a few moments; everyone in the room listens attentively. It made a very impressive *mise en scène*. Gigalov listens to Yat's tapping with a spiteful smile, as if saying: "Here he goes again, showing off his education." Aplombov listens with envy and displeasure; he is irritated that Yat is attracting the guests' attention again. The bride stares at her plate, a dull expression on her face, and continues chewing her food, like a grazing cow in a meadow. Dimba the Greek listens as if he were hypnotized, his mouth wide open. The General, who is hard-of-hearing, puts his hand to his ear, saying: "Please, louder. I can't hear you!"

What was it Yat tapped out on his plate? He tells them: "The first telegram reads, 'I respect you, your Honor, for your goodness.'" That explanation arouses a respectful, modest, servile murmur, the sign of great pleasure. "The second sentence means, 'Madame, I am so happy holding you in my arms.'" That brings a light laugh from the more tactful people and a gross guffaw from those less delicate. Once more Yat turns out to be the cause of misunderstanding, which ends with a complete catastrophe. He forces old Revunov to tell the story of his profession, that of captain of a military ship. From that moment until the end of the play the old naval officer, excited by his recollections, talks ecstatically about how remarkable life in the navy fleet was. He goes on and on, even illustrating the captain's behavior when he gives the most varied orders to the naval crew. In the beginning the host and hostess and all the guests listen patiently, out of respect. The story holds no interest for them, being about things completely unfamiliar to them. But after a while they grow tired and begin to express their displeasure.

Here again Vakhtangov displays the richness of his imagination and the resourcefulness of a fine regisseur. For this second squabble which is brewing, Vakhtangov uses completely new colors. While the first squabble erupted spontaneously, irrepressibly, in the second, displeasure is expressed first with restraint. After all the General is talking. The hard-of-hearing General does not of course hear that murmur. But finally Gigalova, losing her patience, speaks up: "Even though you are a general, you are behaving outrageously. You should be ashamed of yourself at your advanced age!" The General hears this outburst and, slightly intoxicated, he announces candidly: "In the first place, I am not a general, but a captain of the second rank, which, according to the military table of ranks, is equal to a lieutenant colonel."

At those words, an ominous silence falls. Everyone is strained, anticipating a dreadful outburst. All feel disgraced by this unheard-of deception, this swindle. Attention, honor, and respect have been extended not to a general but to an ordinary captain. Retribution is due and it is coming. Madame Gigalova, whose idea it had been to invite a general to the wedding, is the first one to attack "the culprit." "If you are not a general, what did you take the money for? We didn't pay you money to see you carrying on like this," she says. Aplombov steps in more resolutely: "However, with your permission, you received twenty-five rubles from Neunin."

Revunov does not immediately grasp what it is that he is being accused of. But at last he understands, and Basov (the performer who played the role of the "General") delivers with strength and profound emotion the fiery monologue of an honest, undeservedly insulted man. The General's phrase: "Man! help me out of here. Man!" Basov exclaimed with tremendous power, at Vakhtangov's suggestion. One got the feeling that Revunov was calling for help, addressing mankind as a whole. Wrongly accused, crushed by suspicion, the General is asking for a man to come forward and defend his honor and re-establish justice. But this outcry remains unanswered, suspended in mid-air. A long pause follows. The miserable old man, humiliated by these emotionally sick people, gazes around him, looking for support, for compassion, for protection. But no one moves. After a moment, he gropes his way from the table, crosses the room as though in pain, and exits on the far side of the stage as though going into oblivion. All those on stage turn their backs to the audience and with their eyes follow the departing figure of the old captain. Another weighty pause ensues. Then Madame Gigalova turns to Neunin and asks him very directly, even with a trace of sincere sadness in her voice: "Andrushenka, where are the twenty-five rubles?" Neunin, who kept this money, has no way out but to turn this tragic event into a joke: "Does it pay to talk about such nonsense? It does not matter in the least. Everyone is enjoying himself, and you carry on about trifles." He raises his glass: "To the happy young people! Musicians! Music! A march!"

The musicians do not play a march, but execute the same quadrille with which the play commenced. This time they play it sadly in slow tempo. Zmeyukina repeats the phrase she used earlier: "I am suffocated. Give me atmosphere. I am suffocating, people, near you!" But this time she delivers her speech in a melancholy tone, without a shadow of coquetry, as if summing up all that had been lived through that evening of the wedding. And Yat exclaims: "Wonderful one! Oh, wonderful one!" The characters of the play now stand motionless with their backs to the audience; the dream is no more. In this world one cannot attract a genuine general even with money. Softer and softer sounds the sad quadrille. The feast is over; the working week begins. Thus Vakhtangov brought to an end the remarkable one-act play, *A Wedding*, by Anton Chekhov.

There are two plays created by two great Russian writers, Chekhov and Dostoevsky, on the same theme—a general at a wedding. The same plot is used, but the plays are completely different in both the essence of the basic idea and its realization. Chekhov's *A Wedding* is imbued with a subtle and, at times, bitter humor; the one-act play by Dostoevsky, *A Nasty Joke*, is written with a cruel, sarcastic, and merciless pen. In this play Ivan Ilyich Pralinsky, a general, is forced to walk home because his driver is delayed. Passing the house of one of his subordinates, Pralinsky decides to make the small functionary happy by attending his wedding. From that moment, a chain of incredible events begins. On the threshold of the functionary's house, the General treads upon a galantine placed in a passageway to cool off. That is the beginning of the mishaps and the bad luck of the General. With his usual consistency Dostoevsky unfolds the gradual downfall of the General from the heights of his grandeur. Dostoevsky misses no detail, not one characteristic trait, not one chance to horsewhip the General in a most painful manner. He brings Pralinsky (the General) to a "nasty joke," putting him deadly drunk on the bed of the newly-weds, and thus forcing the bride and groom to spend their first night on chairs. We are in complete accord with the manner in which Dostoevsky deals with his high-ranking nonentity. The petty small officials—the host, hostess, and their guests at the wedding—were treated by Dostoevsky with the same intense, biting, and implacable condemnation. The result is an irreparable, black picture of human degradation.

*A Nasty Joke* needs for its scenic embodiment a sharp, grotesque form, similar to the expressive art of Goya. For the scenic embodiment of Chekhov's *A Wedding*, a remarkable Russian painter, Fedotov, with his creative singularity would be the right person. We see that different styles of literary work prompt different forms for their scenic embodiment, even though the theme chosen by the writers is similar and uses the same social background. The sustained, definite style of Vakhtangov's interpretation and embodiment of *A Wedding* made his production a true masterpiece.

## A Wedding

That production played a very important role in the development and the formation of the Vakhtangov Theater. In the process of work on that production the young group understood Vakhtangov's discovery of the application of the Stanislavsky Method to plays of striking theatrical character. The organic justification of images created by means of exaggeration and grotesque became clear to us and seemed natural. That spectacle taught us to appreciate and value the mastery of the inner and outer technique in all its aspects; mastery without which the complete accomplishment of various genres of dramaturgy and their embodiment on the stage is impossible.

The production of *A Wedding* had a tremendous influence on a number of works directed by Vakhtangov's disciples. In the first instance, we see a kindred tie between *A Wedding* and *Egor Bulitchev and Others,* by Gorky, as produced by B. Zakhava, in 1932. In *A Wedding* Vakhtangov depicted that blind alley, that airless atmosphere of the petty Philistine environment of old Russia; in *Egor Bulitchev and Others,* Schukin, who played Bulitchev, extended the tragicomic line of Vakhtangov's *A Wedding* and broadened its scope to show the agony of the old pre-Revolutionary class in its death hours. The manner of the actor's execution and the regisseur's conception and realization of Bulitchev one may define as realistic, but it also at times included both stressed and grotesque treatments. The routine activity in the life of the Bulitchev family was broken by the demented explosions of Bulitchev's irrepressible, despotic temper. Recall Bulitchev's dance scene, also his scenes with Trubatch, Zobunovoy, and Propotiem.

The influence of Vakhtangov's *A Wedding* was also visible in such productions as *Front,* by A. Korneytshuk, in 1942, of which I was the regisseur. There was no curtain. The audience upon entering the auditorium saw a large oval table with chairs placed around it, the setting for a meeting or perhaps for a lawsuit. The character of Gorlov was the central figure, around whom there was an exciting discussion. Alexey Diki portrayed that character in the best tradition of Vakhtangov's conception of theater art. Gorlov was the epitome of the man who cannot see himself objectively, cannot see his defects, his limitations. Gorlov symbolizes the penetration of the Philistine psychology into the Soviet mode of life; he represents a kind of contemporary general who feels he is above Soviet society. Because of that, he surrounds himself with people who encourage that quality of a "General" in him. In the party scene in Gorlov's apartment, we see the following guests: a tenor who sings a romance to please the "General"; a correspondent who participates in a sycophantic procession-march in honor of "General" Gorlov and zealously beats the cymbals to the rhythm of the music. We see, directly subordinate to Gorlov, the military men who create an atmosphere of rank-worshiping and idolization around their "General."

What I had learned from Vakhtangov during the rehearsals of *A Wedding* helped me to find the correct scenic embodiment of the play *Front*. The traditions of Vakhtangov's production of *A Wedding* live also in the work of the theater of the present day in the play *On the Golden Bottom*, adapted from the novel by Mamin-Sybiryak.

Vakhtangov considered that a narrow professional attitude in the theater was not permissible. The theater for him was life itself; he served humanity through the theater. One of the sicknesses of contemporary acting is "professionalism." Students who came into the theater merely to show off and achieve a cheap success Vakhtangov used to criticize severely and in front of the whole theater collective, and he spared neither time nor himself in order to straighten out a student who had lost the high aim of true art. The high, exalted aim of creativity gives birth to a singular atmosphere in the theater, an atmosphere of great spiritual uplift. Vakhtangov strove for such atmosphere and because of that all the little things of everyday life in the theater were extremely important to him. He knew all the workers in the theater, and he personally selected each one of them for his job. We, the eldest Vakhtangovites, remember how once upon leaving the sanitarium he brought with him Feodor Alexeyich. When he introduced Feodor to us he told us that Feodor had kept the sanitarium immaculately clean and that he was a very reliable worker. And true enough Feodor kept our studio on Arbat Street in ideal order.

To build a theater one must be concerned with every little thing in the theater. When Vakhtangov was alive, we had an excellent tradition of duties: behind the stage, in the halls, and in the wardrobe student-actors had their duties. I love to recall my first work in the studio before I appeared on the stage: my duty was behind the stage in the men's dressing room. The main person on duty at that time was Schukin, who instructed me in all my responsibilities during a performance: first, to watch for order and silence; second, to distribute make-up, vaseline, powder, and other essentials. I also had to provide props needed during the day. After the performance, Schukin gave his approval of my first "appearance" in the studio; he informed me that I had fulfilled all my duties very well. His praise made me very happy and I felt that I had executed a good deed for the studio, even though it was a very small one. A month later when I played my first acting role, I understood how important the backstage atmosphere is for an actor. That atmosphere helps an actor to concentrate on the vital creative process. I realized then how those on duty backstage contribute to this atmosphere. The individual on duty at the stage door entrance was also considered very important. His obligation was to prevent anyone not involved in the play from entering. One evening a very young student was on duty at the stage door when Nemirovitch-Dantchenko was about to enter, but the young student, true to her duty, would not let him in. Dantchenko asked her, "Do you know who I am?" The young student answered, "You are Nemirovitch-Dantchenko, but I cannot let you backstage. Such are our rules."

Nemirovitch-Dantchenko did not take it as an insult. On the contrary, after the performance he praised the young student in the presence of the whole collective. Nemirovitch-Dantchenko knew only too well that most responsible commandment—"Theater begins from the cloakroom."

Did not this atmosphere of silence backstage during performances and rehearsals, the strict order, the thoroughly trained attending staff, administrators, box-office people, wardrobe attendants, the way in which the audience was received in the Moscow Art Theater, contribute to that extraordinary impression that the performances of the Moscow Art Theater made on the audience when Stanislavsky was alive? There can be no doubt that it did. I am sorry to say that those high standards are no longer observed by many theaters. We must restore that atmosphere that reigned in the theater—on both sides of the footlights—revive the strict rules and principles that existed in the Moscow Art Theater and the Vakhtangov Studio when our teachers were alive. Vakhtangov, in the first years of the Revolution, appreciated collective management of the theater. A theater created in the name of one person, be he an actor or a regisseur, will necessarily become the theater of the guest-actor. The provincial traditions of one guest-actor subjecting the whole company to his personal advantages and success deprive the theater of an ensemble; hence, of an artistic value. Apart from the "legitimate" guest-actors, when a famous actor surrounds himself with inferior actors, there exists a concealed form of the same phenomenon. This happens when the guest-performer, in so-called ensemble, sets himself above the collective, shows no consideration for the rest of the company, breaks working discipline and ethical standards of behavior. While we do not have in our theaters now the actor-guest of the old provincial kind, we certainly have those actor-guests of the new formation. One hears often in our theaters about young actors who after two or three years of working in a certain theater, or after their first successful role, begin to shout at a wardrobe attendant, the make-up artist, or the stagehands. It could never have happened while Vakhtangov was alive. He would have expelled that kind of actor on the first provocation. We also see actors now who perform in a slipshod manner, sparing themselves during performances. What disrespect for the audience those actors exhibit who consider themselves indispensable; hence, immune from punishment. It could never have happened while Stanislavsky and Vakhtangov lived. It could never have happened because those two great artists considered the moral make-up of an actor as important as his talent.

Our work on Chekhov's *A Wedding* was significant for a number of us because in the period of preparation for that play we began to learn from Vakhtangov the art of a regisseur. In our studio a special regisseur's group was set up, which Vakhtangov directed. He always used to say that in order to become a regisseur one must go through an acting school and for a certain time "live in the actor's skin"; that one must understand through one's own experience what is a correct and what is not a correct scenic state of being, and to experience the communion between actors. Vakhtangov held that a regisseur must know at first hand everything that is connected with the theater: all that complicated and vast "household" behind the scenes; the art of producing a play; everything that has to do with sets, wardrobe, props, the electrical department, and so on. A regisseur he believed must be acquainted with all his administrative and other working personnel; he must know how to meet his audience. But, most important, a regisseur must be up to date; he must have an all-around education, be well read, have a thorough knowledge of social and political science as well as aesthetics, and be acquainted with the history of art, painting, sculpture, and architecture. Vakhtangov considered that it was very important that a regisseur should have a knowledge of National Russian and Western European literature and dramaturgy. Literature widens the horizon and enriches the fantasy of an actor and a regisseur. In order to recreate on the stage the mode of life, the costumes, the morals and manners of different epochs, one must know the national peculiarities and the culture of each nation. How can one understand the characters, let us say, in Shakespeare's plays without knowing Shakespeare thoroughly, without knowing the literature written about him, as well as the rich galaxy of dramatists of the Shakespearean epoch; also the artists and painters of the Renaissance who were kindred to Shakespeare. How can one play Pushkin's *Boris Godunov* without first studying the conceptions of the different Russian historians, which throw conflicting light on the figure of the Tzar and on the complicated question regarding the death of Tzarevitch Dimitri? Vakhtangov strongly opposed the formula, "I, in given circumstances," as an end in itself; a formula that gives an actor the right to play himself in Shakespeare's *Hamlet* or Chekhov's *Treplev*. The knowledge of the singularities of a given dramatist, his epoch, its customs and morals, and a special preparation for the embodiment of that genre in which the play was written—those were all requirements which Vakhtangov demanded of his student-regisseurs. He was an enemy of the regisseur theorists who, acquainted with actors' work solely through book-knowledge, during rehearsals read to their cast scientific lectures which contribute nothing to the actor's mind or heart. Our schools for regisseurs should increase the number of hours of the regisseur's practice instead of having them spend excessive time on theoretical subjects.

At that period of our theatrical youth, Vakhtangov taught us one more important art—the art of listening to criticism.

| 76

Vakhtangov himself was a magnificent critic; his analysis of performances and the notes he gave to actors contained useful, constructive comments which helped an actor find the right path. At that period *The Miracle of St. Anthony* and *A Wedding* ran on the same evening. Often he would come to see the two plays and then remain and talk to the performers, thoroughly analyzing the work of each actor. And he gave his time and attention not only to those who played leading roles, but also to those who played episodic roles or were only in group scenes. His criticism had one aim: to help the young actor. But he used different means with each one. Criticizing the new productions in other theaters, Vakhtangov examined the production and the acting from the standpoint of the aims established by that creative collective. This perceptive perspective is often lacking in the critical articles of our day. Only too often we read reviews or hear remarks made by our critics in discussing plays in general, regardless of a particular theater's handwriting. Vakhtangov held that one should not evaluate all the productions from the same standpoint without taking into account the direction and the creative singularities of the theater, whether it were the Moscow Art Theater, the Maly Theater, the Kamerni Theater, the Theater of Meyerkhold, or any of the others. Finding merits and demerits in the productions of these various theaters, Vakhtangov first determined whether the given direction of the particular theater brought out to the full the actor's potentialities in his work on a character. For example, Vakhtangov severely criticized the Kamerni Theater for their neglect of the actor's inner qualities, for their concentration on the visual to the detriment of the content, which, from his point of view, resulted in a soulless, mannered form. He asserted that the skill of a director is to unfold the content of the play and to find a corresponding form for the given dramatic material.

What was Vakhtangov's position in regard to theatrical

criticism? That under no circumstances should an artist place his head under the axe. An artist, in the question of principles, must uphold his creative·position and never give in, no matter how much the pen of the critic may flay him. Vakhtangov himself was subjected to merciless, petty criticism for a number of his productions, including *A Wedding*. We, his students today, can only admire the staunchness of our teacher who in spite of everything courageously accomplished on the stages of the theater a tragic *Dybbuk* and a sunny, buoyant *Princess Turandot*.

After the death of its teacher, the Vakhtangov Theater continued to live and flourish. It had failures and successes, creative joys and deep disappointments. At times we lost the path outlined by our teacher, but the fault was not always ours. At that period when the trend toward conformity was widespread in theatrical direction, there were even those among our comrades who thought that Vakhtangov's theater should accept those faceless positions. We went through periods of stagnation and complacency; but the ashes of Klass knocked at our hearts as they knocked at the heart of Till Eulenspiegel, reminding us of the passionate fire of love for our people, the art of Eugene Vakhtangov.

Vakhtangov's work on *A Wedding* was to us, the witnesses of his work and participators in it, a theatrical university. During the rehearsals of *A Wedding*, we learned from our teacher how to create characters both true and grotesque; we learned about the inwardly inspired and outwardly expressive mastery of an actor. We understood the enormous significance of the penetration into the singularities of the style of a given dramatist, and how only precise art can reveal the essence of the creativity of one or another dramatist in the contemporary form of his play. We absorbed the unique conception of Chekhov's comedies and tragedies. We were exposed to lessons in the sphere of working with an actor by a most articulate regisseur. And above all, we were learning to

build a theater, to be true to our principles in critical evalua-
tions of the works of other artists and our own. Vahktangov
was training our taste in all areas of theater life.

We often recollect the title of Vakhtangov's remarkable
essay "The Artist's Responsibility," and this title is a constant
reminder to each one of us of our responsibility to our audience—that responsibility which is ideological, artistic, and
ethical. Let those words, "artist's responsibility," live in our
hearts and be indelibly imprinted in our memory. We are
passing on to the young generation the scepter of Vakhtangov's service to the theater, and we are repeating for our
youth's edification the words of our teacher, "artist's responsibility." When the feeling of contemporaneity leaves us, when
we forget what we are giving our life to the theater for, let
those words be lit up before our thoughtful gaze—"artist's
responsibility."

For Stanislavsky and Nemirovitch-Dantchenko, who so
convincingly produced Chekhov's plays in the Moscow Art
Theater before the Revolution, Chekhov was the dramatist
who struggled against commonplaceness and Philistinism,
and who dreamed of a better life. "That struggle for a better
life and striving for it became the overall aim of many of his
works," wrote Stanislavsky. For Vakhtangov, who directed
Chekhov after the great October Revolution, the overall
problem of Chekhov's plays was a struggle with the entire
regime of life that was carried over from the old Russia, a
struggle for the assertion of the new human relationships
that came to life with the Revolution.

# Part II

# Vakhtangov Directs

# *The Miracle of St. Anthony*
## by Maurice Maeterlinck

THE ANTEROOM in a rich bourgeois house in a small provincial town. Against the white wall is a clothes rack on which hang black coats, black hats, and black derbies. The house is in mourning. An old aunt, Mademoiselle Hortensia, has passed away. In the dining room, a funeral repast is in progress; all the relatives are gathered for the mourning dinner. In the anteroom, a maid, Virginia, scrubs the floor with a large brush and now and then wipes her tears with the corner of her apron. The bell is heard. Virginia opens the door. On the threshold stands a tall, emaciated old man, barefooted, with no hat, and dressed in a long sackcloth garment that is colorless and in many places patched. This garment looks like something between the traditional garment of a saint—as is shown in pictures of the Renaissance— and an old dressing gown. The opening dialogue between Virginia and Anthony immediately introduces the audience to an unusual event.

VIRGINIA: Well, what is it? God bless us! Another beggar! What are you after?

ST. ANTHONY: Let me in.

VIRGINIA: No, your feet are muddy. Stay out there. What do you want?

ST. ANTHONY: To enter.

VIRGINIA: What for?

ST. ANTHONY: To restore Mlle. Hortensia to life.

VIRGINIA: To restore Mlle. Hortensia to life? Go along! Who are you?

ST. ANTHONY: Blessed St. Anthony.

VIRGINIA: Of Padua?

ST. ANTHONY: The same. (*His halo glows and brightens*)

VIRGINIA: Jesus! Jesus! And his mother Mary!

Well! Well! (*The old maid lets* ST. ANTHONY *in, kneels before him and begins to pray*) Blessed St. Anthony, have pity on us. Pray for us, blessed St. Anthony. Pray for us. (*Suddenly her religious outburst changes into a severe order*) Well, wipe your feet there on the mat!

She promptly adjusts herself to the unusual guest and tells him all about the death of her mistress and about the two-million inheritance left to the two nephews, M. Gus and M. Achilles. In her chatter she almost forgets to ask the most important thing: Why did Anthony come? But at last she gets around to it.

> VIRGINIA: What do you want for her?
> ST. ANTHONY: To raise her up from the dead.
> VIRGINIA: Then there will be no heirs.
> ST. ANTHONY: Yes.
> VIRGINIA: But what will M. Gus say to that?
> ST. ANTHONY: I don't know.
> VIRGINIA: And my three thousand three-hundred that she left me! Will she take it back?
> ST. ANTHONY: Yes.
> VIRGINIA: That is too bad.
> ST. ANTHONY: If you are afraid you will lose three thousand francs . . .
> VIRGINIA: Three thousand three-hundred francs.
> ST. ANTHONY: If you are afraid you will lose them, I will not resurrect Mlle. Hortensia.
> VIRGINIA: Couldn't you arrange it so she could live and I needn't lose the money?
> ST. ANTHONY: No, one thing or the other. I have heard your prayers and returned to earth, Virginia, and you must choose.
> VIRGINIA: Well, then . . . resurrect her!

The exposition of the play introduces the spectators to

extraordinary events, unheard of in everyday life. At the same time, the scene between St. Anthony and Virginia sounds realistic, very simple, as though it were not about the resurrection of the dead but, let us say, about the visit of an attending doctor. Virginia's relation to St. Anthony quickly takes on a completely friendly character. She even begins to use him as a helper, ordering him to bring a pail of water and to rearrange the furniture. The lonely old woman has no one to talk to and now she's glad to have the opportunity for a friendly chat. She tells the visitor about everything: about the dead woman, about her numerous relatives who have gathered for the funeral, about the menu for the day's mourning dinner, and even what kind of wine is being served. One feels her enjoyment in the conversation, her delight in having a chance to communicate with an attentive listener. In this episode one is aware how very lonely this woman is, how seldom she is accorded any attention. But then comes the moment when she loses this attentive companion. The dinner nears the end; the manservant, Joseph, carries a partridge to the dining room. Virginia kneels in front of the Saint.

VIRGINIA: Now, Sir, I would like to ask you . . .

ST. ANTHONY: Speak, do not be afraid.

VIRGINIA: Give me your blessing, Sir, now, as we're alone. When the company comes in, I'll be sent out of the room, and I won't see you any more. I'm old and I need your blessing badly.

ST. ANTHONY: I bless you, my daughter, for you are good, guileless of heart, of an open mind, without fault, without fear, without reticence before the great secrets, and faithful in your humble duties. Go in peace, my child.

The character of Virginia, with its inner purity and humane charm, reminds me of the character of the maid Félicité in *Simple Soul,* that remarkable story by Flaubert. Félicité —the simple soul—is seemingly not impressive in any way. There were many such women with a similar bitter fate in the bourgeois society of that time, which was founded on social inequality. Loneliness is the lot of many women in such an environment, forced as they are to serve someone else's happiness, someone else's joys. Félicité is denied even the happiness of bringing up other people's children. But she finds a comfort for herself, she buys a parrot to whom she is deeply attached. But a cruel fate suddenly robs her of her only joy—the parrot dies. The only thing left to her then— which she keeps in her room—is the stuffed bird, eaten by moths, the remnant of her one friend with whom she shared so many years of her life. We are deeply touched by the finale of Flaubert's highly humane creation. The scene of Félicité's death is written very movingly: When the parrot comes to life in her dying consciousness, he suddenly rises from his stand and flies high beyond the clouds, up into the blue sky. These "simple souls," deeply humane souls, crushed by the hard circumstances of life, arouse a strong feeling of compassion in us. We have an urge to help them, protect them; we feel like rebelling against the laws of a society that insults human dignity, a society in which a simple, good woman is denied happiness and doomed to loneliness.

Naturally every humanistic work is dear to us because it arouses in us love for simple people and compassion for their miserable lot. Sometimes tears are brought to our eyes, so touched are we by their warped lives. Sometimes anger and indignation are aroused in us. How often we, the workers of the theater, dream of finding a play—a contemporary play— which will touch and excite people's hearts. Our sympathy for the hero of a play is usually born of the author's skill in creating a true picture of life, in painting distinctive characters which are dear to us and for whose fate we tremble. The more deeply the author can capture us by the authenticity of what takes place in a play, by his creation of true-to-life characters, the stronger is our emotional reaction to the art that helps man to perfect himself, to become spiritually richer.

I wanted to mention this because of the strong emotional influence *The Miracle of St. Anthony*, under Vakhtangov's direction, had on the spectators. In Vakhtangov's interpretation, the "simple soul" of Virginia was strongly contrasted with the numerous images of Mlle. Hortensia's relatives. In the last version of the play (I was fortunate first to observe the rehearsals and then later to be actually involved in them), Vakhtangov created a most captivating, humane relationship between the Saint and the maid in the just recorded exposition of the play. During the rehearsal of that scene, Vakhtangov demanded of Zavadsky (Saint Anthony) and Kotlubai (Virginia) the maximum simplicity, sincerity, and humaneness. Virginia handled dexterously the objects she used—the pail, the brushes for washing the floor, and the small rug that she laid down at the entrance door. The work that Virginia executed was carefully scrutinized from the point of view of correctness of the physical actions. The pail that Zavadsky carried to fetch water was empty, but when he returned he had to carry it as though it were filled to the brim. Vakhtangov made him repeat this action again and again. First Zavadsky could not handle the task correctly—either the pail seemed half full, or Zavadsky did not feel the weight of it, or he lacked the concentration that a person would have if he were afraid of spilling the water. Finally, Vakhtangov gave orders for the pail to be filled to the brim and be given to Zavadsky and for him to carry it through the room without spilling a drop. Vakhtangov constantly demanded the correct physical actions of all daily-round details. These were absolutely necessary—as we understood later—for the realization of the concept of his production. He was building the beginning of the play in that way in order to achieve a greater contrast with the fantastic, incredible appearance of the Saint. In those contrasts—between the simple exposition of the play, its emphasized ordinary beginning and sharply dynamic development of the action which followed—lies the directorial principle of Vakhtangov, who thus discovered an interesting form for *The Miracle of St. Anthony,* a brilliant form, plastically expressive and precise.

Now M. Gus, one of Mlle. Hortensia's heirs, enters. He is a short, round little man. He rests his surprised and displeased gaze on the "tramp," who not only is dressed in torn clothes, but barefoot in addition.

M. GUS: What's the meaning of this? What do you want? Who are you?

ST. ANTHONY: Blessed St. Anthony.

M. GUS: Are you crazy?

ST. ANTHONY: Of Padua.

M. GUS: What kind of a joke is this? I am not in the mood for laughing. Are you drunk? What are you here for?

ST. ANTHONY: I want to revive your aunt.

M. GUS: What? Revive my aunt? (*To* VIRGINIA) He's drunk! Why did you let him in? (*He loses patience*) You annoy me. My guests are waiting for me. There is the door—get out quick!

ST. ANTHONY: I shall not leave until I have revived her.

M. GUS: Well, we'll see whether you will or not. (*He opens the glass door and shouts*) Joseph! (JOSEPH, *a pert, quick lackey rushes in. Upon receiving the order from* M. GUS *to throw out the unwanted caller,* JOSEPH *tries first to appeal to* ST. ANTHONY *to leave the house.*)

JOSEPH: Come on, old codger, didn't you hear? You're in the wrong house. Come along with you! Get out! . . . Oh, you won't, eh? (JOSEPH *tries to throw* ST. ANTHONY *out of the door, but his attempts are of no avail. He grasps* ST. ANTHONY *firmly in an effort to swing him out, but the* SAINT *stands rooted to the spot.*)

M. GUS: What's the matter?

JOSEPH: I don't understand what happened to him! There he stands like he was rooted and growing there. He won't budge.

M. GUS: I'll help you. (*The boss and the lackey take hold of the rope that serves* ST. ANTHONY *as a belt. They try to drag him to the door, but* ST. ANTHONY *remains immovable, staring at the room where the dead Hortensia is laid out.* JOSEPH *bends over and puts his shoulder against* ST. ANTHONY'S *stomach. Behind him* M. GUS *pushes his heavy body against the lackey, but that does not help either. Finally, the boss and the lackey realize their helplessness. Exhausted, furious, staggered by the enormous strength of* ST. ANTHONY, *they collapse on the stairs.*)

M. GUS: He's got the strength of Hercules. We had better deal gently with him. (*He changes his rough tone to a polite, almost servile, one. With exceptional courtesy and softness,* GUS [*Basov*] *begins the following conversation with* ST. ANTHONY.) Now listen to me, my friend. You understand, don't you, that on such a day as the burial of my aunt, my poor revered aunt . . .

ST. ANTHONY: I came to revive her from the dead.

M. GUS: But you surely understand that this is scarcely time for it. The partridge will be cold, my guests are waiting, and we are not in the mood for laughing.

This second scene is built on the clash between the practical bourgeoisie, who are ardent Catholics, and St. Anthony, who is a representative of the world which is supposedly sacred to them. That scene made the conflict more pointed. In portraying the role of Gus, the actor Basov was French to the bone. Short, round in build, agile, he kept the animated rhythm and tempo typical of that impetuous people. Quick-tempered, he would lose his self-control during the emotional clashes with St. Anthony, but then realizing the difference between his social position and St. Anthony's he would get hold of himself. It does not become him—M. Gus—to show any weakness in the presence of a stranger, or of his guests and relatives. Gus, to quote a popular French proverb, "put a good face on the matter," but his attempt to veil the absurdity of his situation did not succeed.

The cast of *The Miracle of St. Anthony* excelled in the vocal execution of their roles—spontaneous intonations, vocal duels, bickerings, all typical of French dialogue. Basov, a Russian actor, acquired the melody and character of the French language. That skill we all learned from Vakhtangov. Basov's movements were those of a short, plump figure with short legs; he moved always in a dance-like manner, and he was never still. All the adjustments Gus used reminded one of the type of person that in the salons of provincial France is referred to as a "shuffler": a man with external good breeding, but with poor taste, an inner emptiness, and a lack of genuine culture. Such was the character created by the intelligent and talented actor, Basov. Vakhtangov used a satirical, theatrically graphic means for the design of this episode—as well as for the rest of the play—that revealed the essence of the bigoted bourgeoisie.

I first played the role of the lackey, Joseph, then later on that of Gus and then Achilles. I was compelled to fulfill the outward designs of the roles given to me by Vakhtangov; also to follow punctually the *mise en scène* outlined by him. Here Vakhtangov was expressing theatrical satire by means which

I would call "graphic." I have in mind distinct molding of the body, when each movement, each turn of the head, and each glance has a particular significance. Many theater scholars thought that Vakhtangov used the grotesque style merely as an external expression of his idea. I cannot accept that assertion; neither as a student who saw the play from out front, as a witness of all the rehearsals, nor as the creator of a number of roles in that play. The character of the acting in that play was realistic. Vakhtangov demanded of us a complete belief in the given circumstances of the play. The situation in which the characters were placed was a singular one; there was no need to enlarge it, to sharpen it with some special excitement on the part of the actors—that would only distort the scenic truth. But on the other hand, it was necessary to avoid formlessness, looseness, unrhythmicality of actions.

In the first post-Revolutionary years, this satirical play had to be performed in a style corresponding to the times, so that the spectator would see and feel the wrathful exposure of the vices of bourgeois society: bigotry, heartlessness, Philistine narrow-mindedness. We tried to accomplish this by means of satirical comedy. There were two methods of procedure required: one, the psychological analysis of man's intentions, thoughts, and behavior; two, the expression of these in plastic, clean-cut *mise en scène*. Actors and directors, when analyzing man's thoughts and feelings, become psychologists and subtle observers not only of the inner manifestations of man's psyche but also of his physical body. This second means —the *mise en scène*—is a very important part of satirical art. Often the inner psychological process—the first means—is expressed by people spontaneously; sometimes their behavior is in direct contradiction to their inner state of being—which can be completely contrary to what they seem to be. That very contrast between the psychological state of being and its physical manifestation opens up tremendous possibilities

91 |

to the actor's creative fantasy in the comic and satirical planes and he must avail himself of it. In the scene mentioned above, between Gus, Joseph, and St. Anthony, the satirical and ridiculous came about as a result of the disparity in manner in which well-bred people would be expected to behave and the way they actually do behave. The first impulse of the "respected bourgeois" was to throw out the self-invited visitor—the tramp—who was upsetting his sense of well-being, while poor Virginia—the maid—is ready to lose her three thousand three-hundred francs to have her mistress brought to life. Gus is petrified just by the thought that his aunt might be revived; to lose the inheritance is a terrifying thing to him. That is why, forgetting his dignity and his respectability, he enters into a hand-to-hand fight with St. Anthony, using every means to get rid of this dangerous visitor who may prove a threat to his future.

Gus, in his immaculately clean frock coat, with his dazzling starched high collar, his patent leather shoes, and with a lackey elegant in a tail coat, presents a striking contrast to St. Anthony's composed and dignified figure dressed in rags. That disparity is heightened the moment that Gus, losing hope of overcoming St. Anthony by force, begins to use a polite, servile tone. The audience is aware of what is taking place in the hearts of Gus and Joseph, who are still enraged from the fight, and yet at the same time there is the sweet kind smile and the caressing intonation of Gus's voice. Such contrast brings laughter in the auditorium. What does one expect from irate people, people who have been fighting each other? The determination to continue to fight, of course. Instead we see Gus and Joseph trying to ingratiate themselves with their enemy. What do the eyes and face of a fighter-loser usually express? Hatred and hostility. Instead, we see angelic, conciliatory, sugary glances thrown at the enemy with tenderness. To set off this contrast, make it not only understandable but also visual, is the scenic task, the fulfillment of which requires a chiseled and graphic clarity in the development of the action, and most expressive *mise en scène*. Vakhtangov was striving to accomplish that graphic theatricality.

As long as I have used the word "theatricality," I would like to explain my concept of that word. Theatricality, as I understand it, is a scenic truth born out of the inherent expressive means of the theater and conveyed by the artist, who reveals life in all its complex many-sidedness, as a result of his profound knowledge of the epoch and the people of the play. An artist should never attempt to imitate life—copy its outward signs, its outward manifestations.

I will try to define later the style of the production of *The Miracle of St. Anthony*. Now I will continue the story, to help my reader see clearly the extraordinary scenic situations and understand the singularity of Vakhtangov's treatment of the play. We left M. Gus and the lackey, Joseph, sitting on the steps. In that position, the second nephew, Achilles, finds them. Achilles is played as slow-going, slow-witted—a complete contrast to the animated and keen-witted Gus.

> M. ACHILLES: What's the matter, Gus? What's wrong? We're all waiting for partridges.

At that moment, M. Achilles notices the vagrant standing in the entrance hall. The relatives begin to leave the funeral repast and come into the entrance hall. Men have their napkins tucked in behind their collars; some of them are grasping forks in their hands and in some instances there are remnants of food on the forks; some men are carrying half-filled wine glasses, and are chewing their food and drinking the wine as they enter. Confusion begins to grow. Someone suggests: We must send for the police.

> M. GUS: For God's sake, no scenes! I don't want the police in the house on a day like this.

Suddenly, the attention of Gus, and then Achilles, is attracted by something other than St. Anthony. Now what could attract their attention away from the cause of the commotion? The state of disrepair that the floor is in. That upsets the future owners of the house.

M. ACHILLES: A moment, Gus.

M. GUS: Well?

M. ACHILLES: Have you noticed that two or three tiles are cracked there on the left side, at the end of the corridor?

M. GUS: Yes, I did. And I'm going to have a mosaic floor laid there instead, in place of the tiles.

M. ACHILLES: Good. It will make it look more friendly.

M. GUS: Yes, and more up-to-date. And in place of this door, with those white curtains, I have this idea— a window with a symbolic picture of a hunt, of industry and progress, with a garland of fruit and wild animals.

As you will notice, they have not yet buried the aunt, her dead body is still in the house in which she lived for seventy-three years, and her nephews are already planning changes in her home. The death of the old woman has given them pleasure, which they make no attempt to hide. The joy of a two-million franc inheritance is their predominant feeling. The funeral repast is turning into a gay holiday, as so often happens in life.

Now the entrance hall is becoming filled with more and more of the participants of the repast. The curé enters. He is an excessively fat man, and his face shines from too much food and drink. Achilles tries to shove the curé toward St. Anthony.

M. ACHILLES: Ah! Here is the pastor! He knows you, and he wants to pay you his respects. Come on, Pastor. Saints are your business. *(Under his breath he says to the pastor—)* We want you to get him quietly to the door without his being aware of it. As soon as he is outside, goodbye and Godspeed to him.

At this point, I would like to describe the manner in which Schukin handled the role of the curé. Schukin was broad-shouldered, stocky, thick-set; typically Russian. A large forehead helped to create the impression of a very fat man, and he used heavy padding which gave him a large stomach and round shoulders. When a young actor plays an old man, it is the slender young neck that betrays his youth. Schukin raised the shoulders under the curé's cassock and covered his neck with the curé's collar, and thereby cleverly masked the danger spot. With the help of special make-up he widened his cheekbones, and made up his eyes in such a way that they appeared to bulge, as they usually do when a man eats and drinks too much. Schukin was creating the prototype of Gargantua, that life-loving, healthy glutton who indulged in all the joys of living. All Schukin's behavior made one feel that here was a man with many vices. Probably after a delicious dinner the curé lifts the end of his cassock, fetches his golden cigarette case, and smokes a fine Havana cigar—being careful to enjoy its aroma in some far-away room, because priests were not allowed to smoke in front of people. Schukin's curé gave the impression of being a man who loves women. With all his stoutness, he attempted to be graceful. It sometimes happens that fat people, in spite of their excess weight, are very graceful. Schukin's gracefulness was coquettish, and the coquetry was almost feminine.

The outward appearance of the curé showed with what graphic precision this still very young actor molded his role. But in working on a role, creating an outward appearance is

95 |

only half of the actor's task. The outward appearance must be supplemented by a speech that blends with it organically. Schukin adopted an inspired device: he talked with a high-pitched, thin, tenor voice, in a sing-song tone. Beginning the speech with a melodic, mellifluous voice, Schukin gradually reinforced the sound, imperceptibly changing it into the church recitative, and then went into singing. That reinforcing of his voice was done indiscernibly; we would suddenly notice that at the end of a phrase the curé was not talking but singing. That device, courageous, unusual and brilliant, was executed by Schukin with extraordinary artistry.

Now, remember that M. Achilles suggested to the curé that he use a "military ruse" to get St. Anthony to the door. The curé approaches his task in a roundabout way.

CURE: Mighty St. Anthony, your vassal in all humility bids you welcome to this world, which, we praise God, you have elected to honor with your presence. What does Your Holiness desire?

The last words were on the verge of recitative, changing into song.

ST. ANTHONY: I wish to revive Mlle. Hortensia.
CURE: Poor lady! However, such a miracle would assuredly present no difficulties to the greatest of our saints. The dear deceased had a particular cult for you.

Now here Schukin interchanged glances with the surrounding relatives and guests. And unnoticed by St. Anthony he shrugged his big shoulders ironically and hid a smile.

CURE: I will conduct you to her if Your Holiness will take the trouble to follow me. (*He goes to the* street door and beckons to ST. ANTHONY) This way, please.

ST. ANTHONY: (*Pointing to the door, right*) No, that way. She is there.

The curé is embarrassed. He glances at the guests and at M. Achilles, and upon receiving from them a silent suggestion to act further, he tries to convince St. Anthony that the body of the deceased, because of the overflow of mourners, was placed in the house across the street.

CURE: To convince yourself, Your Holiness has only to follow me a moment into the street and from there you will see the candles and black hangings.

ST. ANTHONY: (*Immovable, pointing to the door on the right*) There will I enter. There! (*The guests are outraged. They grumble. Someone suggests to them that they combine forces and throw* ST. ANTHONY *out. The scandal thickens and, as usual, one looks for the person who caused it. For sure, it must be Virginia, the maid. Everyone begins to attack her.*)

M. ACHILLES: But who told him the corpse lay in there?

M. GUS: Virginia, of course. She's babbled about as much as it was possible to babble.

VIRGINIA: Me, Sir? No, Sir. Not me. I was attending to my work. I answered Yes and No, nothing else. Didn't I, St. Anthony? (ST. ANTHONY *does not reply.*) Well, speak up when a body talks to you friendly like.

ST. ANTHONY: She told me nothing.

VIRGINIA: There! Now, you see! He's a blessed saint. He knew it all beforehand. I tell you, there is nothing he does not know.

Suddenly M. Achilles gets the idea of inviting the doctor,

one of their guests, to solve the predicament. The doctor is still in the dining room eating his trout.

M. ACHILLES: Crazy! Of course, it is a doctor's business.

The role of the doctor was one of the best roles created by Zakhava. He made up with carefully scattered hair on his forehead and affixed a "walrus moustache" so that it covered his upper lip. He wore a black frock coat, and his thin legs appeared to be shaped like the letter X. His elbows pressed tightly against his waist and his hands spread to the sides with the palms up. (In the way a surgeon, after washing his hands, waits for the towel.) Zakhava entered, still chewing his trout, his napkin around his neck. He fixed his professional gaze on St. Anthony and for a few seconds scrutinized his "patient."

I must note here that for this role Zakhava made a close study of doctors—their habits, their manner of treating the sick, the manner of conversation typical of a prominent physician, slightly protective and slightly familiar. The Moscow audience of the twenties could recognize familiar physicians in Zakhava's doctor. The image of a doctor as created by Zakhava was faultless from the point of view of external embodiment of the role. The speech of his doctor was completely in harmony with his movements and gestures. All that blended together the plastic and vocal sides and defined the characteristics of that image.

Incidentally, there exists a long-standing argument as to whether in working on a role one should begin from the speech or the movement in order to master both the characteristics and the whole image. I will not undertake to resolve that argument. I can only say a few words about my personal method which, of course, I do not consider the only correct one. In almost all my work on a role I have looked first for

| 98

the movements and gestures that are characteristic of my image—the manner of behavior of my character when he is in front of other people. I first see clearly the outward appearance of my character: his figure, his dress, face, hairdo, nose, eyebrows, eyes, his way of observing those who surround him. Then only do I look for his manner of speech. In *The Miracle of St. Anthony,* because we had to portray the French, the character of movement was of great significance to us. The tempo-rhythm of the movement of the French is roughly twice as fast as that of the Russian. Hence, the speech must be in keeping with the tempo of the movement.

But to get back to our play. The doctor appears still chewing on his trout.

> DOCTOR: What's up? Is he mad? Is he sick? Is he drunk? (*He looks the saint over*) Oh, a beggar! I can do nothing for him. . . . Well, my friend, what is the matter with you?
> ST. ANTHONY: I wish to revive Mlle. Hortensia.
> DOCTOR: I can see you are not a medical man. (*He feels his pulse*) Do you feel pain anywhere? (*He begins the medical examination.*)

Zakhava executed it professionally, faultlessly. It took him two minutes to take the ear trumpet, put the mouth of it on the neck, then hold it to the heart and the lungs; afterwards to feel the head, then count the pulse. A categorical diagnosis followed:

> DOCTOR: The man is mad. He is a maniac, and to avoid unpleasantness it is better to allow him to enter the room of Mlle. Hortensia for a moment. Such a small compromise will hurt nothing and no one.

Silence ensues. They all look at Gus. It is up to him to make a decision.

M. GUS: Well, as far as I'm concerned, put an end to the matter. But don't let anybody talk about this ridiculous incident, will you?

M. ACHILLES: (*Sotto voce*) Auntie's jewelry is in the chest of drawers, Gus.

M. GUS: I know. I'll keep an eye on it. (*To the Saint*) Well, then, come on this way. We haven't finished lunch yet, so hurry, please. (*They all go into the room on the right, followed by* ST. ANTHONY.)

That is how the first act of the play ends.

So far I have talked only about the interrelationship of the leading characters. But the episodic roles—those of the relatives and guests who were on the stage and participated in most of the act—occupied an important place in the directorial score of this play. They formed a distinctive orchestral ensemble which masterfully accompanied the solo instruments—the leading characters. Vakhtangov was a remarkable regisseur-conductor. He built the group scenes brilliantly by coordinating their action with the action of the leading characters, thus achieving a perfect ensemble. By what means did he accomplish such magnificent expressiveness of the group scenes? He assigned concrete scenic problems for each person in that group scene. But Vakhtangov's secret was not in that —or rather, not only in that. He devoted enormous attention to the dynamic design of the whole scene: the increase and decrease of movements, the culmination point of the scene, and the tempo-rhythm of each actor. In his lessons with the young Vakhtangovites, participators in this play, he discovered very interesting principles of scenic movements and rhythm. I was very much interested in these questions from the very first steps in my acting and directorial work. Later on, I was fortunate to be chosen by Vakhtangov as his assistant in precisely this line during the work on *Princess Turan-*

*dot,* where I conducted the classes in scenic movement and rhythm. When working on scenic movements, I learned that in the dramatic theater scenic movement is tied up organically with sound and it is an integral part of the actor's skill. When the movement becomes an end in itself, then we have involuntarily entered the realm of ballet, which while most valuable in the art of choreography is absolutely unacceptable in dramatic art. In order to understand this correlation between the movement and the sound, one must study thoroughly the nature of the spectator's attention.

In the process of my pedagogical practice, I kept notes of my lessons. In these I endeavored to systematize my observations and make some deductions. While we are performing on the stage the spectator gives us his attention. This we must value, be mindful of, and respect. Give the spectator too much or too little to watch, and you will lose his attention. And we know only too well that to lose his attention is a catastrophe, to both the director and the actors. To recapture that attention demands the mobilization of all the means of an actor's mastery. We are given the oral and visual attention of the audience; the audience while listening to us receives the text, phrases, words, and pauses. The actors and the regisseur in the process of working on a play must not only interpret it but must achieve an expressive modeling of the phrase, clarity of diction, the melody of speech, and colorful intonation. When these seemingly elementary problems are neglected, then the play just does not ring true. This happens especially often when the play is written in verse. Almost all our drama schools fail to teach students thoroughly how to pronounce verses and how to bring out their meaning. Our young students do not know the difference in reading Pushkin, Mayakovsky, or some other poets. To reveal and interpret the uniqueness of a poet is a difficult art, and it demands exceptional mastery. That is why it is absolutely necessary that work on verse be included in the curriculum of drama schools in the very first years. Mastering the form of verse an artist unavoidably learns to treat an author's thoughts with care; he learns the form of verse, its movement. It is essential that an actor learn to convey the temperament peculiar to each author-poet and his images. Voice training is given in our schools, but the modulation of the voice is not taught. As far as the visual attention of our audience is concerned, we impress our audience through our movements, the color of the sets, the costumes, and the lighting. The actor's movement is one of the most essential factors in his performance.

Imagine the following episode: An actor is alone on stage. He does not say a word. His scenic problem is to find a letter in which he will learn the fate of his whole life. The stage represents one room, which he has just entered. It is furnished with a great number of objects, including a bookcase, a dressing table, and a writing desk that has a great many drawers. You watch the actor's movements: he glances first about the entire room, then he scrutinizes each object, trying to figure out just where the letter might be. Your attention follows him. He goes to the bookcase and begins to look through it—there is no letter. He moves to the dressing table and goes through all its drawers; next he goes to the writing desk and begins to pull out first one drawer and then another. Now you watch only his hands. The room does not interest you at this moment, nor does the rest of his body. At last! The letter is found! He takes it out of the drawer. Now it is the envelope that interests you; the envelope that contains the important letter. The actor, with a quick movement, opens and throws away the envelope, then unfolds the letter. He does not, however, read the letter immediately; he is too nervous. Besides, he does not want to be caught reading it. Suddenly he hides it behind his back, and for a second his eyes are fixed on a definite spot. Your attention is attracted to that spot, and then back to the actor. You watch the expression of his eyes. Abruptly he moves to a door, then to another door, to make sure no one is there to catch him unawares. You follow his movements, and here again your attention is on the whole room. There is no one coming. The cherished letter appears once more, and again your attention is narrowed to that small piece of paper in his hands. His reaction as he reads it is an exclamation—one word—a happy or unhappy verdict. The scene is finished. Thus, we followed the actor through all the *mise en scène* of this episode, now widening, now narrowing our circle of attention. The actor "conducted" our attention, showing us how to address it.

How can one control the attention of the audience in a play like *The Miracle of St. Anthony* that has twenty people on the stage at the same time during both acts? The same way as in a symphony. There the richness of the orchestration never prevents one from sensing the main theme; the accompanying instruments do not drown out the soloist. So in the same way in our dramatic art the arrangement of the group scenes should be skillfully planned so as to establish the basic line that develops the play. The regisseur's art in composing the group scenes is similar to that of the painter, who at times is faced with the task of arranging a large group of people on his canvas. We know that talented painters work diligently and devotedly on their compositions. In Leonardo da Vinci's "The Last Supper" and Alexander Ivanov's "Appearance of Christ to the People" the entire composition of the pictures is focused on the figure of Christ, yet we are aware of the figures surrounding Christ at the same time that we look at Christ. The process of attention is divided into four stages: (1) Spontaneous perception of the painting in its entirety; (2) Concentration on a central episode; (3) Concentration on the group scenes; (4) Perception of the picture in its entirety, but with a new and meaningful quality. A similar process takes place in the consciousness of the spectator in the theater. There are various principles to be observed in building the group scenes. The most typical are two: (1) The group scene behaves as a single whole; (2) Each episode, every figure, is carefully worked out in detail and yet, at the same time, subject to the basic thought that the regisseur carries out as a central theme of the given episode on the stage. In *The Miracle of St. Anthony,* Vakhtangov made the participants of the group scenes behave as a single whole, so that the group expressed the conformity of the Philistine morals. The oneness of the reactions of the provincial bourgeoisie was revealed in the clash with the Saint. Gus, Joseph, the curé, the doctor, all the relatives of the deceased Mlle. Hortensia, have the same reaction to the visit of St. Anthony. Only Virginia stands alone. The method for the *mise en scène* of the play was frontal, bas-relief. The group of main characters was arranged in the center; on their left and right were the rest of the relatives of the deceased and the guests. The *mise en scène* in this play was molded sculpturally. Each participant in a scene was given a concrete sculptural molding of his body that expressed feelings in plastic movement, in a definite rhythm. The participants of this mass scene had to express feelings of anger or displeasure, of grief, of impatience, of curiosity and so on in definite poses with definite gestures and with their whole body. Here again Vakhtangov's principle was followed: It is important not only to feel this or that, but to express what one feels spontaneously in a definite form. All communion between partners is not limited by scenic relationship, as some of the interpreters of Stanislavsky state, but demands a masterly combination of figures in an expressive *mise en scène.* An actor was obliged to consider the partner, or partners, who stood next to him and compositionally form with him, or them, a harmoniously completed group.

All the groups in *Miracle* were born on the stage, spontaneously. The knowledge and understanding of the regisseur's principles and his methods of forming *mise en scène* aroused the actors' fantasy, and they developed a feeling of responsibility for having every moment they were on stage graphically expressive. We, the participants of those scenes, improvised the most intricate group combinations, always intelligently emphasizing the essence of what took place on the stage.

Those who are in the theater, or in some of the other arts, know how much the artist draws from life, always being careful to observe all events that take place before his eyes. Those not associated with the arts should learn to look with our eyes at the phenomena of life, observe the *mise en scènes* created by life itself. Let us imagine a place where one may observe a large number of people—the waiting room of a railroad station. Notice how life molds here the most complicated designs of *mise en scène,* cleverly and whimsically distributes people waiting for a train. We see people sitting, strolling, sleeping in the waiting room; some are taking a bite of food, some are reading, some checking their luggage, some restlessly watching the clock, and so on. The place itself prompts their actions: they are all waiting for the train. But look attentively at first one group then another and people's lives and their relationships will open to you. You can easily distinguish those who are related: you can recognize the married couples, and brother and sister, the sweethearts, people who are parting from each other. Without even hearing the dialogue you can practically guess what this or that couple is talking about. You can guess in what state of mind they are, what kind of a trip they are undertaking, whether it is a happy or unhappy one. Watching a group of men you can tell who is the leader of the group and who are the subordinates. If you study scenes such as these attentively you will observe that often the natural grouping of people in real life is more interesting than that of people on the stage, particularly since some regisseurs are not concerned with the plastically expressed form of the performance. Take a look at the hands and fingers of persons sitting in a waiting room and you will notice the extraordinary variety in the expression of their hands, even when the hands are not moving.

Vakhtangov paid great attention to hands in *The Miracle of St. Anthony*. It was important for us to use the French manner of gesticulation, and that is very difficult for the Russian. You have all observed the manners and gestures of French people and you realize how vivacious and elegant these agile and sociable people are. Their hands "paint" in conversation. If a Frenchman has an object in his hand—a wine glass, a walking stick, a handkerchief, a watch chain, anything—he will use that in his conversation as he explains something or points something out. And the interlocutor is not idle even during those moments when he is not talking. One can hear his interjections: Oh! Yes? Oh, la la! You will see eyebrows raised in amazement, eyes full of interest and lively, lips now lifted then lowered. There is a constant change in the facial expressions and in the eyes of these effusive and life-loving people. We know that on the stage actions and movements alternate with "stops." We call such stops "periods." Just as in a written sentence a period follows the completed thought, so does the scenic action when brought to a logical end demand a stop. Let us call that cessation of movement, the moment of arrested movement.

It is not out of place here to turn to the art of sculpture for an illustration. Sculpture shows us most clearly what "arrested movement" is. Recollect the "Discobolus" by Myron, or the "Venus di Milo," or "Apollo of Belvedere," or the "Moses" of Michelangelo. All these masterpieces express movements that are unfinished—arrested—as though the dynamics of that rhythm the sculptor had chosen were in the process of completion. So it is in scenic movement. During the period of "arrested movement" we must not lose the momentum of the rhythm but continue to live in it. For example, you are about to light a cigarette. You have already lit the match, but before you put it to the cigarette something unusually striking attracts your attention. The match is burning your fingers, but you don't blow it out. Your hands and fingers freeze in the position they are in: the right hand holds the burning match at the level of your mouth, the left hand holds the match box. If you are attracted by something of tremendous importance you will not change the position of your hands until you feel the match burning them. During that moment of "arrested movement," your motionless body retains all the expressiveness of that movement. Your pose is natural; you are at ease. But if someone had said to you, "Stay motionless for a moment," you would have stopped in a tense, artificial pose.

In our scenic work, nothing helps us more than our observations of life. Life itself is so interesting, so many-sided, so dynamic, that the most refined fantasy of an artist can conceive of nothing more interesting, more surprising, or more brilliant. The marble sculptures of antiquity show us examples of profound feelings. A man is shown as he is, but with penetrating appreciation of all that is splendid in him. The Venus of Milo is not only an ideally beautiful and exquisitely built woman but also a spiritually serene symbol of peace, and in that harmony she is splendid. Apollo of Belvedere is not only a well-built and handsome man but also possesses a spiritual nature as well as a lucid mind, and here again we have an example of the striking harmony of the physical and spiritual aspects. I do not mean to say, of course, that the techniques of sculptural expressiveness are good only to show the harmony of beauty in man. On the contrary, by means of plastic art strong flights of passion can be expressed: hatred, bacchanal ecstasy, greed, and so on. (Rodin.) We took for study the classic examples that are the eternal models of splendor in their artistic perfection. But to the category of the splendid in art belong not only the beautiful and positive; art may also take for its object the ugly and negative. The most important function of art is to elevate people, war with man's vices, oppose all that stands in the way of society's progress. Satirical art, the art that accuses, is of great help. That genre of the theater disrobes the bourgeois ideology, the imperialists' hatred of man. Satire uses laughter as a weapon for attacking Philistinism, complacency, and the petty bourgeoisie. Nowadays hardly anyone thinks that an artist who uses the satirical genre with a constructive purpose contributes less to society than the artist who creates ideal positive characters. Within the many-sided art of social realism all the directions, all the genres, serve to assert advanced and progressive ideas.

In *The Miracle of St. Anthony* Vakhtangov, as the regisseur, was concerned with lashing the bourgeois morale and the mercenary laws of the proprietary society. To accomplish that end, we actors had to use our bodies as clay to mold figures that, in stark movements, would express the petty, pitiful feelings and passions of the Philistine and the bourgeoisie. We had to show people caught in a morass of self-complacency and outraged by the appearance of St. Anthony, who dared encroach on their established order.

One has to remember that this play was produced only three years after the October Revolution, when the struggle between the two worlds was at its highest point and was of fierce character. In March, 1919, Vakhtangov wrote: "The Revolution has divided the world of the old and the new with a red line. There is no isolated corner in human life that the red line has not passed through, and there is no human being who does not feel it one way or another." People were sharply divided by that line of Revolution into three categories: those who wanted to remain in the old world and were defending that old world up to the hilt; those who accepted the new world and defended it up to the hilt; those who were waiting for the result of the struggle between the two—in other words, those who were passively adapting themselves to either side while waiting the results. And when the Revolution marches, how can it miss the heart of an artist?

The agitated heart of the artist dictated to Vakhtangov those passionately accusatory, sharply expressive *mise en scènes* and prompted in his fantasy newer and newer caustic strokes that laid bare the decomposition of the old world. Great spiritual enthusiasm inspired Vakhtangov's post-Revolutionary aspirations. He created his productions with a keen mind and hot blood. Every rehearsal of *The Miracle* was intensive and full of the most interesting discoveries. The scenes of the play acquired precision and completeness from rehearsal to rehearsal. Vakhtangov had an extraordinary ability to enthrall and carry along those who worked with him. Hours flew by unnoticed; the rehearsals sometimes lasted far after midnight.

Let us get back to our play. Our intermission between the first and second act is much too prolonged. Let us raise the curtain and follow the performers into the room where the corpse of Mlle. Hortensia is laid out. All the characters of the preceding act, led by Gus and Achilles, enter the room sedately and quietly. St. Anthony and Virginia follow them.

M. GUS: Here lies our dear departed. Quite dead, you see. Now, are you satisfied? And now I think we are entitled to be left alone. (To VIRGINIA) Lead the gentleman out by the garden door.

ST. ANTHONY: One moment. (*He walks into the middle of the room and standing by the foot of the bed turns toward the corpse and speaks in a strong, grave voice*) Arise!

M. GUS: There, there, that's enough. We can't stand here and have a stranger offend our most sacred feelings.

ST. ANTHONY: Allow me. (*He goes nearer the bed and raises his voice more commandingly*) Arise!!

M. GUS: (*Losing patience*) Now, that's enough. Here is the door!

ST. ANTHONY: (*Interrupting* M. GUS *in a deeper*

*and more commanding voice*) Hortensia! Return and
arise from the dead!

Now the dead woman stirs slightly, half opens her eyes,
spreads her folded hands, and slowly sits up in bed. The
group of guests and relatives stand stock-still for a second,
dumbfounded. Then they panic; they turn and run frantical-
ly from the room. There is a jam at the door. The women
are shouting hysterically; the men are gasping for breath.
They are all terrified. They stumble into each other, into the
furniture; they overturn chairs, scatter floral wreaths. Someone crawls out of the room; others move senselessly in circles.
The panic scene was played with absolute precision, and the
audience's laughing reaction increased gradually. I am recol-
lecting now Vakhtangov's effort to direct the scene. Such a
directorial objective as panic, sudden catastrophes that take
place in front of your eyes, sudden news of unforeseen joy or
sorrow, demands of an actor a sudden reaction. Experienced
directors who are trying to get an actor's reaction with lightning speed prepare so-called "jumping-off places" for the unexpected "jump" into the called-for state of being. In this
case, Vakhtangov illustrated to us what happens to a person
in moments of sudden fright, and he planted in our fantasy
possibilities of future reactions to it. Often before we reached
the resurrection scene, Vakhtangov would shout from the
auditorium his favorite directorial "Stop!" He would again
and again bring us up to that episode, arousing in us each
time a stronger and stronger desire to try it. During one of
the rehearsals he at last let us go, and we "rushed into the
cold water." It was a complete improvisation done with great
enthusiasm. The excited fantasy of each of the participants
in the scene functioned faultlessly; *mise en scène* was born
easily and organically. And only after the last one of us,
frightened to death, left Mlle. Hortensia's room did Vakhtangov shout "Stop" and summon us into the auditorium. He

then suggested that we first look at the stage. As we did, we saw in front of us a room in utter disorder. Vakhtangov then told us that he had liked what we did, that it had been an excellent scene. "We are going to repeat the scene a number of times now to solidify it," he said. "Meantime, I want each one of you to recall what you did in the scene—whom you collided with as you attempted to save yourself, what objects on the stage you stumbled over or dropped as you ran from the room."

Then and there each one of us went through in his mind what his behavior on the stage had been, in every last minute detail. We then executed the scene again, and the effect was just the same. The very complicated "panic scene" with its large number of participants was thereby accomplished in ten or fifteen minutes.

The scene of the "return of the guests" into Mlle. Hortensia's room was no less complicated. With frightened faces the guests and relatives were peeping out of a number of doors to ascertain if the miracle had really taken place. No doubt of it! The aunt is alive. She is sitting on the pedestal scratching spots of candle wax off her nightgown. Virginia hurries to the bed and throws herself into the arms of her resurrected mistress.

VIRGINIA: Miss Hortensia! She is alive. Just look at her, scratching away a grease spot. She's looking for her glasses. St. Anthony! A miracle! A miracle! Kneel down!

M. GUS: (*Surprised, standing by the door*) Listen, keep still! Don't talk nonsense. This is no time!

M. ACHILLES: There is no doubt about it. She's alive.

M. GUS: It is impossible. She will relapse immediately. Who should we appeal to, to have an explanation of this miracle? The doctor! What does the doctor think?

DOCTOR: What do I think? What do you want me to think? This is none of my business. It is quite outside my field; quite absurd and quite simple. She lives: ergo, she was never dead. There is no reason for throwing up your hands and crying "A Miracle!"

The scene develops further as we see the heirs trying to ingratiate themselves with their aunt. God forbid she should learn how unhappy they are to see her alive! After having looked over the people present, Hortensia's eyes come to rest on St. Anthony with considerable hostility.

HORTENSIA: (Sharply) What sort of a creature is that? Who has so far forgotten himself as to allow him to enter my apartment? He has already dirtied my carpets. Get out! Out! Virginia, you know I do not allow beggars . . .

ST. ANTHONY: (Raising his hand commandingly) Silence!

The aunt stops short and sits open-mouthed, unable to utter a word. M. Gus is embarrassed. He asks Anthony to forgive his aunt. He, together with his cousin, is ready to recompense St. Anthony—of course, modestly, in proportion to his means. There is a thought to make a collection from among the guests. St. Anthony refuses all their offers. All he wants now is to leave. But to let him go empty-handed is embarrassing to Gus. M. Achilles, as usual, comes out with a good idea—to lunch together. Anthony and all the guests. Anthony refuses flatly.

M. GUS: Oh, come, you can't refuse us this! And who can be awaiting you, anyway?

ST. ANTHONY: Another corpse.

M. GUS: Another corpse! Nothing but corpses! Well, I must say I hope you don't prefer the dead to us.

VIRGINIA: (*Petrified*) Master . . .

M. GUS: What's wrong?

VIRGINIA: I don't know. Mlle. Hortensia cannot speak.

All rush to Mlle. Hortensia; all are excited. They ask her questions, but the aunt makes a sign that she can no longer speak.

M. GUS: (*To* ANTHONY) What is the meaning of this?

ST. ANTHONY: She will speak no more.

M. GUS: She will speak no more? But she spoke, just now. We heard her. She was rude to you.

ST. ANTHONY: She will speak no more.

M. GUS: Can't you give her back her voice?

ST. ANTHONY: No.

M. GUS: But when will her voice come back?

ST. ANTHONY: Never.

M. GUS: She will be dumb till the day of her death?

ST. ANTHONY: Yes, she has beheld secrets she may not reveal.

M. GUS: Secrets? What secrets?

ST. ANTHONY: Of the world of the dead.

The relatives of Mlle. Hortensia and the guests are furious. Resurrect Mlle. Hortensia and leave her dumb! It would be better if the Saint had not interfered in the affair. Indignation mounts: this impudent tramp should be punished. Joseph is sent to fetch the police, and he returns with two officers and a brigadier. The policemen treat Anthony as a criminal; they handcuff him. They are finishing a bottle of wine, given them by the masters of the house, and are getting ready to leave when the doorbell rings. A commissar enters. He is elegantly dressed in a black coat and a top hat. Shikhmatov played the role of the commissar very well indeed. He portrayed him as a cold, heartless representative of authority and a polished man of the world. I especially remember Vakhtangov's illustration of the commissar's facial expressions: when he looked at the masters of the house his eyes became kind and friendly, but when he looked at Anthony those eyes had a cold, callous, apathetic look, the look that disregards the person who stands in front of him. Regisseurs often resort to demonstration as a means of helping an actor find characteristics for his role, but such demonstrations more often define the form, the result. The actor, grasping the illustration or demonstration, must fill it with an inner justification: he must fill the form with content, decipher the regisseur's intention and make it his own. To imitate the demonstration only outwardly would mean to execute the regisseur's suggestion only formally. Vakhtangov did not tolerate such an attitude and did not permit such a performance. If the regisseur is doubtful that his demonstration will suggest the correct content, it is better that he does not attempt to demonstrate.

Now every regisseur is not endowed with that special talent for demonstrating the character to the actor, but unfortunately almost all regisseurs resort to that means and thus sometimes crudely disturb the natural process of the creation of the role. This is especially dangerous when a director is working with a young actor. I am writing these lines with my young comrades in the profession in my mind. I want them to test themselves and honestly criticize their ability for scenic demonstrations. There are other ways of helping an actor in his work on a role. Vakhtangov used a variety of methods, depending on the material of the role, the style of the play, and the personality of the actor. The method of demonstration is used most economically and with great ingenuity. In the case of Shikhmatov and his role of the commissar, Vakhtangov's demonstration succeeded completely. The elegant entrance of the commissar, M. Mitou, was most effective. The beautiful velvety voice of Shikhmatov, with its insinuating inflections, fused harmoniously with his appearance.

COMM: Good day, ladies and gentlemen. I have heard all about it. (*Looking at* ANTHONY) Yes, I suspected as much. It is St. Anthony himself, the great St. Anthony of Padua.

M. GUS: You know him then?

COMM: I should say I do. We have turned him out of the hospital three times. You understand, he's a little (*he taps his forehead*) and each time he is turned out he plays the same pranks—heals the sick, steals the doctor's work, and all without a license. (*He goes up to the Saint and looks him over carefully.*) Yes, he is the man. Or at least—well, he has changed since his last escapade. But if it isn't he, it's his brother. I don't know, there is something about him doesn't seem to me quite right, but we'll see about that in court. Come on, my children. (*Gaily and playfully*) In court, in court, in court! (*He leaves, tossing his top hat into the air. He opens the door leading to the garden. A swirl of wind and rain gushes in; a far-away peal of thunder is heard. Here the regisseur was finishing the building of the scenic action.* ANTHONY *begins a slow exit.*)

There is an awkward silence. Maybe deep in his heart each one begins to feel guilty before Anthony, who has done no harm to any of them. The policemen push Anthony toward the exit, and there is the sound of the tinkling of the chains on his hands. Virginia is the first to break the silence. She runs to Anthony, stops the moving procession and blocks the policemen's way.

VIRGINIA: (*Hurrying forward*) But, master, the poor man . . . Look, he's barefooted.

M. GUS: Well, what of it? Are we to get him a carriage or a holy shrine?

VIRGINIA: No, I'll lend him my boots. (*To ANTHONY*) Take them, blessed Anthony. I've got others.

ST. ANTHONY: (*Putting on the boots*) Thank you.

VIRGINIA: And aren't you wearing anything on your head? You will catch cold.

ST. ANTHONY: I have nothing.

VIRGINIA: Take my little kerchief—and I'll get you my umbrella. (*She hurries out*)

M. ACHILLES: The old fool.

Virginia returns with a huge umbrella, which she hands to St. Anthony. Then, seeing his handcuffs, she opens it and holds it over his head. Those present regard the strange procession. The brigadier leads, followed by St. Anthony in handcuffs, followed by Virginia with the umbrella, followed by the two policemen. A long pause climaxed the scene. The host and guests feel uncomfortable. Each feels that the unjust development was the result of his actions. Suddenly, Gus remembers Mlle. Hortensia.

M. GUS: Well, Aunt . . .

M. ACHILLES: What's the matter with her? She is falling down!

DOCTOR: (*Hurrying*) I don't know. This time

she is really dying. I told you so. (*Silence ensues. All assume sorrowful poses, burying their beloved aunt for the second time.*)

But now, after that tragic farce that took place on the stage, their sad poses look particularly false and insincere. Crestfallen, with sorrowful glances, sad sighs, hands crossed as in prayer—but behind that sanctimonious expression of sorrow, a secret joy that everything ended happily. The capital remained in the hands of the heirs. Peals of thunder are heard, as if nature itself is angered by the callousness and heartlessness of people.

M. GUS: (*Fearing punishment from heaven, begins to defend himself*) What a day!

M. ACHILLES: Listen, did you ever hear such a storm!

M. GUS: Well, you know we were a bit hard on the poor beggar. When you come to think of it, he really didn't do us any harm.

The spiritual poverty of all those greedy people was pointed out in contrast to the images of Virginia and Anthony, and Vakhtangov made a point of emphasizing their moral superiority. And in this theatrically brilliant and sharply expressed clash between the two different social groups lies the new interpretation of Maeterlinck's *The Miracle of St. Anthony*—Vakhtangov's interpretation.

Miss Kotlubai, who created the role of Virginia, was one of Vakhtangov's closest assistants, both as a regisseur and a teacher. She was a true artist, excellently schooled, who absorbed thoroughly Vakhtangov's method of work on a role. Her relationship—as Virginia—to St. Anthony moved through the play as a contrast to that of Hortensia's relatives and guests. This old woman, simple, unselfish, humane, compelled the audience's sympathy by her extraordinary guile-

lessness. The character of Anthony occupied a more important—one may say more central—place in the spectacle. To
the creation of that image, Vakhtangov gave a lot of attention. The role demanded artistry, impeccable taste, heartfelt
concentration and humaneness. Zavadsky, who played Anthony, created an image of a very ordinary man: modest, shy,
worthy, but by no means a saint. His Anthony was a man of
reality, of everyday life. The more people around him were
seized with passions, the more simple and humane he became. He watched all the fussing and bustling people with a
kind, sympathetic, and at times compassionately patient look.
Only now and then, when Gus or Achilles abused Virginia
unjustly, his look would become stern and penetrating. Then
one felt a strong and uncompromising character hidden
under that simple and ordinary kindness.

One of the most complicated scenes—the resurrection of
Mlle. Hortensia—Zavadsky played with deep emotion. Neither he nor Vakhtangov felt the need for any external effects.
The phrase at the culmination point of the scene, "return and
rise," sounded authoritative and intense. At that moment
Anthony was revealed as one who is capable of standing by
his beliefs and moving persistently toward his aims. Because
of that interpretation of the finale of the role on the part of
the actor and the regisseur, the impression of mildness and
submissiveness in Anthony's character was removed. The
character acquired rather a pathetic quality. Virginia and
Anthony, in the final analysis, emerge as victors in spite of
the factual defeat. Their artless deeds, their honest intentions, reduced the cynical bourgeoisie to an impasse. In the
unequal struggle between humaneness and callousness, simplicity and manipulation, the naïve and trusting Virginia and
the just Anthony turn out to be the victors. Vakhtangov's
interpretation of *The Miracle* was imbued with the spirit of
the time when the play was produced. It was a magnificent
creation of a regisseur in the beginning of the twenties, and

through it Maeterlinck's play was shown in a completely new light.

Vakhtangov's choice of the play was most fortunate. *The Miracle of St. Anthony*, in spite of the fantastic nature and the uncommonness of the plot—the arrival of the Saint on earth—is still the most realistic, from the social point of view, and most pointed work of Maeterlinck, that talented representative of symbolic drama born in the last century. In the beginning of our century, Maeterlinck was most popular. His plays were produced in Germany by Max Reinhardt and in France by André Antoine. In Russia, his very popular drama *Monna Vanna* was produced by the New Alexandrinsky and Maly theaters. The role of Monna Vanna was played by the great Russian actress, V. F. Kommisargevskaya. She played a number of roles in Maeterlinck's plays, directed in her theater by Meyerkhold. *Sister Beatrice* (1906) attracted special appreciation from the press and the public alike. Meyerkhold built his production of *Sister Beatrice* around Kommisargevskaya. Judging from the references of her contemporaries, the roles of the new repertoire were her most successful roles. Decadent, symbolic plays did not present any opportunity for her realistic talent to unfold. That remarkable actress shone brilliantly in plays by Ostrovsky and also in Ibsen's *A Doll's House*. In 1904 Stanislavsky directed a number of dramas by Maeterlinck in the Moscow Art Theater. In 1905 Stanislavsky together with Meyerkhold worked on Maeterlinck's *The Death of Tantigil* in the Theater-Studio on Povarskoy Street. In 1908 Stanislavsky directed *The Bluebird* in the Moscow Art Theater, a spectacle which is still in the repertoire today.

The collaboration of Stanislavsky and Meyerkhold in the Theater-Studio on Povarskoy Street holds a special interest. A number of reasons contributed to the rise of that Studio and these are necessary for us to understand clearly because it was during this period that Vakhtangov was searching for his road in art. The Moscow Art Theater at that time attracted him more than any other theater. But then in the Moscow Art Theater at that time were created such masterpieces as Gorky's rebellious *Lower Depths*, Chekhov's plays with their profound universal truth—with those famous "Chekhov pauses"—and many, many others. A number of productions in the Moscow Art Theater showed obvious traits of naturalism. Chekhov did not accept them; Meyerkhold tried to fight against them with his "fashionable art." It is interesting to quote here one of Chekhov's remarks in relation to naturalism, taken from *Meyerkhold's Diary*. To one of the actors who insisted that everything must be realistic on the stage, Chekhov said smilingly: "Realistic? The stage is art. Kramsky (a Russian painter) has painted human faces brilliantly. What if we cut the painted nose out of one of the faces and insert a real one? The nose will be real, but the picture is ruined. The stage demands a certain conditionality. You don't have the fourth wall. Besides, stage art reflects in itself the quintessence of life, and one should never have on the stage what is unnecessary."

The Moscow Art Theater in its production of *Julius Caesar* and *The Merchant of Venice* followed to a certain degree the principles of the Meiningen Theater. Indulging in the over-emphasis of historical exactness, and authenticity of sets, costumes, and props, the Moscow Art Theater missed that elevated and lofty theatricality, that exalted quality, that is necessary for true and convincing presentation of Shakespeare. Stanislavsky was aware of the danger of indulging in naturalistic copying and in resorting to museums and was anxious to meet with regisseurs and dramatists who were striving for brilliant theatricality. That was exactly what goaded Stanislavsky into attempting to work with such regisseurs as Meyerkhold and Gordon Craig. Stanislavsky was caught by the at-that-time fashionable infatuations with symbolic theater.

*The Miracle of St. Anthony*

The collaboration of Stanislavsky and Meyerkhold did not last long, but one must remember that in their work together Stanislavsky and Meyerkhold made important experiments in the search for theatricality. The union of these two great artists in that theater-studio was instrumental in their pursuing definite aims for the creation of a new theater, a theater in which the actors had first to master a special technique for the expressiveness required by the new repertoire. It was planned to teach actors in that studio a particular manner of working on texts, to train them in a keen sense of rhythm. But in my opinion their choice of repertoire was not always suitable. With Hauptmann's *Schluck and Jau* and Ibsen's *Comedy of Love* was included the symbolic play *The Death of Tantigil,* as well as *Snow* by Pshibeshevsky. While Stanislavsky came to the Theater-Studio with the rich experience of the realistic style of the Moscow Art Theater, Meyerkhold brought to the work such qualities of the regisseur's skill that the Moscow Art Theater had little of. Meyerkhold, as a regisseur, used a brilliant and at times very sharp scenic form. He had an extraordinary feeling for the pictorial. The union between Stanislavsky and Meyerkhold in the Theater-Studio on Povarskoy Street was creatively very interesting, but it was of short duration. Unfortunately, the works of the Theater-Studio never saw the light—or rather the footlights. The performances of the new theater were seen by only a few and they were writers, composers, and actors who attended the rehearsals. Stanislavsky and Meyerkhold parted, and each followed his own road in art. Meyerkhold stubbornly elaborated on the principles and forms of the theater of representation, which according to his thinking would bring us to a theater kindred in spirit and character to the ancient theater. In practical realization of his ideal, Meyerkhold often went off the path, but that thought about a theater kindred to the ancient theater—really mass theater—is interesting to us who live in the second half of the twentieth century.

Today we are fighting actively for the richness and multi-
formity of the direction of the theater. But I repeat that the
fault of Meyerkhold's activities in that period lay in his
choice of plays, which were mainly symbolic. Symbolic dramaturgy led the adherents of the theater of representation
willy-nilly to an aesthetical theater, a decadent theater which
catered to a limited sophisticated-thinking intelligentsia.
That kind of theater was foreign to the democratic theatergoer, who was searching for answers to the important questions of life. In this respect the dramaturgy of Maeterlinck
was not an exception. Maeterlinck's plays made the playgoers
overlook the contradictions of life and lured them into the
world of "lofty and abstract feelings" that promised comfort
in the kingdom of the beyond, the kingdom of good and of
beauty.

Meyerkhold directed *The Miracle of St. Anthony* twice.
First, it was shown in 1906 on the Russian stage in the city of
Poltava, in the Theater of a New Drama; then, in Petersburg,
in the Theater of Kommisargevskaya. How did Meyerkhold
treat these productions? Well, Maeterlinck loved the art of
marionettes—as did Hoffman, a German writer, who in his
witty but paradoxical work *Extraordinary Struggles of the
Director of the Theater* suggests the substitution of marionettes for living actors. Meyerkhold pursued a different aim
in using the puppets; he intended to emphasize the soulless-
ness of people by creating masks for Gus, Achilles, the Doctor,
the Curé, and others. Talking about his production of *The
Miracle,* Meyerkhold complained that he did not accomplish
his purpose because the actors fell into a vaudeville style and
aroused laughter in places where it should not have occurred.
According to his conception, the world of marionettes should
have become an ironic reflection of the world of reality. His
production was interesting, but only externally. He achieved
no social impact in it. That accomplishment took place in a
different time, after the October Revolution, and was the

achievement of another director, E. B. Vakhtangov.

Before I begin the analysis of Vakhtangov's work on *The Miracle,* I want to recall how his creative individuality was formed, how he assimilated the creative heritage of the masters of the previous generation who had exerted a strong influence on him while he was still a young boy. At that period there had been an interesting and complicated struggle between the two extreme directions in the theater—the realistic school and the school of representation—and a young actor could easily have become confused. Each movement contained positive and negative traits of theater culture. The realistic theater was in danger of becoming naturalistic, and the theater of representation was threatened by formalism and isolationism. One of Vakhtangov's instructors, a man of extraordinary personal charm and a great teacher, L. A. Sulergitsky, once said to his very promising student, "You please me very much. As long as I am alive, you will be all right. Only always come to me for advice. I appreciate you. Some day you will enter the Maly Theater." The last phrase defined the young Vakhtangov's aspirations. He was already at that period trying in his own way to assimilate the realistic method of Stanislavsky. He strove intuitively for harmony between content and form. Vakhtangov was much impressed with the skill of the actors at the Maly Theater who came closest to a synthesis of the truth of feelings and the building of the image; they had the most correct path to this result. And that path was followed by the best actors in the world, those who not only lived the role but at the same time presented it. In one of his last conversations with Zakhava and Kotlubai, Vakhtangov said, "There are only isolated great artists—Duse, Chaliapin, Salvini—who while acting are aware that they are acting." His love for actors of such great talent, of such creative many-sidedness, shows his correct understanding of theater technique from our point of view today. Those actors mentioned by Vakhtangov were by their creative quality, school, and method of building their characters similar to the actors of the Maly Theater.

It is interesting to note the names of actors Vakhtangov was exposed to before he became acquainted with the theaters of Moscow and Petrograd—such performers as Robert and Raphael Adelheim and Marius Petipa. I was fortunate enough to see Marius Petipa in 1917 in the role of Cyrano de Bergerac. Though at that time Petipa was close to seventy, he performed the role of Cyrano with extraordinary mastery. He was Gascon from head to foot. French repertoire was familiar to Marius Petipa, since he was a Frenchman by birth, and he possessed an exceptional ability to convey in the Russian language the inimitable peculiarity of French intonations. I am sure that Vakhtangov while working on *The Miracle* was recalling his youthful memories of Petipa and his "tripping on the tongue" dialogue, his intonational finesse, and his extraordinary skill in delivering the melodiousness of French speech. Marius Petipa was one of the most brilliant and talented representatives of the school of representation. He proved the famous words of Diderot: "The power over us is not held by those who lose themselves in ecstasy; that power is the privilege of one who has control over himself." Diderot also used to say that a poet creates man by exaggerating what is in man; an actor, in turn, exaggerates what is created by a poet. Thus portraits created by actors are exaggerated portraits, subjected to certain rules, certain conditionalities. That formula of Diderot was very close to what Vakhtangov pursued in the production of *The Miracle*.

In connection with this, I recall Vakhtangov saying during one of the rehearsals: "Maeterlinck loved to observe bees and their life through a special glass by means of which he could see the whole process of their work. What if, in that bee's work-loving hive, one would let in an alien creature? Can you imagine what would happen in the hive? The same happens among the guests and relatives of Mlle. Hortensia when Saint Anthony arrives."

Now let us go back to those actors whom Vakhtangov observed and admired in his youth. A strong impression was made on him by one of the greatest of the provincial actors, Pavel Orlenev—especially in his best romantic roles, that of Oswald in Ibsen's *Ghosts* and of Raskolnikov in Dostoevsky's *Crime and Punishment.* Vakhtangov also saw a very talented Russian actress, Lidia Yavorskaya, in the role of Madame Sans-Gene, from the gallery of the Vladikavkas City Theater. Vakhtangov was fortunate in his school days. A very important entrepreneur of the old Russia, B. I. Nikulin, who was democratically inclined and contributed a lot to the popularization of the Russian classic repertoire, organized special matinee performances for students. At these, Vakhtangov saw plays by Griboyedov, Gogol, and Ostrovsky. In 1903, Vakhtangov moved to Moscow and entered Moscow University. His summer vacations were spent in the provinces, participating in their theater presentations. Mrs. Vakhtangov stayed in Moscow with her husband some of the time, but for the most part she remained in Vladikavkas. Correspondence filled Vakhtangov's life. This correspondence was conducted in a theatrical manner; he used to send picture postcards of the actors whom he saw currently in a play. On these postcards we find as a rule actors of the Moscow Art Theater, but there were a number of postcards with photographs of the actors from the Maly Theater, the Theater Korsha, and the Neslobin Theater. From those picture postcards, we learn that Vakhtangov saw in the Maly Theater a play by Beaumarchais, *The Marriage of Figaro,* and also a play by Scribe, *A Glass of Water,* with the great Yugin. I can easily imagine what an impression Yugin must have made on Vakhtangov, as I experienced the sensation myself. When I was in the gymnasium, I saw Yugin in the role of Bolingbroke in the play *The Glass of Water.* Yugin was an actor of great taste, and he possessed a perfect sense of timing in comedy. He was a true artist of the stage, a man of enormous talent, and a thoroughly cultured human being. The resourcefulness and elegance of that clever diplomat—Bolingbroke—required of an actor an improvisational ease and the ability for quick-changing adjustment in situations that demanded immediate decisions. I think that Yugin's performance in this role made a strong impression on Vakhtangov. It was imprinted in his subconscious and one way or the other manifested itself in his regisseur's devices in the production of *The Miracle*.

Anyone who has ever seen the great Russian actress Ermolova on the stage of the Maly Theater carried away an impression that lasted all his life. Vakhtangov loved and deeply respected the creativity and the humane image of that great actress. We read in his diary entry of December 16, 1914: "Tonight Ermolova came to see *Cricket on the Hearth*. I was dreadful in my role this evening. I was not concentrated, not collected, I had no objective. I am so ashamed of myself. And when I kissed her hand, I realized how difficult it is to be an actor, how undeserving I am of her polite 'Thank you.' "

The young Vakhtangov saw Ostugev in the Maly Theater. Ostugev was an actor of rare beauty, and he had a fine musicality in pronouncing his text. Vakhtangov loved opera and ballet. He never missed a performance of the Bolshoi Theater, Mrs. Vakhtangov tells us. He used to collect clippings from theater magazines with pictures of scenery and *mise en scène* of different productions. All that was preparation for his future work as a regisseur.

When we talk about the young Vakhtangov, we must not forget that he took his first steps in the theater as an actor. Vakhtangov, as many other young actors, adored V. E. Katchalov of the Moscow Art Theater. We remember the remarkable, bewitching voice of that splendid actor, a voice that sounded like a musical instrument and which penetrated deeply into one's soul. Vakhtangov used to imitate Katchalov's reading of the monologue from the play *Anathema* by Andreev. Once Stanislavsky asked Vakhtangov to participate in one of the "Kapustnic" in the Moscow Art Theater, and he read the monologue of *Anathema*. Katchalov was present that particular evening, and he loved Vakhtangov's imitation of him. At the gathering commemorating Vakhtangov's memory in 1947, at the Vakhtangov Theater, Katchalov told those present at the celebration about Vakhtangov's brilliant imitation of him, and then he read the monologue of *Anathema*, not as he would read it, but as Vakhtangov read it when imitating him. It was a most excitingly interesting parody on parody. Talking about Vakhtangov's ability to imitate, I have in mind not the delivery of an external similarity to the original, not the ability to grasp Katchalov's intonations, but something much more important—the great, artistic tact and taste of the parody performance when an actor showed the original not through the prism of irony and ridicule, but through the prism of love and respect for the art of a great artist, which Katchalov was.

Vakhtangov appreciated deeply Leonidov and Moskvin and spoke about those two remarkable actors of the Moscow Art Theater with much love and profound respect. He wrote in his diary on December 13, 1914: "Moskvin saw *The Cricket on the Hearth* and came to see me after the performance. He told me, 'Good. Very good. You cope extremely well with the characteristics of the role. There was no over-acting. You know yourself when one actor watches another actor, he can't help but expect some over-acting. But no, you did not over-act; you created a singular, unusual character.' One will not find another like him on the stage. Delicate, gentle, and makes such a strong impression."

Vakhtangov was very close to Michael Chekhov, that extraordinarily talented, I would even say brilliant, tragicomedian of the First Studio of the Moscow Art Theater. During their friendship, Chekhov created such roles as Frazier in Berger's play *Deluge,* Malvolio in *Twelfth Night,* Vaphlya in *Uncle Vanya,* and Khlestokov in *The Inspector General.* These performances were considered a striking accomplishment, indicating virtuosity in inner and outer technique alike. Vakhtangov used to talk about the singularity of Chekhov's talent at the time when he was helping him with his role of Khlestokov. It is difficult to imagine a more perfect delivery of that most demanding, exacting role for a comedian. All of Moscow raved about Chekhov's Khlestokov. I do not intend to evaluate in great detail those glorious actors such as Katchalov, Leonidov, Moskvin, Chekhov. My intention is to estimate those artists who were close to Vakhtangov in the spirit and understanding of theater art. In Katchalov, Vakhtangov loved the depth of his mind, his elevated poetic lyricism and musicality; in Leonidov, his elemental passion, tragic ascents, upward flights. In Moskvin, his Russian humor, his warmth. In Chekhov, his rare, brilliant improvisational spontaneity, his virtuoso ingenuousness. But though the actor's art at the time Vakhtangov entered the creative life was understandable and convincing, by the power of brilliancy of the actor's talents, the understanding and orientation of oneself in the problems of contemporary stage directing were considerably more difficult. The names of Stanislavsky, Nemirovitch-Dantchenko, Meyerkhold, Gordon Craig, Max Reinhardt were widely known. Vakhtangov had to pave his own way among those authorities on direction. In his diary, marked January 10, 1911, "I am completely convinced that the Stanislavsky System is a great thing." On April 1911, of the same year, after Vakhtangov entered the Moscow Art Theater, he wrote in his diary: "I want to organize a studio where we can study. The principle—to attempt to achieve everything by ourselves. The leader—all of us. To test the Stanislavsky System on ourselves. To accept or reject it, to correct it, to supplement it, rid it of what we find wrong in it." This notation ends with: "I am planning to introduce study in movement, training of the voice, fencing, reading of the history of art and history of costume. Once a week we shall listen to music all together—invite musicians to come and play for us."

Thus we see that from the first step, Vakhtangov was interested on the one hand in the System as a method of education of the inner technique of an actor, and on the other hand in organizing classes to develop their outward physical technique. He paid special attention to the physical expressiveness of an actor, a subject which, at that time, was not given much attention in the Moscow Art Theater.

Vakhtangov was well acquainted with Stanislavsky and Meyerkhold's attempts to create a new theater, and with their experiences in the production of plays by Maeterlinck. Also, in the year 1910, Vakhtangov was an assistant to Sulergitsky* in his production of Maeterlinck's *The Blue Bird* in the Rejan Theater in Paris. Vakhtangov wrote in his diary in 1911: "I rehearsed 'Night' (the fourth scene of the second act of *The Blue Bird*). Sulergitsky has been concentrated on *mise en scène*. Not too interesting. One thing I am learning, one should not act as French actors do. Technique only—and a bad one."

Vakhtangov chose *The Miracle of St. Anthony* in 1916 for his work in his own studio. On January 11, 1917, he wrote in his notebook: "In *Anthony,* one should feel Maeterlinck's smile—a good-natured, pleasant smile toward the people he placed in such an unusual circumstance."

In his first version of the play in 1916 (in the studio that later became the Vakhtangov Theater), one felt his gentle forgiving attitude toward the French bourgeoisie. In that interpretation, the relatives of Mademoiselle Hortensia were even grateful to Anthony for his resurrection of their aunt.

* Sulergitsky was a co-worker with Stanislavsky in the Moscow Art Theater, and a great teacher.

"Of course, people do not believe he is a saint. Of course, she was not dead as yet. Of course, there is something peculiar about the situation, but they are grateful to that strange man"—we read further in Vakhtangov's notebook. What a difference between that "appeasing, idyllico-kindly" interpretation in 1916 and the sharply satirical treatment Vakhtangov gave the same play in 1920-21. "Now the theatrical means we use in *Miracle*—branding the bourgeoisie—concur with the demands of life in our time," insisted Vakhtangov, while working on the last version of *Miracle*.

While Vakhtangov's interpretation of *Miracle* in 1916 brought into Maeterlinck's drama the traits of appeasement and kindliness (one cannot help but think that this came about through the influence of Tolstoy's ideas, which Suler-gitsky—one of Vakhtangov's teachers—followed religiously), the interpretation of the play in 1920-21, in after-Revolutionary days, by a now mature master, significantly and sharply intensified the conflict in *Miracle*. The active clash between the two antagonistic groups gave the play the character of important social generalizations, allowed the presentation of the play in a sharply satiric plane, and gave it graphically striking form. Satire is the foundation of *Miracle;* it is inherent in the very idea of Maeterlinck's play, in its innermost depth. This was brought out by Vakhtangov with enormous power and distinction.

Vakhtangov discarded the use of masks—which Meyer-khold and Maeterlinck had felt to be right. Vakhtangov's production proved convincingly that the play is much more expressive with live actors and their realistic acting, rather than with marionettes. *The Miracle of St. Anthony* in its satirical form was characteristic of French literature in the spirit of Balzac, Flaubert, and Maupassant, Vakhtangov's favorite French writers.

Vakhtangov's mastery of psychological analysis was based on his thorough knowledge of Stanislavsky's Method. In the comedy style, the process of work on the role according to the Method gives one splendid opportunities to get into the heart of humor, to find the comedy characteristics in scenes. The more thoroughly the suddenness of the comic situations and their paradoxicality is disclosed, the more subtly we analyze the true motives that direct the innermost thoughts of the characters, the more zealously we hide those thoughts from the surrounding characters, the more vividly the audience reacts to the regisseur's conception and its realization.

The basic "through action" of the characters opposed to Anthony is to defend and safeguard their home and their bourgeois property against the visitation of this unbidden guest. Now, what is the acuteness of the scenic situation and the foundation of the paradox that gives us the right to use a satirical and ironical attitude toward such personages as Gustav, Joseph, Achilles, the doctor, and the curé? It lies in their unwillingness to return to the time when their aunt was alive and demanded all their attention without giving anything in exchange. Now the dead aunt gives them all her possessions without demanding anything.

That scenic situation, according to Vakhtangov, provides us with an ample opportunity to "brand the bourgeoisie" because it reveals its characteristic traits: greediness, self-interest, egotism and, especially, bigotry. Anthony in the eyes of the bourgeoisie is not a saint but an "expropriator" who has come to rob them of their riches. Therefore one must fight him resolutely and mercilessly. The whole arsenal of bourgeois "democracy" is used: "angel defenders" of the bourgeoisie—the police—appear. Fetters are placed on Anthony's wrists—a very expressive touch. Fetters symbolize the basic law of the bourgeoisie—everything belongs to them, the masters of that society, everything is subordinate to the defense of their amassed capital.

The uncommonness of the plot of *Miracle*—its fantastic nature, even its paradoxicality, its acute satirical trend—naturally demanded a singular scenic form to help to communicate to the audience as fully as possible the content of the play. In search of such a form, regisseur Vakhtangov turned to the works of a remarkable French artist, the satirist Honoré Daumier. His political caricatures give a merciless analysis of bourgeois psychology. Daumier shows graphically what the "powers that be" represent—beginning with King Louis Philippe and his ministers and concluding with functionaries of the legislative body. Daumier created a large number of caricatures and cartoons on that "king of shopkeepers"— Louis Philippe. One of his most memorable lithographs is "Gargantua." In this, Louis Philippe is pictured as an insatiable monster. The lithograph shows a crowd of officials and dignitaries stuffing a gigantic Louis Philippe with tributes. He sits like some greedy Buddha, with the no less greedy members of his big family behind him, but the throne on which he sits is actually a stool. An abundant shower of medals is pouring out of the royal fundament. Behind the King's throne, next to the building of the French parliament, are clustered pygmies—the "people's representatives."

In another caricature Daumier shows those "people's representatives" on a larger plane, constituting the legislative body. Daumier does not depict them as occupying the respected benches of deputies, but the benches of defendants— those behind bars. Among the "people's representatives" some appear sleepy, some bored; some are gossiping, others seem to be telling each other dirty jokes; a few are listening to the representatives' speeches with indifferent expressions on their faces. We understand Daumier's intention—to disclose the farce of the so-called "legislative body" that is called upon to watch over the people's interests. We also know those works of Daumier which tell us with anger and indignation about brutal exploitation of ordinary men, and of their tragedies. One of the lithographs depicts the room of a worker wrecked by a governmental punitive detachment. On the floor lies the dead body of the worker and the dead bodies of his wife and child. That lithograph is full of protest from the noble heart of the artist-citizen who loves his people and defends their right to a free life.

Undoubtedly, Honoré Daumier was under the influence of Eugène Delacroix, the author of the remarkable painting "Liberty Guiding People." One feels the influence of liberty guiding people in Daumier's picture "Uprising," which calls for a revolutionary fight, with the same pictorial power.

Daumier lived among ordinary men; he knew his people very well and he disclosed their sublimity with much love and great strength. His lithographs "Shaken by Heritage of the Year 1871"—a woman draped in black, bemoaning those perished in the days of the Paris Commune—and "Family on the Barricades" are both on an important, tragic revolutionary theme.

A famous French actor, Frédéric Lemaître, created a typical satirical image of a character he called Robert Macaire—a rogue and a chameleon. Daumier took the image created by Lemaître as a model for his series of social, everyday caricatures—angry, satirical, theatrically expressive. In Daumier's caricature "The Financier Gambler," we see Robert Macaire surrounded by a mob of excited and bewildered stockholders with their arms outstretched, as if saying, "One cannot help it." In other lithographs, we see Robert Macaire as a philanthropist, a journalist, a doctor, and a preacher. All those brilliant, comic, satirical drawings were typical portraits of the bourgeoisie and the Philistines.

The cycle of the Robert Macaire lithographs was exceptionally theatrical. Daumier felt the scenic figure created by Frédéric Lemaître and made graphic variations on this theme.

Daumier's feeling for the theater is clearly seen in his works: "In the Theater Box," "Concluding Couplet," "Complimentary Ticket," "Comedian," and "The Parade of Comedians." For regisseurs and actors, Daumier's creations are a school of *mise en scènes,* the molding of figures, characters, portraits, make-ups, and expressive hands.

Vakhtangov's taste prompted him to dress *The Miracle of St. Anthony* in the style of Daumier's spirit. The arts of painting, music, and sculpture often prompt regisseurs to the form of the spectacle, its complete, integral, artistic image— and actors to their interpretation of their roles and their embodiments. An actor and a regisseur should begin to make their choice of music or scenic design for a given play only after they know clearly what is needed: what the actor wants to say with his role, and what the director wants to say with the play as a whole. For an actor or a regisseur to choose the form first and then adjust it to the content of the role or the play would limit his fantasy and force it.

Vakhtangov first defined for himself the idea of *The Miracle of St. Anthony*—"to brand the bourgeoisie"—and then envisioned for its plastic embodiment the character and manner which would be similar to the creativity of that most fiery enemy of the bourgeoisie, and artist-patriot-revolutionary, Honoré Daumier.

The set and costume designer of *Miracle* in the studio presentation was Y. A. Zavadsky, who studied painting—as did V. V. Mayakovsky—with the artist P. Kelin. Kelin was a student of the great Russian painter Serov. The light background of white walls with the black coats and top hats on the hall-stand and the figures of the guests and relatives in black created a gamut of light and dark similar to the gamut of Daumier. Against the background of white walls and the many black spots, the grayish-brown tones of Anthony's costume and Virginia's stood out sharply.

The style and the form of the presentation of *Miracle* had no direct, or I would say immediate, continuation in the productions of the Vakhtangovites' regisseurs that were created after the death of their teacher. While the characteristic

| 134

singularities of *A Wedding* and *Princess Turandot* found their reflection and development in a number of productions of Vakhtangov's students, *Miracle* until now showed this definite influence only in performances of some of the actors —in their graphic, precise formation, reminiscent of some in *Miracle*. I would like to name the following performers: B. Schukin (Governor), E. Alexceeva (Anna Andreevna) in Gogol's *Inspector General,* M. Sinelnikova (Madame Ksidias in *Intervention*), E. Toltchanov (Magora in *Virinea* by Seyfulina), Michael Chekhov (Chlestakov in *Inspector General*). All those actors worked with Vakhtangov for many years, in a close association. It is characteristic also that the creations of those actors developed on classic material, which demands of an actor precisely that expressiveness that is contained in the plays of Gogol and Dostoevsky *(Uncle's Dream)*. The works of M. Sinelnikova and A. Dikii developed on the basis of talented and daring Soviet plays such as *Front,* by A. Korneychuk, and *Intervention,* by L. Slavin; plays which also give the opportunity for an expressive molding of the scenic image.

Analyzing now Vakhtangov's interpretation and mounting of Maeterlinck's play, I feel that plays by such Soviet dramatists as V. Mayakovsky, V. Vishnevsky, M. Bulgakov, and H. Erdman could be staged with the same mode of treatment as Vakhtangov used for *The Miracle.* That method demands a subtle and intelligent psychological basis in the play: graphically laconic theatrical form, precise design of *mise en scène,* clear-cut scenic figures, exact expressive make-ups and costumes for the actors.

The plastic side of the actor's performance in such plays is as important a component of the actor's creativity as is his inner technique and should be developed by a fine actor to the faultless exactness that allows him to arouse easily in himself the necessary emotions for the role.

In one of my regisseur's works of recent times, on Gorky's

*Phoma Gordeev,* I first intuitively and then deliberately applied the elements of Vakhtangov's mounting of *Miracle.* I was of course changing and remaking those elements in a manner corresponding to the problems presented to me by the realistic work of Gorky, and according to the different ideologically artistic aims of the play as a whole. But in such episodes of the play as "Merchant Club" (especially when lighting the boat), I strove for graphic exactness of *mise en scène.*

In Gorky's description of the appearances of the merchants, dressed in black attire, or of such details as their headdresses flying in the air at the beginning of the church service, or the dynamic scene of the confrontation between Phoma and "important citizens," I saw something reminding me of *Miracle.* I don't know in what degree we succeeded in materializing what we saw, but we tried our best to follow Vakhtangov's principles in the presentation of *Phoma Gordeev,* and to reveal organically Gorky's ideas that are contained in the play.

Undoubtedly, somewhere in my subconscious mind was the same intent that Vakhtangov had for *Miracle*—to "brand the bourgeoisie," but this time it was our Russian bourgeoisie, and my experience acquired during participating in *Miracle* undoubtedly helped me in working on the play *Phoma Gordeev.*

In concluding this chapter on *The Miracle of St. Anthony,* I would like to quote an evaluation of *Miracle* by the newspaper *Trud* (Labor). "The talented and great regisseur of our time, E. B. Vakhtangov, made the production of *The Miracle of St. Anthony* a rich, brilliant spectacle, an important one to be produced at this time. By his distinctive staging of this play he transferred the emphasis from the plane of the religious to the plane of satire on the bourgeoisie devoted to its faith. Thus we have a contemporary thorny satire, which sharply brands the hypocrisy of the Philistines."

Our performances of *Miracle* in Paris had a tremendous

success. They were organized by Firmin Gemier, a man of great culture; the teacher of Jean Villard. Incidentally, we recognized Vakhtangov's handwriting in Villard's presentation of *Don Juan* and of *Mary Tudor*.

The character of Vakhtangov's embodiment of *The Miracle of St. Anthony* did not receive sufficient development and continuation in the Soviet theaters because of the mistakes committed by theater people in their fight with formalism. It is not a secret that at times the fight against formalism was turned into a fight for formlessness, into a fight against any search in line with new expressive theatrical form. These mistakes greatly harmed the Soviet theater, impoverished its means of expression. Together with the truly harmful in art, many fruitful experiments and developments were also suppressed. Vakhtangov's tradition was impoverished and oversimplified. That splendid tradition of the true, great art, most expressive and exact, that tradition of art on a large scale and of subtle taste must be brought back to the Soviet stage—and, in the first place, to the stage of the Vakhtangov Theater.

# Part III

# Vakhtangov Directs

# *Princess Turandot*
## by Carlo Gozzi

VAKHTANGOV created the play *Princess Turandot* during severe years of devastation and hunger—during the years of the civil war, when the young Soviet Republic was defending the achievements of the Revolution against the White Russian Army and the Interventionists. The streets of Moscow were plunged into darkness. The roads were covered by snowdrifts. Cabmen cleared a passage for the sleighs on the tramrails. The trams were not functioning, and Moscovites performed their daily duties mostly on foot. For the transportation of produce—frozen potatoes or dark flour—children's sleighs were used. It was cold in the homes; the rooms were heated by so-called "bourgeoiky"— small-sized tin stoves with pipes which went directly through the fortochka (small, hinged windowpanes used for ventilation during the winter). The times were hard.

I consider the fourteenth chapter of Mayakovsky's poem *Very Well* a most remarkable picture of that period. Describing those difficult years, and viewing the troubled past from the lofty, elevated view of the great ideas that were already triumphing at the time the poem was written, the poet finds in it all an amazingly deep and compassionate humor. Mayakovsky stressed neither the hardships nor the sorrows, but sought for warm, lyric words with which to evoke in his readers a greater understanding of what the people of the country had accomplished and endured.

"Not home,
not for soup,
but to the beloved
for a visit
two
carrots
I am carrying
by the green tail,
I

often presented
candies and flowers,
but more than
all
expensive presents
I remember
that precious carrot
and a half
of the log
of the birch tree . . ."

But at the end of the poem Mayakovsky expresses the innermost feelings that reigned over the hearts of those who considered themselves firmly bound to the future of their ravaged but high-spirited country.

". . . Were left
the clouds
to the countries
clouded.
Behind the cloud
seacoast
lies
America.
Lay
lapped
coffee,
cocoa
in your face
thicker than
pig's whims,
rounder
than
restaurant dishes,
from our
beggarly
country
I shout:

> 'I
> love
> this
> country!'
> Possible
> to forget
> when and where
> my belly grew
> and 'goiter . . .
> but the country
> with which
> together I starved
> impossible
> ever
> to forget!''

When I read these lines, I always see Mayakovsky in the orchestra applauding Vakhtangov's brilliant production of *Turandot*. The urge for social uplift was reflected in all areas of the people's spiritual life, and influenced the youth greatly. About forty years have passed since then; now, glancing over the past, thinking of those heroic days, I am astounded by all that ardent youthful enthusiasm which flooded the numerous theatrical studios at that time. And the thought of that joyous enthusiasm brings me to the name of Vakhtangov, a director who immediately moved in step with the times. He attracted the youth who dreamed of creating a new Soviet theater, a new art. Simply take a look at a list of the theatrical studios and schools which besieged him to teach for them, to work with them, and you will see how the youth gravitated toward Vakhtangov. I will mention only some of the young theatrical collectives with whom he worked: The First Studio of the Moscow Art Theater, The Second Studio of the Moscow Art Theater, The Studio of Vakhtangov (formerly called The Third Studio of the Moscow Art Theater), The Habimah, The Armenian Studio, Studio Chaliapin, The Studio of the

Big Theater, and The Opera Theater of Stanislavsky. He also still worked as an actor in the Moscow Art Theater, and he was invited to head the theater section of the People's Committee on Education.

I remember how after his rehearsals in Habimah, at one or two o'clock in the morning, Vakhtangov, tired and ill, would come to us at the Mansurovsky Studio. He would stay and talk with us for half an hour, then dismiss us. Many of us after those "talks" had to walk home through Moscow's empty streets, hungry but happy, with the joyous awareness that a theater was being created. We would have a theater; Vakhtangov would help us reach our goal.

Even such short discussions with Vakhtangov were as interesting as rehearsals. At times a discussion because of its significance could take the place of a number of rehearsals. He talked to us about the most diverse questions of life and art, and these talks were so much more brilliant than the books and articles written about him by theatrical connoisseurs and historians. Vital speech, sincere and fiery, with that special Vakhtangov temperament, with polemic fervor, with ideas born suddenly, with brilliant comparisons, with enormous humor—naturally such is almost impossible to reconstruct with the usual book phrases, maybe very clever phrases, but nevertheless far from expressing the essence of Vakhtangov's personality with all its facets, all its warm, kindly, dynamic fascination.

There are expressions we use in the theater which on paper cannot convey the exact meaning they have when used in actual work in scenic practice. For example, a "run through" of the play. Hidden in that prosaic term is the infective excitement of the whole collective, including the director, the actors, the propmen, and every individual involved in the production, regardless of the size of his contribution. Or other expressions such as "scenic objectives," "super objectives," "relaxation of muscles"—all the terminology used to

express the various processes of creativity sounds most un-
poetical. Readers who are not familiar with the theater might
think that the creative process in the theater is very dull, but
actually each of these terms is fraught with a deep meaning
and leads to the fascinating, captivating process of work on
individual scenes.

I would like to point out an obviously faulty interpretation
of Vakhtangov's thinking, I might almost say a direct distor-
tion of his ideas, in the writings of some of our theatrical
connoisseurs. For example, let us take one of Vakhtangov's
definitions of what theater should be. Often, during the rehearsals of *Turandot*, in an effort to formulate his creative
credo, he used two words: "fantastic realism." Of course that
definition, to a certain degree, is relative. But almost all the
theatrical historians who wrote about Vakhtangov gave that
definition an interpretation completely alien to Vakhtangov's. They defined the word "fantastic" as fantasticality, as
not representative of life.

One has to admit, however, that theater terminology is not
yet well worked out and is still in the process of formation,
as is the science of the theater. In this respect Vakhtangov
had much difficulty because he tried persistently and with
great pains to formulate in one word that which he had been
searching for in art with all the intensity of his creative
strength. Getting away from the naturalistic, intimate theater
to the theater of the great passions and emotions, to the theater called upon to express the grandeur and sublimity of
the Revolution and the people who created it, Vakhtangov
stubbornly strove for the theatrical basis and purport of his
experimentations.

We know that the problem of fantasy and reality, fantasy
and truth, often stirred the minds of those Russian publicists
engaged in the subject of aesthetics. Chernishevsky, in his
work *The Aesthetic Relations of Art to Reality,* gave considerable attention to the problem of fantasy. Chernishevsky

criticized sharply those philosophers who considered fantasy
as a power which turns an ordinary object into a very splendid one. According to his own philosophic conception that
ordinary object is already beautiful—life is beautiful.

But Chernishevsky by no means expected an artist to copy
reality. He knew too well the significance of the creative
imagination during the process of character formation. Chernishevsky wrote: "The purpose of re-creation is to help the
imagination and not to cheat the feeling, as does the imitation; and it is not a light sport, as the imitation is. Re-creation is a work with a real purpose. There is no doubt that the
theory of re-creation, if it deserves attention, will arouse
strong resistance from the adherents of the theory of creativity. They would assert that re-creation leads to the photographic copying of reality, against which they are only too
often armed." But foreseeing these retorts, Chernishevsky
contended that in art it is a man's right and duty to make
use of all his moral and intellectual faculties, including his
imagination, if he desires to do more than just copy the
object.

Vakhtangov's last discussion with his two assistant students,
Zakhava and Kotlubai, was on the creative fantasy of the
actor. And Vakhtangov's final note completing his diaries
was the note which defined and deciphered the meaning of
his term "fantastic realism." Here is how Vakhtangov put it:
"The correct theatrical means, when discovered, gives to the
author's work a true reality on the stage. One can study these
means, but the form must be created, must be the product of
the artist's great imagination—fantasy. This is why I call it
'fantastic realism.' It exists in every art."

This definition makes it obvious that Vakhtangov spoke of
the artist's fantasy, of his creative imagination, but not of
those contrived fantasticalities that lead the artist away from
truth. Fantastical—or one may call it fantasy's—realism is realism in which the artist's creative fantasy takes the most active

part in revealing the content and in searching for the form of the theatrical work, the play. Of course, any creativity or reproduction of reality by means of art necessarily supposes participation of the artist-creator's fantasy. Vakhtangov, emphasizing the significance of the artist's fantasy, insisted on the maximal expressiveness of those happenings which are natural to life.

When we talk of the role of fantasy in the creative process, this is the procedure we have in mind—and we are speaking now of acting, although all artistic creativity functions similarly. First the artist, stimulated by the play and by his role, visualizes them both in a general sense, perhaps conscious only of some of the aspects of them. Then, gradually, he begins to see the work in its entirety, in all the completeness of its myriad details, in all the richness of its content. His creative imagination helps the artist to find the necessary corresponding form for that image. This imagination when given free play helps him to assemble the details and the partial aspects that have been perceived and accumulated by his fantasy and weave them into a completed form, the final and only possible expression of the idea, born with love. In poetry this process is connected with meter and rhythm. Inspiration is an indispensable ingredient in this process. Without it, art is inconceivable, unthinkable.

Chernishevsky says: "Inspiration is an especially favorable mood for creative fantasy." Vakhtangov understood this thoroughly. His rehearsals were a thrilling example of it. Here he revealed an extraordinary enthusiasm in his work; a sparkling fantasy which would picture suddenly the enormous possibilities of his work and would inspire all those participating; inventive, daring, brilliant ideas for portraying the meaning of the play, which sprang suddenly to his mind; and the courage to discard bravely what he had painstakingly discovered earlier and start again to search for the means whereby he might express the essence of the play more point-

edly, more vividly. As a natural consequence of all this, Vakhtangov had an extraordinary ability to arouse in his actors
the same creative mood he himself had.

The correct definition of Vakhtangov's term "fantastic realism" is of great importance because, when correctly understood, that definition would elucidate the whole function of
Vakhtangov in the field of theatrical art. It would create the
right perspective for true perception of the scenic canvases
he created and for appreciation of the singularity of his directorial art. Vakhtangov loved life passionately. Pretentious-
ness, sentimentality, and superficiality were completely foreign to his nature. Nothing dubious, questionable, or second-
rate was ever tolerated by him; in matters of taste, he was in-
finitely exacting. The actor guilty of lack of taste on the stage
was severely reprimanded by him. Vakhtangov demanded
that an actor possess a real sense of responsibility in his relation to his profession. He demanded that students rise to a
level of true art even during rehearsals. This meticulousness
he had learned inside the walls of the Moscow Art Theater
from his teachers, Stanislavsky and Nemirovitch-Dantchenko.
And, like them, he believed that the rehearsal requires just
as responsible a relationship to the work and to the mobilization of the creative forces as does a performance. Active, intensive work of fantasy during the rehearsals is one of the
most important factors contributing to the creative state of
an actor.

The question of fantasy occupies an important place in
Stanislavsky's teachings. In his book *The Work of an Actor
on Himself*, in the chapter "Imagination" (originally called
"Fantasy") , Stanislavsky says: "Each of our movements on
the stage, every word, must be a result of the imagination in
the correct direction of the life of the play. The creative work
on the role, and the transformation of a written work of a
dramatist into the scenic life, from the beginning to the end,
proceeds with the participation of imagination. That's why I

want you to pay special attention to the development of your imagination."

While exploring the means of scenic expressiveness, Vakhtangov simultaneously was trying to find the definitions which would most correctly interpret his scenic principles. Naming his ideal "fantastic realism," he contrasted polemically his conception of art with the primitive, shallow, small truth that blossomed in the intimate theaters, thanks to those pseudo-followers of Stanislavsky who misinterpreted his method and his teachings. In his search, Vakhtangov strove to correct not only the mistakes others had made, but those he too had made. He felt that the petty problems, the self-analysis, the rummaging in one's soul, so typical of the theaters of the pre-Revolutionary period, must be done away with. Vakhtangov was aware of such mistakes in his own production of Ibsen's *Rosmersholm*, in 1918, and in *Holiday of a Peace*, by Gerhart Hauptmann, in 1913, in the First Studio of the Moscow Art Theater.

After the Revolution, a new audience came to the theater; people seeking an art which would reflect all the grandeur, all the exaltation of Revolutionary events. All art, but particularly the theater, was called upon to express the unprecedented social changes that the Revolution had brought about and to give answer to the problems of life to which these changes had given birth. The pre-Revolutionary theater did not have the flexibility and expressiveness needed by the theater of the first Revolutionary years, and Vakhtangov, as a sensitive artist, felt and understood this. He understood this new audience and its needs.

But how was he to reform the existing theatrical art, since it depended completely on dramaturgy? There were no plays that met the demands of this new audience. Vakhtangov reasoned there were two possible ways in which he could do this. He could read the classics with a new eye, and endeavor to find in them some consonance with the Revolution and its ideology. Or, he could prepare for the birth of a new dramaturgy by developing new forms of theater art—forms which would disclose a theater replete with the great ideas that were closely bound up with the life and struggles of the Revolutionary people.

We all know from our study of history that there are times when it is imperative to break with the old, to destroy it resolutely and relentlessly. In those first Soviet years, a tremendous reconstruction took place in Russia. All art underwent drastic changes. The old was banished because the development of the new-born society created new and different needs. Vakhtangov was in accord with this shifting scene. He fought the old theater, destroying its out-of-date forms and replacing them with new forms which were both brilliant and honest. Such characteristics were essential to a people striving to create a new world. Vakhtangov never betrayed the eternal realistic basis of the teachings of Stanislavsky; he never doubted the validity of Stanislavsky's system. But he criticized it, pointing out some of its weaknesses, and he expressed new thoughts, which Stanislavsky often accepted.

"You are the first fruit of our renewed art," Stanislavsky wrote to Vakhtangov. "I love you for your talents as a teacher, regisseur, and artist; for your striving for the genuine, for the true in art; for your ability to discipline yourself and others, fight and conquer defects. I am grateful to you for your patient, laborious work, for your convictions, humility, persistence, and purity in realizing our common principles in art. I know and believe that the road you have chosen will bring you a great and deserved victory."

Stanislavsky wanted to direct Pushkin's play *Mozart and Saliery* in collaboration with Vakhtangov. As it is known, Stanislavsky had failed as Saliery in 1915 in the Moscow Art Theater's production of Pushkin's play. That failure caused Stanislavsky a great trauma, yet at the same time it paved the way for his important and iconoclastic discoveries concerning the very fundamentals of the actor's skill. The desire to produce Pushkin's masterpiece remained with Stanislavsky for many years. This desire is readily understandable. The complicated material of Pushkin's play taxes the actor's skill to the utmost. It requires perfect control of his inner and outer techniques; the music of its verse—its rhythm—demands irreproachable diction; the passions extend far beyond the range of everyday feelings and call for great intensity and brilliance of expression; the thought demands deep and penetrating perception and extraordinary razor-edged precision of expression; the movements of the body, the gestures, require flexibility and must be clean-cut, arresting. On this play —a most complicated and exciting challenge to an actor— Stanislavsky wanted to collaborate with Vakhtangov.

We can only regret there were just a few meetings between Stanislavsky and Vakhtangov regarding the production of *Mozart and Saliery*. There is much basis for believing that these meetings, particularly those famous discussions between them on the "grotesque style," played a significant role in Vakhtangov's formulation of his directorial principles.

Vakhtangov was deeply involved at that period in the search for new creative avenues in theatrical art. What were his thoughts about the theater? What does the production of *Turandot* represent? Had it the significance and the impact necessary for the people of those turbulent years of the Revolution? Was it breaking the decrepit traditions of the old theater? Did it pave a new way for the theatrical art of the Soviet theater? Is it a departure from the teachings of Stanislavsky? What is its significance in the history of the development and growth of the Vakhtangov Theater? These are the important questions that must be answered in this part about *Turandot*. To do that one must examine the process of the creation of the production of the play.

In the beginning of the year 1920, a young student showed a scene from *Princess Turandot,* by Schiller, in a class at our

Studio. Vakhtangov became interested in Schiller's play and it was included in the repertoire of the Third Studio of the Moscow Art Theater, as we were then called. Vakhtangov entrusted Zavadsky and Kotlubai (his leading students) with the preparatory work on the play. The first distribution of the leading roles was as follows:

> KHAN ALTOUM . . . Schukin
> TARTAGLIA . . . Basov
> PANTALONE . . . Zakhava

Later on, when Vakhtangov took over the rehearsals, the leading roles were redistributed, and the other roles assigned, as follows:

> KHAN ALTOUM . . . Basov
> TARTAGLIA . . . Schukin
> PANTALONE . . . Kudryavtzev
> TRUFFALDINO . . . Simonov
> TIMUR . . . Zakhava
> BARACH . . . Toltchanov
> ADELMA . . . Orotchko
> SKIRINA . . . Laudanskaya
> ZELIMA . . . Remizova

For the role of Turandot, four actresses were tested: Mansurova, Tumskya, Slastenina, and Tauberg. All four eventually played the role in turn, but Vakhtangov began rehearsing the play with Mansurova.

Rehearsing with Zavadsky, the cast of the play was striving to create the atmosphere of the fairy tale with all that naïve fancy which seemed to us to disclose the poetic meaning of Schiller's *Turandot*. Rehearsals took place in all the rooms of the Studio. The action could start in one of the rooms and finish at the other end of the Studio. One room would serve as the forest, a second as the palace (of Khan Altoum), and a third room as the torture chamber. Each one of us tried to recall fairy tales we had heard or that had been read to us in our childhood. We recalled plays and ballets with a fairy tale background that we had seen in our childhood. Traditional masks (Tartaglia, Pantalone, Truffaldino, and Briguella) were worn to represent the usual characters: the chancellor, the minister, the head of the eunuchs—who was in charge of the harem—the chief of the police. Each fulfilled the obligations of his role as the play demanded.

Vakhtangov was ill at that time and was sent to a sanitarium. Upon his return he was shown the preparatory work that had been done, but he did not accept it. Schiller's fairy tale did not meet with his demands at the time. It was impossible for him to create on its foundation the kind of a production needed by a contemporary audience. What was the purpose of the production? To present it, as Reinhardt did—showing China as a fairyland with all the meticulousness of the sets and costumes and props—was not interesting. That would make the production merely stylized. On the other hand, to reveal the psychological subtlety of Prince Kalaf's and Princess Adelma's sufferings, painting the gradual transformation of the capricious princess into the loving woman, could be done, but it did not arouse Vakhtangov's fiery genius. He decided against the production of *Turandot* and started looking for another play.

However, during one of his talks to us, he returned to the possibilities of *Turandot*. "Let us indulge in our imagination," he said. Of course, he was the only one indulging in it. We only listened to him, captivated by his extraordinary, unmatched imagination. I do not vouch for the exactness of Vakhtangov's words, and I will relate only his thoughts as they are imprinted in my memory.

"What if we take Carlo Gozzi's play as the basis for our production, instead of Schiller's? While the Schiller *Turandot* is a play which adheres to all the rules of conventional drama, the Gozzi play is a fairy tale, a continuation of the folk-theater tradition, the theater of improvisation, born on the streets of Italy. Suppose we were to attempt to find a creative approach which would allow us to handle a play of such improvisational character today. Is it possible to create the same fiery passion which inspired the actors who played on the streets of Italy before simple, unsophisticated audiences? We would have to put aside all devotion to detail, all concern about polish, and concentrate on big, spontaneous feelings. These alone would be in evidence on the stage. Brilliant colors would predominate: zest, a joy of living, humor. And what is of great significance, young actors would have to come in touch with the most important moment in creativity— toward which every actor strives in his work, and which is the best guide to creativity—the improvisational state.

"But all I'm talking to you about now will require enormous work by everyone in our theater. The most complicated problems will face you actors, and you must be prepared to solve those problems. You will have to develop your inner technique to perfection, to attain the maximum flexibility of your movements and have them at your command to express the subtlest feelings along with the most violent passions that this play could demand. The placement of the voice must be irreproachable, because the key to this play will be different. It should not be the customary half-tones of our theatrical training. Actors will have to be trained to express their thoughts through sculpturally shaped phrases; to develop their sense of rhythm, of musicality; to handle props skillfully. If the Studio will undertake this complicated work with me, let us dare!" concluded Vakhtangov.

The members of the Studio, of course, accepted fervently the plan proposed by Vakhtangov; and the preparatory work and rehearsals started off in full swing. But Vakhtangov gave us at that time only a rough draft of his conception, only a general outline of his scheme. A way had to be found to a concrete realization of that scheme on the stage. From the moment that he discovered it, the directorial work began.

Now, I am posing myself a question: How was the performance of *Turandot* born? Was it the result of a director's desk work, the outgrowth of the many books read by him? No. Vakhtangov most likely did read a few books on comedy masks. He surely had read the article by Meyerkhold, "Love for Three Oranges," published before the Revolution. But it was not these literary sources that prompted Vakhtangov's inner and outer view of the production of *Turandot*. It is true that Vakhtangov had an extraordinary capacity, after having read one or two books on the subject, to see clearly a whole epoch; its peculiarities, customs, morals, and manners; its characters, the life of the people, their dwellings, their mode of life. This is, of course, one of the qualities of directorial talents in general, but certainly not one of the most basic. The most basic quality is the ability of the director to communicate his vision and his enthusiasm to the actors, to the composer of the music, to the scenic designer, and to each and every one connected with the production. In order for a director to stimulate an actor with exciting problems, to arouse in each one the creative beginning, he must be perfectly clear in his own mind as to the aims of the play. What is the purpose of putting on this play? With what method does he think to excite, or shake, or shock, or cheer the audience? With what contemporary thoughts and feelings will the theatergoer leave the theater? Without these great purposes, Vakhtangov could not imagine work in the theater. But whom does he have at his disposal to fulfill the plan he conceived? He had only the young, inexperienced members of the Studio; many of those entrusted with the leading roles (like Mansurova, Remizova, Schukin, Simonov) had not yet finished drama school, and even so-called experienced actors had only four or five years of actual stage experience. But that did not bother Vakhtangov.

It was such a wonderful time in the life of our Studio when each one of us, in terms of physical work, could do the tasks of two or three people; that strong was our devotion to the work. It was such a marvelous time, when the production of a play was the concern not only of the actors who played roles, but of the whole collective of the Studio. It was deeply vital work performed by all the members of the Studio-Theater. Thus we were trained by Vakhtangov. Each one of those not having roles in the play would necessarily be involved in the production in one or another capacity. And how can one be involved without being technically and creatively prepared? That is why all the studies that were especially organized for the play *Turandot* were attended by all the members of the Studio, without exception.

Pyatnitzky taught voice placement. Rhythm, movement, development of musicality, Vakhtangov appointed me to teach, after he himself gave us a number of lessons and showed us the basic principles of the movement for *Turandot*. Following Vakhtangov's instructions, I gave the actors exercises to develop the necessary scenic lightness, precision, rhythmicality, the ability to behave on the stage to the accompaniment of music, the handling of the stage costumes, etc. Zavadsky, Zakhava, and Kotlubai were appointed to do the preparatory work on the play. After a number of discussions with Vakhtangov, the rehearsals took place on the stage.

The first "baptism of fire" was received by the performers who were rehearsing masks. Vakhtangov sent us (I played one of the masks) onto the stage and told us to entertain the audience, which consisted of the members of the Studio. This experience took place on the small stage at Arbat (Street) 26, where the Third Studio of the Moscow Art Theater had moved from Mansurova Lane.

"What is the theme of our improvisation?" one of us asked timidly.

"It's your choice," replied Vakhtangov from the auditorium. We lived through terrible minutes of shame and help-lessness. We had not one idea, not one theme, for the im-provisation. Thus passed agonizing minutes; minutes which seemed like hours to us on the stage. There was dead silence from the auditorium. We wandered gloomily up and down the stage, lost for something to start with. Suddenly, one of us went backstage and brought out a large basket and arranged it over his shoulder with a rope, like a bread-seller would do. He put a large loaf of bread into it, which we, being able to think of nothing else to do, began to break and eat. Stim-ulated by the pleasure of eating, some sounds were uttered, some exclamations, and finally words. In the auditorium, life began to stir; one of the spontaneously spoken phrases on the stage received a reaction of laughter, which made us—the masks—feel more at ease. Encouraged by that reaction of laughter, another mask ran backstage and returned with a lady's large hat, the kind that fashionable ladies used to wear long ago. The mask put it on most awkwardly. That brought forth some rolling laughter from the audience. We began to feel better and better, more comfortable, now we had those objects to work with. Even people who are not of the theater know how it is when a funny story is well received by the audience. It gives the storyteller a lift, an inspiration. Thus, gradually warmed up by the audience, we were becoming more daring, gayer, more resourceful, easily inventing witti-cisms, funny situations, such characteristics that took us out of ourselves. Our improvisation lasted twenty minutes, or maybe twenty-five; the audience rolled with laughter, and even applauded us. Suddenly, at the peak of our enjoyment, when we were ready to go on and on, we heard Vakhtangov's voice, "Stop! Rehearsal is finished!"

Happy, excited, drunk with our success, we came down into the auditorium. It seemed to us that through this im-provisation we had discovered how to play our roles, and we felt that we were extraordinary, talented, highly gifted actors.

The next day, however, we were convinced to the contrary. The same improvisation, with exactly the same details, failed catastrophically; did not draw forth a single smile from our audience.

For a long time, failure and success came in succession. We even learned to cheat and prepare something at home. Schukin was especially clever at it. He would bring a completely worked-out story from home, and each time adjust it to his dialogue with his partner. The fact that Tartaglia (Schukin played Tartaglia) stuttered, according to the tradition of *commedia dell'arte,* helped him very much. When he was not prepared to answer his partner, he would stutter continuously, and that by itself was very funny. And the "refinement and erudition" of Pantalone sounded especially cute because the performer pronounced his wise sayings with an accent typical of a small Russian town. Briguella, the head of the police, was a glutton, simple-minded, frightened of any trifle, very far from the brave fighter he is supposed to be. Truffaldino, gay, easy-going, ready-witted, liked to tease his comrades, play jokes on them. Thus, little by little, we were "covered with characteristics," as it is called in our actor's language, meaning that we were each closer and closer to our role, and gradually entering it.

An important event that played a great part in our mastering the nature of the humor and temperament of Italian masks was the meeting with the musician and conductor of the Moscow Circus Orchestra, Esposito, an Italian. Vakhtangov was looking for a person who had seen performances created on the principles of *commedia dell'arte,* the acting company that played on the streets and in the squares in Italy. Such an eye witness happened to be the charming maestro, Esposito. He came to talk to us, wearing an ancient frock coat; he was in a gala spirit, ceremonial and majestic. Esposito was an old man with a gray, very pointed Vandyke, and black, young, vivacious eyes, which looked gaily out from under thick gray eyebrows. He spoke very poor Russian, and that made him shy and rather at a loss as how to start. One of us, anxious to relax the old gentleman, prompted, "Have you seen the productions of *commedia dell'arte*? What was their character? How did the masks behave in those performances?"

Suddenly Esposito changed in front of our eyes; the shyness and the gala look were thrown off. Recalling the behavior of Tartaglia, Truffaldino, and Pantalone on the stage, he burst out laughing. "Tartaglia in that spot . . ." He could not continue because laughter was choking him. Recovering, the old man went on, "And Truffaldino answered him . . ."

Here Esposito was completely under the spell of a rush of memories of the performances he had seen. He laughed so much that tears came into his eyes, and it was becoming quite impossible for us to distinguish one word from another. All we heard was his continuous laughter. The old Italian charmed us with his naturalness, simplicity, inner candor, and free young temperament. We finally joined him in his mirth, infected by his gaiety and love of life. He spent an hour with us and left accompanied by fervent and friendly applause.

Vakhtangov addressed us with the following words: "You saw the way Esposito behaved in front of us; you saw his spontaneity, his sincerity. This is the key to the complex character of masks, and it is foreign to us who are used to working with the given text of an author. Absorb and remember that fire and charm, and the loving heart of the old Italian musician."

Vakhtangov started to work with the actors who had the set text in the play. He devoted special attention to the analysis of the content of the verse, the logical construction of a phrase, as well as how to speak it irreproachably from the point of view of diction. He told us we must have a pure

Russian speech, and advised young actors to listen to the actors of the Maly Theater, who excelled in this respect.

"Now we need to find the key to the characters of Gozzi's play and understand how they differ from the characters of Schiller's play of the same name. The traveling companies of the *commedia dell'arte,* from the sixteenth to the eighteenth centuries, played primarily under the open sky on the streets and in the squares of the villages and cities of Italy. The question of sets, costumes, and props naturally did not exist. The principal component of the theater was the actor, his art. The actor's expressiveness, his temperament, his sincerity, his ability to captivate the hearts of his audience . . . that, and that alone, decided the success of *commedia dell'-arte.*

"In a contemporary interpretation of Gozzi's fairy tale, we must make our actor the principal component. But the character of performing in the sixteenth century differed strongly from the character of performing today. Must we revive and copy that manner of acting? Least of all, am I interested in the restoration of the form of acting of *commedia dell'arte.* From the creative armory of the actors of the Italian Theater of Masks, we have to take that eternal quality that was in the Russian Theater actors of the seventeenth and nineteenth centuries: their noble and lofty relation to their profession, their love for human beings, love for everything worthy of their respect. Such actors, who were not afraid to tell the truth to rulers, were favored by the common people. They were the bearers of humanistic morals even then, when they interpreted the roles of villains and made the audience hate them fiercely. The naïve, unsophisticated theatergoer almost always identifies the role portrayed with its portrayer, thinking the character and the actor are one and the same person. These actors were often semi-literate. Their lives were hard: almost all of them dragged out a miserable existence, but they loved their profession and would not have changed it for any other, no matter how advantageous and profitable that might have been."

During the rehearsals, Vakhtangov suggested that we search not only for the special qualities of this or that character of Gozzi's play, but also the singularities of the actor from the People's Theater who would have performed this or other of the roles in *Turandot*. Even in our time, when meeting an actor personally we may guess what kind of parts he plays on the stage. But in the older theater of "emploi," one knew exactly what role this or another actor played on the stage. For example, a tragedian necessarily spoke in a low range of voice, meaningfully, in a sing-song style, no matter what thought he expressed. He was usually a tall man, dignified, with imposing gestures, inclined to assume a noble pose. He moved majestically; he strutted rather than walked. The role of Kalaf would have been played in the old theater by an actor of the emploi of "hero," or, "hero-lover," as it was then called. Therefore, first of all, it was necessary to find the distinct traits characteristic of the actor of the old theater in this particular emploi, and then when this was accomplished to go further into the creation of the image of Prince Kalaf.

This was a big, complicated, and interesting problem for the actor, that double-transformation, which is not, and has nothing in common with, the problem of playing his relation to the image. (Though it was precisely thus that theater connoisseurs understood Vakhtangov's idea of the theater.) To the contrary. We were not supposed to imitate feelings. We had to learn to arouse our feelings with much more intensity, to arouse them with a lightning speed without that psycho-technique of the intimate theater. The second criticism with which the critics often charged *Turandot* was the reproach that the actors of that play did not become one with their characters, but made fun of their feelings and behavior. This is a totally wrong point of view.

Working with Orotchko on her role of Adelma, Vakhtangov

asked her to play the tragic actress of the company, who was in love with the hero not only as a character but also in life. Vakhtangov showed her brilliantly with what depth of feeling the actress Adelma must live the tragedy of unhappy, unreciprocated love. The actress had to cry, to shed tears—not hysterical tears, but those which come to an actor in minutes of inspiration, when he wishes with all his being, with all the depths of his talent, to create for the audience. Let us forgive the actress her desire to exhibit her talent to the audience. Excited by the performance of the actress, we will thank her for the minutes of suffering that gave us artistic ecstasy. That is exactly what used to take place when Orotchko would leave the stage in the last act, after the tragic monologue of Adelma. The audience thanked her with long and stormy applause.

Is it thus necessary to openly and directly communicate with the audience? That is the question I expect to be asked. In the book *Building a Character,* Stanislavsky wrote, "The singularity of our scenic communion consists of the fact that communion must take place simultaneously with the partner and the audience. (With the partner directly and deliberately; with the audience indirectly, through the partner.) It is remarkable that with the first and the second, the communion is reciprocal all through the play."

When an actor says, "I was so completely engrossed in my part that I forgot I was on the stage. I was not aware of the audience," he lies. An actor never forgets that he is on the stage. He makes a pause in order not to break the audience's attention, he is perfectly aware of a cough or any other sound on the other side of the footlights, he is always grateful to the audience for its attention, and he plays his role much better, is more inspired, when there is a dead silence—the sign that the audience is completely involved. The audience, in its turn, also takes part in the performance: applauding during the performance, expressing its enthusiasm for the actor, letting

him feel from the darkness of the auditorium that it is living
with him all the peripetia of the play. There is nothing
wrong in such a communion between the actor and the audience. On the contrary, when there is a close contact between
the two, stimulating and exhilarating art is born.

Striving to achieve fuller participation of the audience
(which is important in a performance based primarily on improvisation), Vakhtangov intentionally widened the actor's
"center of attention" during the rehearsals of *Turandot*. He
moved the "fourth wall" over the footlights to the last row of
the orchestra and gallery. When, according to the content of
the play, the action was spread into the auditorium, the auditorium was lit. This was a sign for the audience that a moment had arrived when a most important communication between it and the actors would take place. Needless to say, all
such moments were organically justified by the action of the
play, and they were realized with Vakhtangov's impeccable
taste and sense of proportion. Joyfully and unconstrainedly
revealing to the audience all the secrets of the performing
art, its "wings and its kitchen," Vakhtangov raised the prestige of the actor, emphasizing the significance and the brilliance, the skill of the actor's mastery. During the rehearsals
of *Turandot*, Vakhtangov never stopped talking about the
magic "if." In *Turandot*, it sounded as follows: "If you were
an actor of the People's Theater, creating the role of Kalaf,
how would you behave in the given circumstances of the
play?"

What was Vakhtangov fighting in the art of the theater at
this stage of its development? He was ridding the theater of
the method of work that encouraged an actor's self-indul-
gence. That method was blossoming in many acting studios
at the time. "Living the part" became its own purpose; the
actors began to indulge in sentimental, petty feelings, in shallow passions, feigning all-importance. The process of accu-
mulating the feelings of a role was much too long; and once

having accumulated a small feeling, the actors were afraid to spill it. The theater was turning into a closed monastery, where the priests were dedicated to the mastery of art. It was necessary to break the lock on the mystery door and show uncompromisingly how foreign and out-of-date that method of work was; then to give the people a healthy art, one of big feelings and passions, one that would correspond to the grandeur of the epoch. It was necessary to tear aside the veil with which many workers in the theater covered their principle of "art for art's sake"—those who were hiding from life and the Revolution under the pretext of serving pure art.

The above may seem exaggerated to the reader. Does it pay, my reader may ask me, to fight the transformation of the theater into a monastery? My reader must recall that it was happening on the third birthday of the Soviet power, when a large part of the artistic intelligentsia was far behind the Revolution and its ideas. Many intellectuals were in the White Russian Army fighting the young Soviet Republic and, as a result, found themselves outside of Soviet Russia. But maybe Vakhtangov, fighting that kind of art, was striving to destroy wonderful old traditions of the Russian Theater, discarding the valuable and eternal, which must be a part also of a new society? Of course not! He never said a negative word or indicated any non-acceptance of the realistic teachings of Stanislavsky, either in our rehearsals or during our discussions with him.

Vakhtangov was discovering new and wider possibilities for the application and concrete use of Stanislavsky's teachings about the actor's creativity. He also consistently reminded us that this particular interpretation of some of the elements of Stanislavsky's teachings, which he used during the rehearsals of *Turandot,* was necessary for the revelation of the content and composition of the form of that play specifically, dictated by the given concrete conception. The presentation of *Hamlet,* for example (Vakhtangov intended to do *Hamlet* soon) , would demand a new interpretation of the same elements of the teachings, suitable to the specific qualities of Shakespeare's tragedy.

One must remember that the rehearsals of *Turandot* took place in the years 1920 and 1921. At that period, Stanislavsky was still at work completing his system. Much was becoming clearer to him; much he was still experimenting with. He was searching to define more precisely the method of the actor's work on himself and on the role. There was nothing in print about his system. Many of its elements, written about in the book *Building a Character,* were completed after Vakhtangov's death.

In order to emphasize once more the point that the work on *Turandot* in no degree indicates any break on Vakhtangov's part from the teachings of Stanislavsky, I quote one more passage from the above-mentioned book: "Let us suppose that an artist feels comfortable on the stage while creating. He is so much in control of himself that he is able to be the character completely and at the same time test his feeling and dissect it into its component elements. Let us suppose all those function correctly, helping one another. Then suddenly there is a break, and the artist looks within himself in order to understand which element of his state of mind has begun to work incorrectly. He has no difficulty, being divided in two: part of him corrects that which went wrong, while the other part of him continues to live that character."

The thought expressed here by Stanislavsky shows again and again how thoroughly the wise teacher knew his actor, how precisely he analyzed the inner being of an actor while on the stage. Vakhtangov had just as delicate perception of the actor's psychology. He never imposed on an actor's method of work that which was foreign to the actor's natural creativity. He believed the highest mastery of the regisseur reveals itself when a regisseur surrounds an actor with conditions on the stage which fully stimulate the actor's creativity.

165

Such conditions from rehearsal to rehearsal were created by Vakhtangov while he rehearsed *Turandot*.

Rehearsals of *Turandot* were nearing the moment when it was time "to gather" all that had been previously worked out in the laboratories. The most remarkable, unforgettable days of the rehearsals had begun. They were taking place on the big stage of the theater. Those were the days of extraordinary and creative enthusiasm . . . the days of intensive work with Vakhtangov. The hours flew by unnoticed. We rehearsed evenings, nights, sometimes until morning. Each of Vakhtangov's students realized that his teacher was not to be in the theater for long. We were hiding our sorrow and our anxiety just as Vakhtangov was hiding his feelings and controlling inhuman physical pain. We were possessed with one desire: to do our very best with all our ability and fulfill all of Vakhtangov's demands. Perhaps thus we might ease his suffering. I should add that, unbelievable as it might seem, our actors were especially joyful and festive in spite of their profound anxiety about their teacher.

....................

The orchestra thunders. The participants of *Turandot* put on their festive costumes. The sets are on the stage. The difficult lighting in the play has been tried out and finally set. The auditorium is almost filled with actors not appearing in *Turandot* and with the technical workers in the theater.

Vakhtangov is persistently working on the beginning and the ending of the performance. He is trying again and again new variations of the first and last scene of the play. How could he begin this unusual and festive performance so that the audience would be drawn immediately into active participation in the actor's creativity?—which is so necessary for the joyous, special character of this production. Most likely it would be necessary to use some device—before the beginning of the first act—for the meeting between the actors and the audience. Thus was born the idea of a "parade." According to the first variation, the actors were supposed to sit among the audience and with the first sounds of music start marching up onto the stage. Later, Vakhtangov rejected this plan, and the actors were to appear before the audience from behind the curtain. The purpose of the "parade" was not only the meeting between the actors and the audience, but to establish immediately the festive character of the performance and bring the audience in to its elated and unrestrained atmosphere. The audience at once was made to understand in what scenic language the conversation between it and the actor was going to be held. In the exposition of the scenic action an experienced regisseur and a competent actor usually draw the audience into the necessary atmosphere imperceptibly and thus prepare it for the right reaction to the activities on stage. I repeat that usually it is done subtly. Vakhtangov, by beginning the action with a parade, strove to accomplish the same purpose openly, directly, without veiling his intention, as though deliberately revealing all the secrets of dramatic art. As though deliberately saying, We are going to play a fairy tale, and the character of the presentation will be fairy-tale like. The audience will see the transformations which take place when the actors change into the characters of the play, when they make up and dress with lightning speed right on the stage during the "parade."

Now, if the beginning of the play is the "parade"—the making acquaintance with the audience—then, naturally, the ending of the play must be the leave-taking of the players from the audience. Vakhtangov searches for the final moment of the play, the most difficult task for any regisseur. In it, in that concluding chord, it is always necessary for the regisseur to give the audience an opportunity to sum up its impressions and once more realize the basic idea of the play. Vakhtangov creates a touching and exciting finale for *Turandot*. Under the accompaniment of the already familiar music—sounding now not so joyous as before but with a lyric sadness—is composed the final *mise en scène*: actors without make-up, holding each other's hands, and with only an inclination of their heads, leave the audience and slowly move behind the curtain. Thus takes place the parting between actors and audience who during the three hours of the spectacle have become friends.

Now begins the last rehearsal with Vakhtangov in the theater. Exhausted with a terrible illness, he reclines in the sixth row of the auditorium (this chair in the sixth row has been reserved in his memory forever). But each time there is a need to show something to the actor on the stage or to correct a *mise en scène*, Vakhtangov with unbelievable lightness, unmindful of his illness, runs from the auditorium up onto the stage. Having made the improvements, corrected the faults, he returns to his seat in the sixth row. At dawn, the first dress rehearsal begins. At last, after long painstaking work with Vakhtangov, comes the run-through of the play, without stops. Afterwards, Vakhtangov is taken home in a cab, never to return to the theater again. Those last *Turandot* rehearsals took place the night of February twenty-third of the year 1922. But a bedridden Eugene Vakhtangov continues to guide the work of the play. He is visited daily by his assistant regisseurs—Zavadsky, Zakhava, Kotlubai—who take from him directions and corrections for the play. Vakhtangov calls the "masks" to his home, and tries changes with us, tries again a witty, funny text for the opening scene. He is anxious about the building of the theater. He plans the repertoire for the near future. With great excitement, he is anticipating the day when *Turandot* will be shown to his great teacher Stanislavsky, to Nemirovitch-Dantchenko, and to his artist friends of the Moscow Art Theater and its First Studio.

At last the significant day comes. Behind the wings there is enormous excitement. The fate of the Third Studio is being decided. This is the test for creative maturity, and, most important, each participant of the play feels a great responsibility to Vakhtangov—not only for his own performance, but for the performance as a whole. Here! The majestic figure of Constantine Sergeyevitch Stanislavsky appears in the auditorium along with the always elegant figure of Vladimir Nemirovitch-Dantchenko. The backstage grapevine buzzes with the news that new guests have arrived at the theater, that well-known actors and directors of the Moscow Art Theater and its First and Second Studios have come to our theater.

The actors of *Princess Turandot* are already gathered on the stage behind the curtain, shaking each other's hands, embracing each other, and plucking up each other's spirits. But all have one unexpressed thought—Vakhtangov! We all know that before the opening of the play, Zavadsky will read Vakhtangov's letter to the assembled Moscow Art Theater members.

An assistant regisseur gives the signal to begin. Joyously and festively sounds the Turandot march. The first to appear are the "masks" who with their clear ringing voices announce: "The presentation of the fairy tale of Carlo Gozzi, *Princess Turandot*, begins." "Parade!" cries out Tartaglia, and together with Pantalone partly opens the curtain, leaving a narrow passage for the actors—characters of the play. On the left, actresses; on the right, actors. All advance to the footlights, each taking his designated place. Zavadsky is to introduce each member of the cast, but first he reads Vakhtangov's letter.

"Our teachers, our old and young comrades! You must believe us that the style of today's performance is the only one which is possible for us—The Third Studio. This form is not only the form for the *Tale of Turandot,* but for all the tales of Gozzi. We searched for a contemporary form expressing the Third Studio in its theatrical stage of development today. The style demanded not only the story content of the tale but also the scenic means—maybe not noticeable to the audience—but absolutely essential for the training of an actor. Any play is an 'excuse' to organize in our Studio the six months' special necessary studies for the given form. We are just beginning. We have no right to offer for your attention a play performed by excellent actors, because they are not sufficiently developed to be such. Many years are required in order for actors to become masters of their skill. So we select young people—we search the stage laws, absorb all that Stanislavsky gives us, and do not even dream of showing you a finished theatrical presentation until we have our actors trained according to our demands. Until then, we show you only the laboratory work.

"Now we are searching for contemporary forms for plays by Ostrovsky, Gogol, and Dostoevsky. The three plays by those authors are again only an 'excuse' to search for form. Therefore, we look for means to explain it. Also, *Hamlet,* which we are working on, is such an *'excuse.'* We know that we are not up to playing *Hamlet,* but we also know very well that work on *Hamlet* will excite the members of the Studio and will teach them a lot that they need to know."

Further along in his letter, Vakhtangov introduces the actors. He informs the audience that the actress who plays Turandot—Mansurova—and the actress who plays her friend Adelma—Orotchko—are playing their first roles, and the actress who plays Selima—Remizova—is a student of the school. Vakhtangov was anxious about our young actors, and he wanted to give our much experienced audience and critics the right criteria for evaluating the talents of the young taking their first steps on the stage.

Slowly, with the accompaniment of the waltz of *Turandot* (by the way, that waltz was somewhat plagiaristic, being a variation of the song used in Vakhtangov's production of *The Deluge*), the stage is revealed. On it, thrown around in a carefully planned "disorder," are vividly colored strips of material. Truffaldino lightly jumps onto the platform and in circus style orders "Hop!" On this signal the actors quickly run onto the platform, and, on a command from Truffaldino, lift the colorful strips of material, and in the rhythm of the waltz, gracefully toss them into the air before wrapping them around themselves. This game with the brilliant colored pieces of cloth thrown into the air in the rhythm of the music, and the plasticity of the actors' movements, immediately brought thunderous applause from the audience. It took just a few minutes for the actors to make up and "dress" in front of the audience. Here in this short time of two or three minutes, by the magic of theatrical transformation, the actors changed into the personages of the *Tale of Princess Turandot*. Then they ran down to the footlights and lined up in front of the surprised and charmed audience.

"We are ready," Truffaldino informs the audience. The orchestra plays the introduction to the song which the whole company sings:

> Here we begin
> With our simple song.
> In five minutes China
> Will become our rough platform.
>
> All of us in this tale,
> Your servants and your friends
> Among us four "masks"
> It is I, I, I, and I.

The "masks" bow in the rhythm of the song while pronouncing the text of the last line. The difficult, rhythmical abruptness of the passage "I, I, I, and I" had to be said in a fast tempo. Further on, the song develops into a more flowing tempo:

> We will open the curtain
> And under the storm of rags
> Show you how with the hero fell in love

171 |

I and I (confiding in us, Adelma and Turandot).
Here we are beginning
With our most simple song
In five minutes China
Will become a rough platform.

Speeding up the tempo with every bar, the actors finish their ditty-song. Then in a rhythmically coiling snake-like line, lightly and gaily, they run off the stage. The four masks are the last ones to leave the stage. They prolong their exit in a round-about way, intentionally going astray, bumping into each other, not going in the right direction. The lightest one, Truffaldino, leads the foursome, followed by the gray-haired, respectable Pantalone. After him hops Briguella and last comes corpulent Tartaglia, with small mincing steps, afraid to be left behind without his comrades. At last, the masks reach the wings to the accompaniment of rolling laughter and unanimous applause by the audience, which is captivated by the exuberance, the festivity, and the joyousness of the parade.

A short pause ensues; then we hear the sound of a gay polka that accompanies the action of the "stage servants," our young actresses who are dressed in blue theatrical overalls, each with a number on her back, like a member of a football team. The stage servants change the set to the rhythm of the music, transforming the empty sloping platform into the streets of Peking. They let down the ropes with colorful weights. Three very wide drop-curtains are hung on the sticks. On the curtains there is an appliqué picturing a Chinese town. The stage servants pull the cloth-made scenery, which is simultaneously flying up, and with fairy-like speed, we find ourselves in Peking. There is no doubt that we are in Peking because we are so informed by very large letters reading PEKING on the curtain. Anticipating the possible criticism of emphasizing the non-realistic presentation of *Turan-*

*dot,* I would again like to quote Stanislavsky. Analyzing one of the études done by a student, he expressed the following important thought.

"Here is one of the many examples showing how, with the help of the imagination, one can inwardly change for himself the world of things. One must not fight the imagination. On the contrary, one must utilize whatever is created by it. Such a process always takes place in the beginning of our rehearsals. From the Vienna chairs, we construct houses, platforms, ships, woods . . . anything that the imagination of the regisseur can conceive. Now, we do not really think that this particular chair is actually a tree or a rock, but we believe in the authenticity of our relation to the constructed objects, and we behave as if they were tree or rock."

I think when the actor believes completely in the circumstances given to him, he is already taking a big step toward passing this belief on to the audience. Recently, I saw a play done by a group of visiting Chinese actors. The strongest impression was made on me by a scene in an inn. For twenty minutes, two highly talented Chinese actors were looking for each other in "darkness," with a full, dazzling light on the stage. The behavior of those actors made us believe that they were trying very hard to find each other in complete darkness. The scene was supposed to be in a large room in the inn, which was represented, by the way, with only one table in the middle of the room. Yet we all saw clearly where the door was, where the window was, where other non-existent objects were, against which the actors constantly stumbled. We got so used to the "complete darkness" that when that amazing performance, in its subtle mastery, ended, we felt as if we had been sitting for a very long time in a dark room that was suddenly flooded with brilliant light.

Now, on the streets of Peking, appears Barach, the tutor of Kalaf. He hums a melody (a variation of the song "Indian Guest," from the opera *Sadko,* by Rimsky-Korsakov). The lyric song is suddenly interrupted by an alarming chord, foretelling something mysterious. And then Prince Kalaf, Barach's ward, appears. (Barach and Kalaf were separated for a long time by a cruel fate; now they are happily re-united.) The dialogue between the two is Barach's account of the self-willed Princess Turandot, who has plunged the whole country into sorrow and terror. She has been sending all the pretenders to her hand to execution, one by one. That scene could have been a boring exposition, during which the audience, yawning, would have waited for the beginning of the play. But Vakhtangov had staged it with brilliant changes from one scenic problem to another—like the joy of meeting, questioning, the telling of horrible events that took place in the city—with such mastery of the dialogue and exchange of thoughts between the two characters that the scene is listened to with great intensity of interest.

The character of the communion between those two on the stage in that scene could be defined as "a communion with the audience through the partner." The action develops further. Ismail, a friend of one of the executed daredevils, enters, crying bitterly and mourning his lost friend, who could not solve the riddles of the cruel princess. In a fit of des-peration, Ismail throws Turandot's portrait on the ground, trampling it, while continuing to lament and wail pitifully. Under the accompaniment of the music, which sounds like an odd musical complaint, Ismail runs off the stage. This is the culminating point of the first scene.

Prince Kalaf snatches the portrait out of Barach's hand— Barach was trying to hide it from him—looks at it and falls in love with the Princess Turandot. This moment was built directorially to perfection, if we remember that it was neces-sary to show convincingly the feelings that overpower a man who falls in love at first sight. Movement-wise, the scene was directed in such a manner that Kalaf, while admiring the portrait, moves it from one angle to the other, giving the audience the opportunity to see the portrait. They can see it is the portrait of a woman of great beauty, though the portrait was painted by one line, reminiscent of the cameo with its classic nose. The pleadings of Barach, not to give in to the temptation, are in vain. Kalaf runs off to look for Turandot and happiness. Barach remains on the stage in complete despair. He cries, and his outburst brings his wife, Skirina, a servant to the Princess Turandot, on stage. She is a woman whose character is well defined by Barach's short remark when she tries to wring from him the name of the Prince: "Don't be curious, woman." Skirina would give anything to learn the name of the newcomer. Her pleading is of no avail, and she runs off.

The stage servants change the set into the palace of Khan Altoum, where the next scene takes place. Truffaldino and Briguella appear. At their command, a curtain made especially for *Turandot* comes down; and the change of the set takes place behind it. The audience is getting more and more excited. "Why are you late?" asks Briguella of one of the latecomers in the audience. A more quick-witted theatergoer enters into a dialogue with the masks. The less resourceful hurry to their seats to remain just theatergoers and not actors. Such spontaneous communion brings actors and audience closer to each other. Now the late-comers are seated; the masks resume their places on the stage. But it turns out that the shifting of the set behind the curtain is not completed. The dialogue begins between Truffaldino and Briguella. During the thousand performances of *Turandot,* the theme and witty remarks of that dialogue would differ at each performance. During some performances, that dialogue was full of comments on topical issues of the theater and of new productions in the Moscow Art Theater. There were witty comments directed at the critics and some of the well-known theater personalities. Some of the remarks satirized political figures in foreign countries. For example, at the time of the international conference in Genoa, on the stage of the Maly Theater the première of Schiller's play *Conspiracy in Fiesco* was taking place. On that day, Truffaldino passed a winged comment: "In Moscow they are giving a play in the Maly Theater, 'Fiasco of the Conspiracy in Genoa.' " Also there were frequently sarcastic remarks referring to the shortcomings of life in Soviet Russia. The two actors ridiculed narrow-minded officials who indulged in petty bureaucratic administration. Many other topics of the day were cleverly satirized. It is necessary to say that each new text, composed just before the performance, demanded of the actor a special concentration at the moment when he told his joke from the stage for the first time. To tell a new joke is always frightening. Will it or will it not bring forth the desired laughter? So-called "running in" or "rolling the road smooth" caused much concern to the masks. If any role makes an actor nervous to a certain degree before the rise of the curtain, that role that has an improvisational text will deepen his nervousness. There were brilliant successes in those improvised scenes, but there were also dreadful failures that aggravated the actors greatly.

Well, the set for the next scene is ready. Truffaldino and Barach announce: "The second scene of *Turandot* begins!!" The main curtain goes up. We see on the stage the palace of Khan Altoum. We named this scene the "divan scene," the place of the meeting of the sage old men. There are two thrones on the stage: one for the Khan and the other for the Princess. That completes the luxurious set of the palace. To the accompaniment of a march, resembling national Chinese music with its characteristic of loud formation of percussion instruments and the buoyant singing of the flutes, begins the procession of the sage men of the divan, advisers of the great Khan. They leave no doubt that they are sage men: they strut, deep in thought, ceremoniously greeting those who greet them. They are full of concern and they sigh heavily, spreading out their hands and thus obviously revealing their loss of a solution for the tragic problem of the Khan. Not one of these sage men has found the way to save his country from the misfortunes into which the stubborn and cruel Turandot has plunged her people.

Now begins festive music, which announces the approaching Khan. The sage men take their respective places, with their backs to the audience, raise their hands in prayer-like manner and respectfully bend their heads, waiting for His Majesty's entrance. This solemn behavior culminates in the entrance of the Khan. Out of breath from walking fast, he hobbles (far from solemn), with the gait of a very old man, to his throne and with great difficulty scrambles up the steps and settles down with his ministers, Tartaglia and Pantalone. He has a handkerchief in his hands, with which he continually wipes the tears which he sheds on the slightest provocation. Here now, with tears in his eyes, he begins his speech: "Oh, my loyal, faithful ones, how long will I suffer? How long will I be thus tormented?" The Chinese ceremony, of course, has to be respected and each phrase of the Khan's is interrupted by music and the ritual of ceaseless deep bows by the sages and the Khan's ministers:

> "No sooner one unhappy prince
> parted with his life
> and his decease is bemoaned
> then here another appears
> and my heart is wrung with new grief."

Having lamented thus over his difficult life, Khan Altoum draws an unpleasant conclusion concerning his advisers: "And there is no one to help me with advice."

Now comes the time for Pantalone's statement. The old Pantalone begins in a drawling manner, and deep in thought, but obviously not knowing what to say, "Ah! Yes, yes, yes, and yes."

"P-P-Pantalone, what did you s-say?" stutters Tartaglia.

"I said, 'Yes, yes, yes, and yes.'"

"Magnificently said!!" concludes Tartaglia.

Here begins the scene between the masks. They talk about the Roman Pope and about the fact that Pantalone comes from the city of Ryazen. This is just a gay, short acting scene, brilliantly executed by Schukin, who is continuously stuttering and who finally ends the scene by a direct question to the Khan: "Generally speaking, are you a Tzar or are you not?"

"I am a Tzar," meekly answers Altoum.

"Well, if you are a Tzar, then reign to frighten your enemies. Something has to be done!" the hot-spur Tartaglia says, as he rushes upon the Khan.

Of course, the ministers are now completely mixed up. They can think of nothing sensible to advise; therefore, it is necessary to invite Prince Kalaf, the next victim of Turandot, to enter.

"Let the next prince enter, and let us try to dissuade him," announced the good-hearted Altoum. But all the attempts on the part of the masks to persuade Prince Kalaf to give up his claim to the hand of the Princess fail.

"Turandot or death!" the Prince declares solemnly and irreconcilably.

"Let the Princess enter, and let her revel in the new victim," says Altoum hopelessly, waving his hand.

The ceremony of Turandot's entrance begins. First, floating in a dance (a parody on Isadora Duncan), come Turandot's slave girls. They are followed by her two friends, Adelma and Zelima, and finally, Turandot herself. Her face is covered with a light veil, so as not to overwhelm the pretender to her hand by her beauty. The Prince is now facing the complicated problem of guessing the three riddles. According to the ritual a decree is announced, which is right then and there translated from the Chinese language into the Russian. In that decree, the brave man is warned that if he does not guess the riddles he will lose his head immediately.

All are ready to hear the first riddle: Khan, the ministers, the sage men, and the slave girls prick up their ears so as not to miss one word Turandot speaks. Kalaf stands still in expectation. His head is bent as he tries to concentrate, his hands outstretched to the crowd as if pleading with them to be as quiet as possible so as not to disturb him. The text of the first riddle is pronounced, rhythmically measured, with a clear and very musical voice, by Turandot (Mansurova). All present repeat the riddle, imitating her intonations. The riddle is told. The cymbals clash. Dead silence. All eyes are glued on Kalaf. The divan, the hall of meetings, is still. Kalaf, covering his face with his right hand, thinks over the riddle. Suddenly his face brightens. All present grasping that the riddle is guessed, still cannot believe such good luck, do not believe he has guessed it correctly. But Kalaf, with joy in his voice, begins to explain the meaning of the riddle, and then loudly shouts out his answer: "Fire!" The wise men open the large envelopes containing the answer to the riddle. "Fire! Fire! Fire!" they exclaim together happily three times, showing to the audience a piece of cardboard on which the word "Fire" is written in large letters. A general rejoicing takes place. The Princess Turandot is somehow lost; she is upset, thrown off balance. This is the first man who has solved the riddle. Her pride is wounded. All right, let him rack his brains over the second riddle!

After a supreme effort, silence in the hall of the palace is restored, and the Princess, as if in a hurry to break the Prince's obstinacy, announces the second riddle immediately. Excited courtiers now repeat it in a whisper; one hears only fragments of the phrase, told with hushed, tense voices. All look at Kalaf with hope and anticipation. But this time, Kalaf seems to be lost. There are whispers of desperation: "Oh, he can't guess it!" . . . "He doesn't know the answer." But suddenly there is the clash of cymbals and kettle-drums and everyone is startled. This is the signal for the Prince's answer. He has found the answer. "Rainbow!" triumphantly exclaims the Prince.

Princess Turandot does not allow the general joy to break out. Instantly with a powerful, energetic tone, she attracts the Prince's attention and everyone else's. Now, she will use the strongest weapon, and that will surely strike down this prince. Nervously, in a quick tempo, Turandot tells the third riddle. As she finishes it, she suddenly half-opens her veil, as if saying: "Look at my face, and dare not tremble!" Prince Kalaf almost faints, he is so startled by her heavenly beauty. By now, the members of the divan, the slave girls, the masks, and the Khan himself, all adore the Prince, and they bustle around to prevent his collapse. Tartaglia and Pantalone especially are very agitated. Finally, with a great effort of will, the Prince summons the last of his strength and begins repeating the riddle slowly. With every word the impatience around him grows. But the characters become transformed before our eyes when Kalaf answers: "Lightning!" with all the power of his voice, not concealing his happiness and triumph. Now begins such rejoicing that "neither fact nor fancy can describe." The wise men pick up the Prince and rock him in their hands, Altoum cries—but this time from joy. Suddenly Kalaf sees his beloved Turandot fainting, and Adelma and Zelima trying to revive her. Turandot, recovering, throws herself on her knees before her father, saying, "Father, I beseech you in the name of your love for me, and if my love is dear to you, I beg of you, appoint another day for a new testing!"

"No more tests. Now, to the temple for the wedding!" orders Altoum, gaily.

She answers, "Let us go to the temple, but your daughter will die from sorrow and despair there." Forgetting her pride, losing control over herself, Turandot bursts into tears. The tears and the words of his adored Turandot arouse Kalaf to pity, and now he offers her a riddle to solve. If the Princess guesses whose son he is, and what his name is, he will give up that great happiness which he has won with such difficulty. Turandot, catching at a straw, the only chance to preserve her reputation for being inaccessible and invincible, accepts this challenge.

Accompanied by special music, the magnificent exit of all the participants who have lived through so much at this meeting begins. Turandot, followed by the noble and amorous stares of the generous Kalaf, passes the youth without looking at him, proudly holding her head high. But, who knows, maybe love is born already in her cruel heart. Slowly the curtain comes down. "Entr'acte," Truffaldino announces to the audience.

When the curtain comes down, we hear applause that surpasses anything we have ever heard in the theater. Shouts of "Bravo!" grow stronger and stronger. Now, what shall we do? According to the tradition of the Moscow Art Theater, there are no curtain calls. But we know Vakhtangov's feeling about them. He had been telling us during the rehearsals, that the tradition of the old Russian Theater should be revived, that an enthusiastic and gratified audience had the right to express its appreciation to the actor.

So the curtain went up. Among those in the audience applauding most heartily we recognize the familiar figures of Stanislavsky and Nemirovitch-Dantchenko. They are applauding, their hands outstretched towards us on the stage. Is it all real? Is it true? Everything that Vakhtangov had created with such love during the rehearsals is accepted so heartily by the actors and directors of the Moscow Art Theater, whom we always worshiped, who were our teachers. The names of Stanislavsky, Nemirovitch-Dantchenko, Katchalov, Leonidov, had been the dearest to us and most greatly esteemed. This is not the usual applause, out of politeness and condescending encouragement, from teachers to students. This is the fiery applause of an audience enthralled and ecstatic, deeply moved by a great theatrical event.

How desperately we all miss our glorious teacher, Vakhtangov. It was he alone who had created that production, making it a unique, great, and joyous holiday of the old and young generations of the Moscow Art Theater.

Entr'acte has to be prolonged. Stanislavsky is driving to Vakhtangov's home, where Vakhtangov is on his death-bed, to congratulate him on an overwhelming success.

Stanislavsky returns to the theater, and the play continues. The second act begins with Adelma's monologue, from which we learn that she is in love with Kalaf. Many years before, Kalaf, under an assumed name and dressed as a pitiful slave to hide his identity as a Tzar's son, used to work in the palace. She fell in love with him then, and her heart had belonged to him ever since. Before us, the tumultuous and passionate nature of Adelma, Turandot's closest friend, reveals itself. In the monologue of Orotchko (she played Adelma), one felt the ebullience of true passion. Adelma would do anything for the sake of love. "Victory or death!" the actress emphatically concludes her monologue. Then we hear Turandot and her retinue approaching (Adelma is hiding).

"Whose son, and what is his name?" Turandot repeats again and again.

"Whose son, and what is his name?" echo the slave girls after her. No one knows his origin, no one can help the Princess. Adelma begins to put her own plan into motion. She must prevent the marriage of Kalaf to Turandot. For that purpose, she must learn his name. She succeeds in finding out that Kalaf is staying with Barach and Skirina, the mother of Zelima. There is the possibility of unwinding Kalaf's riddle. The scene culminates in Adelma's monologue, which sounds like passionate pleading:

"Oh, love, give me strength.

All-powerful, you shatter everything.
Help me to break my fetters,
To cast off my bondage."

The stage servants are now re-setting the stage for the next picture, named "Arrest." Kalaf and Barach enter. Barach pleads with the Prince to be careful. He tells him that the walls and the trees and all things have ears. As if confirming his words, at that very moment Tartaglia appears and he is followed by Pantalone. Like the rest of the courtiers, they are most anxious to learn the name of the Prince. Their behavior is quite obvious. They offer to photograph the Prince, if he will autograph the picture. They then ask him to fill out a questionnaire. Instead of his name, Kalaf, who quickly sees through their intentions, writes the laconic words: "Give up the attempt, tomorrow you will learn everything." The masks accept their failure good-naturedly and leave.

Briguella, the head of the guards, invites Kalaf to the palace, where the apartment is ready for him. For a minute the stage remains empty, then an old man in rags appears. This is Timur, Kalaf's father. He sees Kalaf led by the guards, and he begins to shout his name. Barach throws himself on the old man like a tiger, slapping his hand across his mouth, raising his dagger over him, fearful that someone might overhear the name of his ward. He is even ready to stab the old man, but, Oh horrors! before him stands Khan Timur, his sovereign. Barach falls on his knees, asking forgiveness for not having recognized his sovereign, and explains to the confused old man why it is necessary that the Prince's name remain a secret. Barach hardly finishes explaining the situation to Khan Timur when the guards appear and arrest Barach and Skirina, and while they are about it, they even arrest Timur—on Turandot's orders.

After tying their hands, or to be more precise, forcing the arrested ones to take the rope in their hands, Truffaldino,

assisted by his slave, leads the arrested from the stage. Entr'-
acte is announced.

The success of the play grows with every act. Many of the
actors and regisseurs of the Moscow Art Theater come backstage to thank and congratulate the young actors. The audience and everyone backstage know about Stanislavsky's visit
to Vakhtangov after the first act.

The third act begins with the "torture scene." Khan Timur and Barach are being tortured. The cruel Princess uses
every means to learn the name of the Prince, but all her
efforts are of no avail. With all the torture, neither Timur
nor Barach utter the name of Kalaf. While the re-setting of
the stage takes place, from the "torture scene" to the next
one, the "night scene," the stage servants are playing a witty
pantomime in front of the curtain. The theme of the pantomime is a cut version of the play *Turandot*. There is the
parade, then the meeting between Barach and Kalaf, the
riddle scene, Kalaf's guessing of the riddles, then the unexpected, pantomimic prophecy of the end of the play: Turandot victoriously announces at the meeting of the divan
the name of the Prince. (Apparently she learns it in some
way.) She chases Kalaf out. Her wrathful speech is illustrated
by the movement of a kerchief that covers her face; the kerchief waves to the rhythm of the music, as she breathes. Then,
each servant stabs herself with her dagger. In the pantomime,
as you see, the ending of *Turandot* is tragic. But how is it
going to end actually? Though there is no doubt in the mind
of the audience that there will be a happy ending, still it is
extremely interested in the development of the play. Over
which peripetia will our beloved heroes have to go to arrive
at a happy ending? The "night scene" is one of the most
remarkable and one of the best scenes in the play. The poetic
talent of Vakhtangov, which is the essence of his regisseur's
style, reveals itself most powerfully in this scene. This scene
demonstrates clearly his basic principle of play presentation.

Apart from working with actors to bring out the inner life of the characters, Vakhtangov considered music, the rhythm of words and movements, as the stimuli of the actor's feelings.

Here once more I like to emphasize the kindred creative views of Stanislavsky and Vakhtangov regarding the role of rhythm in the creation of a production. In his book *Building a Character,* Stanislavsky maintains that tempo-rhythm can arouse the feelings, help to create a character, and finally help to create not only the individual characters, but the complete scene. Let us see how Vakhtangov realizes in his production many possibilities of tempo-rhythm.

The "night scene" is simple enough as far as its super-objective is concerned. In it, Turandot manipulates Barach, Zelima, Truffaldino, and Adelma, in order to get Kalaf's name. But Vakhtangov develops the scene so subtly, so poetically, that while watching it the audience experiences an excitement that is caused by the use of excellent verses and music. Vakhtangov discloses the meaning of that scene, starting with rhythm and music, and uses these to arouse the actor's—and his own—fantasy. From that music are born *mise en scène,* intonations, and inflections. In the beginning of the scene, the night chimes are heard. They sound very softly, as if to remind us that everyone in the palace is asleep. Briguella, yawning, passes by carrying a lighted Chinese lantern; thus indicating the night atmosphere.

After a tumultuous day, crowded with extraordinary events, everyone is tired. Kalaf is also very tired and sleepy. Skirina, dressed as a guard, appears, and the sound of march music, played very softly, is heard. She passes before Kalaf's eyes as an apparition. Half asleep, Kalaf sees the young Zelima and Truffaldino, and it is only with the appearance of Adelma that Kalaf overcomes his tiredness and jumps up.

This whole situation, which Vakhtangov created for the actors, has sharpened their scenic problems, and made their

simple behavior most expressive. Next Briguella, the coward-
ly head of the guards, enters. His responsibility is to protect
Kalaf, but he is panic-stricken by the dark corners of the
stage, where he thinks a crafty enemy is most likely lurking.
To arouse in oneself a feeling of fear, and to express it sincerely on the stage is most difficult. How is an actor to stimulate this feeling in himself? One may of course use "the emotional memory"; that is, arrive at the feeling by the long
road of finding a kindred memory in one's life and in that
way "accumulate" that feeling. But it would hardly be right
in this case, would scarcely be in keeping with this fairy-
tale-like play. Vakhtangov was accomplishing the necessary
results by purely directorial devices. He created a mysterious
night atmosphere, which was expressed by perfect silence,
moonlight, and deep darkness which made the corners of the
stage mysterious. He used the right rhythm, alternating
hushed conversation with the excited exclamations of Briguella, who was frightened to death. Kalaf is half asleep, but
Briguella's panic infects him, too.

Stanislavsky says: "All the tempos and rhythms together
create either a monumental, majestic, or a light and gay
mood. In some plays, more of the first kind, and in others
more of the second kind of tempo-rhythm. Whichever pre-
vails gives the tone to the play. Just try to play tragedy in the
tempo of vaudeville, and vaudeville in the tempo of tragedy."

While the regisseur and the actor search for the right
rhythm in the comedy, the gay action must be tuned up in
a special way—the characters must react to the events with
more energy than the normal logic of such behavior demands. Then the comical is born on the stage. Recall how
funny a child finds the grown-up who pretends to be frightened by the child's knitted, angry little brows and who runs
from the room in horror. The child laughs because he thinks
that the grown-up took his joking threat seriously. By the
way, almost all grown men—who could never be actors—do

these make-believe scenes of fright quite sincerely. The most untalented people, not trained for the stage, are able to arouse in themselves easily one of the most difficult feelings for a professional actor—the feeling of fear. These grown-up men playing with the child are guided by the correct and lightning-speed tempo-rhythm which communicates fear. In the given example, there is another interesting circumstance. In this game, the child is the actor and the audience at the same time. He succeeds in behaving as an actor and immediately reacts with laughter as the audience. Instinctively his tempo-rhythm of the imaginary is switched into the tempo-rhythm of reality.

Stanislavsky writes: "Tempo-rhythm helps actors to live their roles truly when they don't know anything about psycho-technique. This is an important discovery. And if it is so, then we learn that the correct tempo-rhythm of the play or the role, by itself, subconsciously, almost mechanically, may arouse actors' feelings and thus the true living of a part."

Telling us that the word and the overall problem act upon our mind and will, Stanislavsky adds: "Tempo-rhythm acts directly upon our feelings. Isn't that an important gain for our psycho-technique?" These thoughts, which came to Stanislavsky in his declining years, summing up his enormous experience, were only burgeoning during the years of *Turandot*. The problems of rhythm had been worked on simultaneously by Stanislavsky, Vakhtangov, and Meyerkhold. Stanislavsky was working out the problems of musicality—or tempo-rhythm—during his lessons in 1921 with the students of the Vakhtangov, Habimah, and Armenian Studios, which we had the good fortune to attend; and also, in his creative function, especially when he directed *The Marriage of Figaro* and *Hot Heart*. Meyerkhold showed his accomplishment from the point of view of the rhythmical score in the direction of the plays *Forest, The Bug, Mandate,* and a number of others. But the experiment of Vakhtangov on *Princess*

*Turandot* had an exceptionally important significance. The mastery of Vakhtangov's staging undoubtedly gave Stanislavsky much food for thought in probing into tempo-rhythm. Vakhtangov possessed extraordinary skill in using such subtle means of building a scene that it involved the actor's whole being into "the music of action and words." In the scene of Kalaf and Adelma, the tenseness of passion and feeling reaches its peak. The scene embodies the elemental, violent love of Adelma for Kalaf, and the unreciprocated love of Kalaf for Princess Turandot. The danger may even mean death for Kalaf from the treacherous hand of his beloved Turandot. The scene is filled with that gamut of emotions which the audience took in as a musical composition, in which one melody, following the other, grows, widens, joins with a new melody; then finally all the thoughts, all the melodies and feelings, fuse into one powerful and tender melody. By what means can a director express such a scene? How can one express the most refined transitions—one moment lyrical, the next full of profound dramatic intensity? A poet, we know, expresses his spirit by using measured forms of speech, musical measures, rhythmic verses.

Moments of exaltation and inspiration sometimes visit the regisseur during his creative work, and then the image is born of him as though it were being born of a poet.

> "The daylight is extinguished,
> The evening mist is rising over the blue sea,
> Roar, roar, obedient sail,
> Surge, turbulent ocean, under me."

Pushkin addresses the elements as if commanding them. How does one command the waves of the sea? There is no everyday truth in this expression, but there is the profound truth of poetic feeling: the truth of a disturbed heart, looking for solace in the terrible and splendid primordial forces.

These lines are deeply agitated, the poetic accompaniment to other quickly changing themes running through the conscience of the genius-poet. Here is the theme of the Motherland, from which Pushkin was exiled by the Tzar. Here is also the lyric world of the suffering poet:

> "But former heart wounds,
> Deep wounds of love nothing could remedy,
> Roar, roar, obedient sail,
> Surge, turbulent ocean, under me."

Directors endowed by nature with their own poetic vision of the world should be called director-poets. And that, in my opinion, is the highest praise that could be given a director.

The last act of *Turandot* takes only twenty minutes. The action takes place in the "Hall of Meetings," as does the second scene in the first act. Vakhtangov's handling of this scene could be compared with a conductor who orchestrates a symphony—so harmoniously does he tie in all the themes at the end of the play.

Turandot guesses the Prince's name. Kalaf is to be sent away from the palace, and he is about to commit suicide. Turandot, at the last moment, stops him by confessing her love to him. Her father and the courtiers are very happy. Adelma is in despair. She gives voice to a magnificent, tragic monologue, then exits. Everyone is filled with compassion for her. The meeting between Khan Timur and his son, Kalaf, takes place. Then there is a happy engagement. How many important events are taking place? If the regisseur presented every episode with all its details, the finale of the play would be too long and it would be overburdened. In such scenes, filled with action, the art of the director consists in his ability to create an overall mood of the joyous events and tie in the diverse themes of the play. The regisseur at this point must allow the audience to complete with its imagination that which the regisseur sketches with a few strokes and suggestions. To express the thought more precisely, the audience—now in possession of all the facts—completes the play for the actors. It is this way: the audience, once involved in the play, begins to create it together with the actors, begins really to feel itself the author of the play. The ideal audience is the one that accepts the performance spontaneously, like a child.

Now in order to be able to bring the audience to that kind of child-like spontaneity, it is necessary for the performance to be skilled, masterful, captivating. I do not remember a more spontaneous audience than that elated one of this public rehearsal of *Turandot*. Each scene, each detail of the last act, was reacted to with roars of laughter and storms of applause. And when, after it was all over, and the actors were removing their costumes and their make-up and starting to leave the stage, the narrow line between the actors and the audience was completely erased. The audience did not want to leave the theater, and the actors were exuberant at hearing their repeated applause and seeing their joyous faces.

At that moment, all the thoughts of the whole company were on Vakhtangov, who had created such a remarkable holiday for everyone. "Bravo! Bravo!" was heard from the auditorium. There were tears of joy in the eyes of the performers and the audience. Finally the applause ended. For a long time the members of the Moscow Art Theater, headed by Stanislavsky and Nemirovitch-Dantchenko, remained in the auditorium. The musician-students moved onto the stage and played the musical numbers from *Turandot* again and again. Friends, comrades in the theater, and students were composing a telegram of gratitude and love to Vakhtangov. Stanislavsky telephoned Vakhtangov. Since Vakhtangov was bed-ridden, Stanislavsky spoke to Mrs. Vakhtangov. "Please tell him that the 'old' of the Moscow Art Theater are standing by the telephone, and we want you to tell him that we are all excited and most enthusiastic about his production. This performance is a holiday for all the collective of the Moscow Art Theater. For art's sake, we demand that he take good care of himself. In the life of the Moscow Art Theater, there are very few such victories, such accomplishments. I am proud of such a student, if he is my student. Tell him, 'Please wrap up in the blanket as if it were a toga, and sleep with the sleep of a conqueror.' "

The play is finished, the audience has departed, the footlights are dimmed, the auditorium is plunged into darkness; but it seems as though the feelings and passions that had been lived through this remarkable evening still continue to fill the air.

Our hands filled with flowers, we are hurrying to Vakhtangov to share with him our joys and our moments of creative happiness. We are walking through the dark street—the street lanterns are not lit. Now and then one sees light through the curtainless windows. There is a deep silence. But in this silence we feel the enormity of the events of historical significance, the birth of a new society. In this Moscow night of 1922 we think of the people who, with unmatched heroism, defended the Soviet Republic. Weapons in hand it was defended by the working people, peasants, and that fine part of the intellectuals who tied their fate with the revolutionary people. To defend the Republic now meant to rebuild the ruined factories and plants, to build the foundation for new socialist constructions. To defend the Republic now meant to spread culture to the broad masses, to the people at large. In spite of all the difficulties the Soviet Union lived through, regardless of hunger and deprivation, there was no despondency. There was unshakable faith in the future, in this victory of the Revolution. The process of the birth of a new life was organic, majestic, and it inspired all sincere artists in the country.

And in that night we all wanted to believe that we, too, worked honestly, that we too brought at least some contribution to the common task of the entire country. We wanted to believe that our audience would start their working day tomorrow with the memory of those happy hours it had spent in our theater the previous night. Significant artistic impressions do not fade away; they remain and live in the conscience of men. This is why our work in the theater is of great importance and responsibility—it influences the conscience of men.

From that point of view, I would like to emphasize the significance of Eugene Vakhtangov's last work, *Princess Turandot*. Life itself had prompted the necessity for this performance, which asserted its joys and optimism. At that period, I repeat, there was not one contemporary play that would have answered Vakhtangov's demands. *Turandot* was given only some possibility along that line. The regisseur, Vakhtangov, turned out to be much stronger than the play. On the foundation of the fairy tale about Princess Turandot, he created an important work of the theater, in which a passionate, fiery love for a man, filled with lofty and beautiful feelings, captivated contemporary theatergoers. What were the basic creative principles, the basic creative problems, which he used as a foundation to direct *Princess Turandot?* I would like to name three: (1) the affirmation of the artistic credo of the theater for the given collective; (2) the definition of the dramatic genre of the play and the means of expressiveness which most precisely met the demands of that given genre; and (3) the subordination of the performance to the demands of the times, of their social significance and their spiritual value. Does the performance answer the artistic needs of the people and its new ideology?

Let us see what the genre of *Princess Turandot* is. Gozzi's play is a comedy fairy tale. Vakhtangov's staging of this fairy tale followed the principle of the writers who write fairy tales and the storytellers who tell them to the people. A fairy tale demands of the teller a complete faith in all the events of the tale. The moment the teller doubts his story, he is no longer convincing to his listeners. Vakhtangov, in presenting *Turandot,* was seeking the principle of scenic action and theatricality which applied to that specific genre. In creating this make-believe world of kings and princesses, Vakhtangov wanted his actors to behave as though they were the members of a strolling company. The personal feelings and passions of these strolling players had to be intermingled with those of the characters of the play. And that second theatrical sphere was no less exciting. It gave a more simple folklore tint to it, because the actors were then of the common people, playing on the streets and in the squares.

In the articles about *Princess Turandot,* one is aware of a tendency to consider the amusing details of the performance as its main accomplishment, an innovation of Vakhtangov's direction. The beard of old Timur was made out of a towel, a tennis racket served as a scepter for the king, a knife for cutting the pages of a book was used as a dagger. Of course, Vakhtangov by no means saw the key of the comedy in these amusing details. He tried to accomplish the comedy by the overall joyous tone of the actors' behavior on the stage. The singularity of this comedy is its improvisational foundation. The masks were improvising a new text on the stage. But still, the most important is the improvisational state of being of all the participants of the play. Stanislavsky demanded of an actor, even after having played his role a hundred times, that he play it as if he were playing it for the first time. Vakhtangov, following Stanislavsky's demand, taught the participants of *Turandot* to be in a creative, improvisational state during the entire time they were performing their roles on the stage. That is, to create each time a new interrelationship with their partners, new adaptations, new adjustments. Every improvisation demanded a skilled and finished technique.

This technique must be called upon to help the artist in the moments of his improvisational state of being. Improvisation is the road to inspiration, to priceless creative behavior on the stage. As we see, Vakhtangov's demands were based on his knowledge of the fundamental principles of theatrical art, and not on the small, easily changeable adjustments. These may be substituted, even thrown out of the performance altogether, without changing its essence. But when the actors are robbed of their improvisational state of being—of the festivity—the performance is deprived of its essence, its soul.

Vakhtangov considered characterization equally important. He told us during the rehearsal that all roles are character roles. The characteristics of the comedy role are the guide to the comic element in it. Vakhtangov tried to develop in actors that unique creative state which he called "the imminence of humor." At the same time, he was very strict in his demand that an actor have a sense of proportion in comedy scenes and stay within reasonable limits. The comedy genre requires impeccable taste. The young actor is inclined to be tempted by the audience's laughter to repeat again and again whatever made them laugh. Vakhtangov used to say: "It is always better to underplay than to overplay." That which is truly funny is born spontaneously, without any effort to call for a laugh. The true humor is in the idea, never outside of it. It is common knowledge that the actor must be inwardly serious when he is playing comedy, and that seriousness must grow proportionately with the laughter of the audience. The more active the theatergoer's receptivity to the actor, the more the latter must be involved in his scenic problem. God help the actor when he begins to enjoy himself! He loses the interest and involvement of the audience right then and there. Vakhtangov used to tell us that we are praying to the God to whom Stanislavsky taught us to pray; he was perhaps the only artist of the theater on earth who had his own Lord's Prayer.

In the criterion is the System of Stanislavsky, then we students of Vakhtangov must be able to answer the question that is disturbing us: Is *Princess Turandot* a deviation from this system, or is it the product of a scenic art built entirely on its foundation, as absorbed and applied by Vakhtangov? As we said before, Vakhtangov, while cherishing the teachings of Stanislavsky, in his own creative search found it necessary to widen and to develop some of the elements of that System. Let us take for an example one of the most important elements of the System—communion. Stanislavsky was asserting that the character of communion on the stage is just as manifold as communion between people in life. Analyzing various kinds of communion, he finds for them a common denominator. The communion on the stage between the partners, he calls direct communion; it is understood, of course, that communion must be continued through the pauses and speeches of one's partner.

But there is another kind of communion. For example: there are two persons in the room who are not on speaking terms with each other. They obviously take no notice of each other, though both of them inwardly are acutely aware of each other. There is also communion with oneself (a monologue), in which the mind of the actor talks to his heart, usually when the character has to make a decision or find an answer to some question disturbing him. The mind has its reasons, its pros and cons; while the heart may appeal or protest to the mind, and has its feelings on the subject. The actor carries on an inner dialogue with himself. Then there is another kind of monologue, in which the actor addresses the audience directly. A classic example of this kind of communion is a famous one from Gogol's *Inspector General*. "Whom are you laughing at? You are laughing at yourselves!" That device was used in dramaturgy before our epoch, at the birth of theatrical art when the writer sent heralds or a chorus on stage to tell the audience about important events that took place off the stage. Stanislavsky learned much from the galaxy of actors of the Maly Theater, who resorted daringly to direct communion with the audience and yet did not violate the truth in any degree. I remember the great Sadovskya, sitting in an armchair at the footlights, addressing many of her lines in the Ostrovsky plays to the audience. Stanislavsky advised actors to make this "coming forward to the audience" courageously and boldly. Vakhtangov followed his advice, thus being true to Stanislavsky's principles also in the question of scenic communion.

We established two more kinds of communion in our studies for the preparation for *Princess Turandot*—the communion in rhythm and the communion in movement. Think of a symphony orchestra. The conductor gives a set rhythm and tempo to the members of his orchestra. A very fine process takes place in the orchestra when one musician has to sense the other, coming in during the great number of different measures of a given composition, passing the melody from one instrument to the other, changing the tempo. The artist-musician while reading the music sheet must at the same time watch the conductor out of the corner of his eye and catch all the nuances of his conducting and execute them. In the group scenes of the play the actors are like a symphony orchestra, if the scenes are staged by a fine regisseur. The actors of the group scenes must not only feel the general rhythm of the scene, but they must also be tuned in to its conversation, and they must time their cues perfectly. If the actors of the group scene are divided by their contrasting relationship to the event taking place on the stage, they must be perfectly organized in their behavior. Every member of the group scene must follow the *mise en scène* given them by the regisseur: enter, withdraw, step forward, or join another group; at some precise moment leave the stage and re-enter. The performers' movements must be set during the rehearsals to a minute detail—a regisseur creates a precise score for the group scenes—sometimes called "mob scenes"—but also for scenes between two or three performers.

There exists an expression among experienced actors: "Not in tone." Our fathers and great-grandfathers loved that expression. It had a deep meaning. If a certain scene required a quick tempo, for example, in a quarrel scene, or squabble or wrangle (so often used in Molière's plays), that scene was ruined if one of the participants dragged it out. He irritated us; he was obviously not in tone with the light, elegant French dialogue. Nowadays when an actor is "not in tone," we say he is not in rhythm, or not in the tempo of the scene.

Life gives us an enormous number of examples of communion in rhythm and in movement. In sports—tennis, boxing, wrestling—each movement of one sportsman must be a proper response to the movement of the other. Tennis balls sent to the corner of the tennis court bring the other player to that particular place. Incidentally, watch the behavior of the onlookers during the match, and you will see the rhythmic movements of their heads as their eyes follow the ball and the players.

Though the "amplitude of movement" of the players and of the onlookers is almost incomparable (one is measured by scores of meters and the other is counted by centimeters), the communion still exists and is expressed in movement. Often a similar situation takes place on the stage when the actors communicate with each other in a fighting, dancing, or fencing scene: that is to say, they communicate with each other in rhythm and movement. The actors know only too well that this kind of communion on the stage gives them a special sense of great creative joy because they are controlled by dynamic rhythm.

Let us take another thesis of the Stanislavsky System, that which deals with the sense of truth and believability on the stage. Stanislavsky says: "In life, the truth is that which exists in reality, that of which man is sure. On the stage we call

197

truth that which does not appear in reality, but which might and can happen." Many people of the theater, as well as some art connoisseurs, oppose that statement of Stanislavsky's. They insist that the exact copying of life is truth. That is the kind of error that brings dramatic art to naturalism, reduces it to a petty verisimilitude. When we worked on *Turandot* that tendency still existed. It was the heritage of the theater of decline and of social stagnation. Vakhtangov led an irreconcilable fight with such pseudo-followers of Stanislavsky, those preachers of naturalism. Vakhtangov was striving to bring the theater into the theater—looking for a new form that would express the life-truth in the theater-truth. In this respect, the art of Vakhtangov moved in the channel of true development of the realistic traditions of Stanislavsky and Nemirovitch-Dantchenko. According to Vakhtangov, we must enrich the theater art of social realism with new means of expression in the sphere of its content and form.

*Turandot* had a triumphant success all through the Soviet Union and also abroad—Berlin, Stockholm, Paris, and many other cities. The play carried in itself, let us say, one-millionth part of the faith in a bright and happy future which permeated the conscience of the Soviet people. Mayakovsky's words come to memory:

> "Joy forges
> not for you
> shall we share
> it with you?
> Life is splendid
> and
> astonishing.
> Until a hundred
> to grow
> we will be
> without old-age.
> Year from year

to grow
will our courage
glorify
hammer
and the verse,
Earth of youth."

I dare to think that if Vakhtangov had still been living
when Mayakovsky wrote his plays, he would have been their
best regisseur. Vakhtangov wrote: "Humanity does not have
one great work of art which is not the personification or completion of the creative force of the people. That which is
truly great in the soul of the people is always overheard by
the artist. The artist creates not for the people, not outside
of the people, but with the people."

The performance of *Princess Turandot* was a sort of challenge to naturalism, facelessness, and grayishness in art. Vakhtangov was striving to destroy moodiness, sentimentality,
pseudo-psychological significance, and to discrown all the
"howling of the wind" backstage and the "cricket on the
hearth" sounds that created an atmosphere of Philistine cozi-
ness, when he directed *Turandot*. It is true that sometimes
he went too far in his fight with naturalism, but I am sure
that the mounting of *Turandot* was one of the first stages of
what would have been for him a further development. He
was not happy with the platform as a part of the set, but the
progressiveness of his fatal illness made inroads on him every
day. There was no time to change things. The production
had to be finished. A year before *Turandot*, Vakhtangov had
directed *Marriage Proposal*, by Chekhov, where the mounting of the production was realistic. Also, his production of
*Deluge*, in the First Studio of the Moscow Art Theater, was
given realistic treatment. Vakhtangov was a true realist and
a strong enemy of the naturalistic.

Experimentation was typical of the first period of the Soviet Theater. Many experimentations of that time have disappeared completely, leaving no traces of themselves, although in their day they caused a sensation and were proclaimed as examples of outstanding proletarian art. Such was the fate of the Theater of Proletcult and a great number of studios now completely forgotten. *Turandot* had a great influence on the subsequent creative life of our theater, and I am not exaggerating when I say that it had a definite influence on the Soviet Theater in its entirety.

We may see the immediate influence of *Turandot* in a number of plays of our theater: comedies of Mérimée, from the cycle of *The Theater of Clara Gazul, Leo Gurich Sinichkin,* and many others. And after a special analysis of the Revolutionary plays in our theater (*The Break,* directed by A. Popov, and *Intervention,* directed by R. Simonov), we will see the great influence of *Turandot.* In those plays, one observes the influence not only of the school and creative method of Vakhtangov, but also the attempt, dictated by the new demands of the times, to realize certain scenic problems first tried in *Turandot*—the problem of style and genre of the play, the problem of realistic theatricality in the true spirit of Vakhtangov.

*The Theater of Clara Gazul* was created by the brilliant fantasy of Mérimée. Short one-act plays, *The Carriage of the Sacred Gifts, Paradise and Hell, African Love,* and *The Woman Devil,* are distinguished by intensity of passion and also by their demand for a great comic temperament in the actor. The unexpected turns of intrigue in those plays required of an actor the utmost sincerity, spontaneity, and an improvisational state of being on the stage. The Turandot school had helped our actors to master the swiftness characteristic of the French theater, whose brilliant dramatist Mérimée was. The sharpness of the dialogue, the fast tempo of the speech, the musicality, the gracefulness of movement, the sweeping gestures—all the mastery needed to express the comedies of

Mérimée—were learned at the rehearsals of *Turandot* and also during the lessons given by Stanislavsky in 1921 in the Habimah Theater for a number of studios. The production of *Comedies of Mérimée* was produced by Vakhtangov's Studio two years after the death of our teacher. The influence of the master on these young actors and student-regisseurs was profound. The student's personal store of knowledge was still small, his experiences were limited by his few years of adult life; his artistic experiences were not filled with enough observation and knowledge, and his personal criterion was not yet formed. A master's effects on the student at that period influence almost all his future: his understanding of life, his creative method, his artistic taste, and his moral make-up. All we teachers and regisseurs remembering that must feel a special responsibility for the future of the theater youth, eagerly absorbing all our words. Our pedagogical, educational work must be deeply thought over, and our creative credo must be a matter of principle. We must not only teach, we must also educate our young. Writing these lines I feel a deep gratitude to Vakhtangov, who succeeded in making the theatrical youth of our generation so interesting and so resplendent. Vakhtangov gave his students a correct understanding of the present in its relationship to the past, trained our artistic tastes, based our creativity on the foundation of the realistic school, taught us to love the mastery of acting and to fight professionalism, dilettantism, and amateurishness.

The production of comedies of Mérimée showed the result of the excellent training Vakhtangov's students had received. Also, the young regisseur met his challenge when the Vakhtangov Theater gave plays by Mérimée and Maeterlinck in the Theater Odéon in Paris with tremendous success.

*Leo Sinichkin* was the first important production in the vaudeville style on our stage. (In Russia, vaudeville is a theatrical piece of light and amusing character, interspersed with songs and dances.) Vakhtangov believed that every actor

must have Russian vaudeville training. Each student was required to work on one or two one-act "vaudevilles." For our
public examinations, we showed Chekhov's vaudevilles—
*A Wedding, The Boor, Anniversary, Marriage Proposal*—as
well as a number of other Russian and French vaudevilles.
It is characteristic of vaudeville on the Russian stage to inter-
mingle the comic, the dramatic, the gay, and the lyric. Vakhtangov even used to say a vaudeville must end with a sad
melody. In this interpretation of vaudeville, we recognize the
tradition of Schepkin and Martinov, two great Russian actors,
who, when playing vaudeville, used to move their audience
not only to hearty laughter but also to compassionate tears.

In those great traditions of Russian vaudeville, we were
striving to realize our production of *Sinitchkin*. Schukin,
playing the role of Sinitchkin (an old Russian actor), took
Schepkin as a model. The character of the old actor, with his
bitter fate, his inspiring dedication to art, reminded Schukin
of Schepkin—of his noble fight for the purity of the Russian
stage, for young talent, and for the dignity of an actor. This
approach to the role gave Schukin a deep insight into the
character of an old, honest toiler in the Russian Theater, and
it brought remarkable results. Along with vivid comedy
scenes, we saw in the last act a genuine drama of a cruelly
insulted and undeservedly humiliated little man. We were
anxious about him, and our hearts were filled with compassion.

Vaudeville used to allow the actor the right to stop the
action of the play by addressing the audience on burning
topics of the day, sometimes even in satirical couplets. In the
thirties and fifties of the last century, the period of vaudeville's hey-day, the patrons of art, and theater habitués, often
recognized themselves in the characters created by the actors
on the stage. Producing *Sinitchkin*, we found it appropriate
to include in the performance a contemporary observation of
theater life in the years 1924-25, and a number of the coup-

lets of the original play, which were of interest only because
they contributed an insight into theater life of the last century, were replaced by couplets on the contemporary Soviet
theater.

The influence of *Turandot* on the production of *Sinitchkin* is obvious. It is also obvious from the remarks above that
the classic tradition of performing vaudeville as practiced by
our theater fathers and forefathers, the actors of the previous
century, had an influence on our production. The interlude
and the couplets of *Sinitchkin* were always changing during
its ten-year run on our stage. I am sure that Mayakovsky
would have changed the staging of his play *Russian Bath* had
he been living in our day. In fact, Mayakovsky did have the
foresight to suggest to the theaters that if they found it
necessary they might add to or alter the text in *Bath* and *Bug*
to fit the times.

When I am asked why we do not present *Turandot* now on
our stage, I answer: "Because I do not know how Vakhtangov would have directed it in our day." I only know that the
basic principle of the production would be the same, because
the principle is always young. But the form of the play, most
likely, would be different, because the aesthetic demands and
tastes of the theatergoer have changed considerably during
the last thirty-five years. The production of *Uncle Vanya* that
had been realized by the older generation of the Moscow Art
Theater at the dawn of the creative life of the theater is different from the same play created by the same theater in our
time. Even its content is treated differently—also the interpretation of the characters. We ask ourselves: How would
Stanislavsky have treated *Uncle Vanya* today? Most likely altogether differently, though I personally would have liked
very much to see the production of *Uncle Vanya* done in our
time a little closer to the original, which probed deeply into
the life of the Russian intelligentsia in the pre-Revolutionary
years. I, as a spectator, who had seen *Uncle Vanya* played by

the brilliant galaxy of Moscow Art Theater actors—Stanislavsky, Knipper, Vichnevsky, Michael Chekhov—am interested in seeing today those characters of Chekhov's as I first saw them. Maybe it is a debatable question, but experience has proved to us only too often that the overweening desire to revise old plays often brings undesirable results. It seems to me that the right to revise the plays that entered the golden fund of the Russian Soviet Theater should be given only to the artist who has discovered a thoroughly new directorial conception, one which would disclose the given work of art in a new light for the contemporary audience.

The play *Much Ado About Nothing*, produced twenty years ago by the regisseur Rapoport, the stage designer Rindin, and the composer Chrennikov, is still on our stage. Shakespeare's unfading text is the same on our stage, also the *mise en scènes* are still unchanged, there are the same brilliant sets, the same beautiful music; but we cannot say that the production as a whole has not changed. The play has been re-evaluated and has gone through a number of changes by the cast. I would like to tell you about my personal experience as an actor who has been playing Benedick for over twenty years. When I started to work on the role of Benedick, I tried to take the fate of my hero most sincerely, consider all the feelings, passions, thoughts, and behavior of Benedick (who became very dear to me) as the great dramatist conceived them. By correctly interpreting the text, I could project the epoch and the inimitable conditions of the remarkable times: when humanity was being liberated from feudal oppression, when ethical standards, morals, and customs were undergoing a drastic change, and when women had begun to demand equal rights with men.

In having equal rights lies the charm of the conflict between Beatrice and Benedick. Their attraction for each other is obvious even through their dissensions, their exchange of caustic remarks, their battle of words. At the end it brought the obstinate pair to a happy outcome—marriage.

In playing Shakespeare, the actor must strive not only for an exceptionally true and rich psychological life in his role but also for the most brilliant plasticity, rhythm, and speech. The comedies of Shakespeare demand of an actor a correctly placed voice, masterful delivery of verse, poetical speech, lightness in dialogues and monologues, precision in movement, and so on. All these qualifications must be polished, worked out to a high degree of skill, in order to reveal the inner content of the role more fully. In my work on Benedick, I had the opportunity to realize how important it is for an actor playing Shakespeare to study paintings of the Renaissance period. The portraits of Velasquez helped me especially. An acquaintance with the art of painting reveals to an actor and a regisseur the epoch in its visual images. Of course I do not mean that one should literally copy the gestures and poses of those marvelous portraits of the Spanish, Italian, or Flemish schools. That would make an actor a formal, soulless—though perhaps externally beautiful—figure. It is necessary to understand the essence of the Renaissance, that magnificent upward flight of human talent that gave the world superlative beauty. Also, it is necessary to absorb its feeling of life—splendid and terrifying, elated and prosaic. The basic character of my Benedick has not changed in its outward form, but every year the work on my role has brought subtle changes, born of my perception of the audience's reaction. The audience is different each evening; each audience has its unique character. We, the actors, know only too well a "difficult audience": cold, observing the performance without much response. This is usually the audience of the dress rehearsal and opening night. To break through the thoughts and feelings of the connoisseurs of the theater is very difficult —they know everything beforehand. Here one has to forget that kind of reaction and "get away" from it as far as possible —not expect any help from the audience at all. One has a peculiar feeling during such performances. On such occasions, an odd sensation is born, the sensation of having a duel with the audience; the actor needs extraordinary self-control to know how to conduct himself on the stage at such a time. The further we move away from that opening night, the happier is our state-of-being, and the more natural becomes our communion with the audience. The audience will accept our work of art with an open heart if our work is pithy, artistic, and inspiring.

What did change in my role during those twenty years? My perception of contemporaneity was changing with the times. My understanding of the tasks and aims of theatrical art, my experiences as an actor, naturally were changing as I grew older. I started to play Benedick when I was a very young, inexperienced actor. Naturally, then, my spontaneity, temperament, gaiety, and buoyancy were suitable to the character of my hero. With the years the actor grows, and also the image he is playing grows. My Benedick after ten years became more enriched. In place of spontaneity and youthfulness, my image had deepened psychologically. The necessity of keeping the sense of proportion became more and more clear to me, especially in comedy scenes. Shakespeare's comedy allows the actor direct communication with the audience. For example: after the scene of "manful interacting" (after overhearing a dialogue especially staged by Don Pedro), Benedick begins to think that Beatrice really loves him. In the first years of playing, I addressed the monologue directly to the audience. But then came a time when the audience—fearful of obvious theatricality and under the influence of a widespread understanding of realism—shied away from direct contact with an actor during a performance. At that time, I addressed the monologue to myself—and I felt more comfortable because of doing so.

Years went by. The demands of life prompted new perspectives in the development of the theater. The theatergoer ex-

pected new genres, a variety of genres: courage, a vivid expressiveness—and most important—the cessation of the boring
"leveling" that made theaters much alike, depriving them of
their own creative handwriting.

There came a new period in the art of the theater, and
again I felt the need to address Benedick's monologue directly to the audience. It stands to reason that the manner of my
direct communication with the audience had changed. What
were the differences in my rendition of the same monologue
while addressing it directly to the different audiences? The
difference, I think, lies in the degree of the "openness" of the
device. If before, the device was completely bare, straight-
forward, now it is restrained and not obtrusive. One of the
characters of Ostrovsky's play says: "A right degree is art."
That will always be an unchanging precept.

In the year 1952, exactly thirty years after the production
of *Turandot,* an original Chinese play was added to our
repertoire. The name of the play is *A Grey Maiden,* by Che-
Tzin and Den-He, and it is directed by Gerasimov. *A Grey
Maiden* is distinguished by the traits of the traditional Chinese dramaturgy, specifically the monologues of the characters telling the audience what had happened to them right
before their entrance on stage. There are monologues when
the performer talks to himself of joys and sorrows, of his
happy or tragic fate. Music is its inherent component; it
accompanies and sustains the action. The sets are conditional.
They are subjected to the actors' needs. The regisseur, Gerasimov, kept the acting realistic without the traditional masks
of the old Chinese theater. He treated it as a folk-heroic
tragedy. The combination of the realistic means with the traditions that spring from the traditional folk theater gives an
extraordinarily strong effect and impresses the minds and
hearts of the audience most powerfully. Also, in the tragic
genre, the introduction of theatrical elements intensifies the
impression the play has on the audience. It could not be

otherwise. The theater is always, first of all, the theater. Its past explains much to us. In the Greek theater, the chorus did not divert the audience's attention from the actors, nor did it keep the audience from participating in the spectacle. The absence of sets in Shakespeare's theater did not prevent the great dramatist from creating masterpieces. In Molière's time, the presence of the public on the stage did not interfere with the brilliant French comedians' living their roles fully. We watched with admiration the sketch *The King of the Monkeys* given by the ensemble of the Chinese People's Army—a unique masterpiece of theatrical-dramatic, plastic, and musical art. Only the true understanding of people's feeling for art, of people's spontaneity and fantasy, could help to create such a brilliant work of art as *The King of the Monkeys.*

But why did we, experienced workers in the theater, enjoy so much the folk art of China? I think because we had missed for so long the brilliant theatrical spectacle. The theater often lacks festivity. The audience hears the old truisms, spoken poorly, performed passionlessly and prosaically, by mediocre actors. We all talk about the necessity of daring, about theatrical experiments, but at the same time we are afraid of them. Our talk and our calling on the regisseur for courage remain on the pages of the theater magazine. Vakhtangov's outstanding service to the theater is in his daring, in his courage. While preserving all the richness of realistic art he went further, widening the scope of the realistic theater, its means of expression, its poetic essence—creating the theatrical spectacle *Turandot,* the satirical pamphlet *The Miracle of St. Anthony,* and the realistic tragicomedy *A Wedding.*

If *The Grey Maiden* gave us the opportunity to create a vivid theatrical production in the tragical-heroic folk play, the other work of art closer to our point of view, to Vakhtangov's *Turandot,* is the play by Marchak, *Fearing Sorrow*

*One Escapes Happiness.* Directed by Eugene Simonov, this production introduces the genre of the folk theater. It is a story about a noble soldier, Ivan Tarabanov, who fights misfortune, ill fate; a fairy tale about two hearts, unjustly separated. We were trying, within our abilities, to impregnate it with the poetry of Pushkin's fairy tales. But in addition to the lyric theme of this fairy tale, there is also a satirical theme, in the characterizations of the Tzar, the general, the merchant, and the woodcutter. Here, also, we have before us brilliant examples of Pushkin's creativity in *The Story of the Village Goruchina,* a chronicle that paved the way for the great satirical works of Russian literature and led us to the necessary approach in creating negative images. Pushkin's creativity taught us the objective approach in portraying a human being, without emphasizing one particular trait of his character, without tendentiousness. Pushkin admired Shakespeare tremendously, because of that master dramatist's great ability to do just this. Tendentiousness results from the behavior of a given character and his reaction to the events and other characters in the play. The actor's conception, and his relation to his hero, marching shoulder-to-shoulder with the conception of the production as a whole, will necessarily prompt the desired result.

Here, interpreting Vakhtangov's ideas again, we approach once more a very important matter—the actor's attitude toward the role. In the play *Turandot,* we were striving to enrich the images, by use of all possible means of theatrical expressiveness to paint them with vivid colors so that they would imprint themselves on the audience's consciousness. But various aims have various means. "The Religious Procession in Kursk Province," by Repin, if done in watercolor would have lost its power to impress the onlooker. Illustrations of Don Quixote—masterpieces of graphic art—would be unthinkable in a means of expression such as painting. Enlarge the "Madonna Litta," by Leonardo da Vinci, to the size of Raphael's "Sistine Madonna" and the essential proportion would be broken: the philosophical idea of that masterpiece of painting depicting the elevated theme of motherhood, the charm of femininity, the purity of infancy, the eternal poetry of blue sky, would be lost. As we know, each chef-d'oeuvre of art is a striking illustration of that indissoluble, unbreakable bond between content and form, between the thought and the means of its embodiment. Among the most memorable works of art, we always cite the images created by the great Russian singer and actor Feodor Chaliapin, who for each of his roles found a new means of expression, not only in sculptural plasticity, but also in the unique timbre of voice necessary for the specific character. The richness of an artist's conception is always the result of the artist's experiences, the artist's life. Conception is born of the artist's ability to perceive reality profoundly and sensitively, and from his own point of view; then in the works created by that artist with enthusiasm and creative excitement, one feels the artist-man asserting his innermost ideals.

Vakhtangov found an inner aim for himself in the purifying storm of the October Revolution. We, the participants in the Vakhtangov production of *Turandot,* were in the first dress rehearsal the witnesses to his courage, his tremendous will power, and his dedication to the art of the theater as a tribunal for the propagation of ideas vital to humanity. When we say that the theater is the school of life—or utter similar high-flown phrases—we automatically see in our mind's eye the image of the typical professor-philosopher mounted on a platform for the purpose of teaching "the great science of life." However, we know very well from the history of art that artists whose only purpose was to propagate, to teach, were not artists of the highest caliber.

Leo Tolstoy had no intention of preaching from the pages of his plays, his novels, his romances, or his short stories. But his philosophico-Christian work, written with the specific intention of teaching, could not be compared with his artistic prose, since it lacked both poetic power and conviction. And Gogol, so great in his works of art, is most disappointing in his philosophical writings. The art of the theater has little liking for didactics and deliberate preaching. Its elements are thoughts, passions, feelings, images, action, laughter, and tears.

The art of the theater is to convince the theatergoer of what takes place on the stage. The means the theater uses to convince can be most diverse: from tragedy to vaudeville, from revolutionary heroics to the popular fairy tale. All these thoughts agitated us during the period we worked on the production of that fairy tale by Marchak. In the first place, we had to understand, to create, the image of "Misfortune—Bad Luck." That "Misfortune" is a kind of house-sponger, one of which the master of the house cannot rid himself. The "misfortune" enters a man's life, becomes a part of his life. This image must be plastically vivid, and at the same time there should be nothing out of the ordinary about it. All the other images of this fairy tale must be multi-sided characters and must be most expressive. To produce such images one needs perfected skills, and one must maintain an improvisational state of mind while on the stage—and one should also possess a sense of musicality. The poetical atmosphere of the Russian mode of life and Russian nature was created by Mr. K. Yona by his excellent sets, which revived the tradition of fine culture and the decorative art of the Russian theater. The production of this fairy tale by Marchak was remarkably kindred to that of *Princess Turandot*.

Until now I have been talking about plays which in my point of view were kindred in spirit to Vakhtangov's *Turandot,* and which truly developed his teachings. But I must also mention the productions of classics that were utter creative failure. Such a defeat was *Hamlet,* produced in our theater in 1932, ten years after our teacher had passed away. The basic fault in directing *Hamlet* lay in a misinterpretation of Shakespeare's concept of the play. In our theater, the play was interpreted as a struggle between Hamlet and King Claudius for a throne, whereas the cardinal point of the play is the struggle of the humanistic ideas of the Renaissance epoch—which is represented by Hamlet—against the obsolescent ideas of the feudal way of life, represented by the King's court. In our production the deep philosophical essence of this tragedy was rendered vapid. The tragic fate of Prince Hamlet, who fought for high and noble ideals, lost its meaning. Making a mistake in defining the basic idea of the play, the regisseur consequently misconstrued separate scenes. The appearance of Hamlet's father was treated as a fabrication invented by Hamlet, and in this scene in our production Hamlet spoke the father's lines as well as his own. The brilliant monologue "To be or not to be" was delivered while Hamlet was trying on the crown. The very fact of casting a talented comedian, A. Gorunov, in the role of Hamlet was a tragic mistake in itself. A number of the most important scenes in the play had comic implications, when they should have had tragic ones. Neither the remarkable music by Shostakovitch nor the interesting mounting of the production by N. Akimov could save it. A critic, R. A. Makov, wrote: "Vakhtangov allowed such a treacherous weapon as irony only as the means of expressing a deep philosophical problem. *The Miracle of St. Anthony* and *Turandot* certainly are not senseless trinkets, but plays containing affirmation of one or another position. *Hamlet,* raising the ironic device for the sake of the device, outside of the philosophical content, was doomed to inner emptiness."

We students of Vakhtangov knew very well that the task of producing Shakespeare's plays always excited him. Even in his first years in the Moscow Art Theater, Vakhtangov was recording the discussions on *Hamlet* that took place between Stanislavsky and Gordon Craig. Those discussions, no doubt,

| 212

strongly influenced Vakhtangov's thinking on the art of the theater. He was facing two alternatives, which seemingly led to two contrasting trends in the theater. It looked as though one had to choose between art that was true-to-life but not sure of its form, and art rich in form but poor in content. Vakhtangov did not attempt to fuse these two positions, nor did he look for a compromise between them. He simply decided to take the strong side of each position and search for his own stand in the theater—which he defined as "theatrical realism." Developing the traditions of the realistic schools, Vakhtangov sought ways to fully express the richest resources of theater art. There are artists who, once having defined their credo, adjust and work on dramaturgy in one manner, afraid to abandon their "personal handwriting" and attempt something new. One may say that such artists keep themselves in "cotton-wool." But then there are other artists who courageously keep seeking new resources in art. They are like those astronomers who do not rest on discoveries already made but continue to search in the infinite household of heaven's universe. The means of scenic expressiveness, which is many-sided and bountiful, is inherent in the nature of the theater and art in general. Tchaikovsky wrote symphonies, operas, romances, and marvelous musical stories for children to express his world outlook. In the creative genius of Pushkin that bountifulness is most evident: poems, lyric ballads, novels, fairy tales, plays, satirical writings. But bountifulness in the theater does not manifest itself only in the versatility of genres. The question of diversity is first of all the problem of brilliant, interesting, fresh forms, of multi-sidedness in devices and means of scenic expression. Vakhtangov never meant the principle he discovered for the presentation of *Turandot* to dictate the creative direction of the theater; he never expected that the following productions of our collective would be like *Turandot*. His works of the same period were the satirical spectacle of *The Miracle of St. Anthony*, which had a sharp and laconic form, and Chekhov's *A Marriage,* which excelled in its tragicomic pointedness. Vakhtangov, while creating sunny *Turandot,* was at the same time directing the tragipathetic play *The Dybbuk* in the Habimah Studio, and he was also dreaming of doing *Hamlet.*

Just at that time, our teacher spent two or three sessions discussing the presentation of *Hamlet,* and recalling those sessions I see how gross an error we committed in not using Vakhtangov's suggestions in our production of *Hamlet* in 1932. In his letter to the spectators of the dress rehearsal of *Turandot,* Vakhtangov wrote, "The forthcoming work on *Hamlet* will be only 'a motive' to search for a form; and consequently to seek for the means to express it. We are not ready to play *Hamlet,* but working on that great play will entice the Studio and we shall learn much."

How shall we interpret the word "motive"? At that period of the formation of Vakhtangov's young company, it was necessary to train the beginning actors in such a way that they would be ready to carry on the future repertoire: multisided, diversified genres, together with the gay, buoyant, lyrical comedy *Turandot.* Vakhtangov was preparing his company to master the peak, that acme of theater art, the tragedy *Hamlet.* The first task in order to play this tragedy was to develop actors with the necessary inner psychological and emotional technique and a mastery of all the elements of the actor's skill in the sphere of speech and movement. The deeper the content, the more accomplished must the actor be. No matter how perceptive and fine the ideas of the regisseur of the tragedy may be, he cannot realize these without the solid, fundamental skill of the actor; this is necessary to embody the tragedy. And the technical work becomes so much more exciting and engrossing for the actor when he is preparing himself for a definite play and anticipating the applicability of his work. That is why organizing studies around a play from the point of view of teaching and educating the actor is especially purposeful and fruitful. In that case, the play naturally becomes a "motive" for the actor to master his skill. The other, deeper meaning of that expression "motive" is an opportunity to disclose the work of a dramatist in the way it can be understood today, to apply today's attitudes. And Vakhtangov in his discussions with the students was first of all defining "the purpose of our producing *Hamlet.*" Without a mature and solid conception of what constitutes the world and man in it, it is impossible to play and produce *Hamlet.*

I want to make it perfectly clear to my reader that neither now nor further on am I delivering Vakhtangov's thoughts literally, but only as my memory has retained them. *Hamlet,* he used to say, is a most truthful tragedy. It is close to and understood by every man. That makes *Hamlet* a work of genius. Each one of us, at some time in his life, has been confronted with the conditions in which Shakespeare, the greatest psychologist and the most thorough explorer of human thoughts and feelings, placed his Hamlet. The conflict takes place both outside and inside the hero, who is young, inexperienced, and a noble and trusting human being. His honesty and purity do not allow him even to suspect egocentricity, cruelty, or insidiousness in another. Avidity and greed move people to crime. Young and fiery, the youth Hamlet grows from day to day confronted with a morbid reality. Romantic thoughts are dissipated; life presents him with cruel facts. His train of thought is colored by a deep personal sorrow over his father's death. Suddenly the scene with his father's ghost turns the action into an altogether different channel. His father was killed by his own brother—Hamlet's uncle—and his mother knew it. What could be more terrifying, more shocking, more inhuman? Hamlet's noble outlook on life becomes groundless and "time is out of joint." Inexorable proof seems to be in Hamlet's hands. It gives him every right to judge the villain. But—is a mistake possible?

Dare he act? The youth decides first that he must be completely convinced of the deed, that he will evoke a confession
from the criminals. Hamlet would be happy to be wrong in
his horrible suspicions, and he does everything possible to
give the criminals a chance to clear themselves. These are,
by no means, the doubts of a weak character. This is a passionate, clever man embarking on a fight with evil, which is
represented by a cruel, narrow-minded and obtuse feudal
world. But Hamlet has been brought up in the same world,
so he is also fighting himself. That struggle is deep and significant. As the play grows, Hamlet is transformed. He must
face bitter disillusionment in his friend, deny himself happiness with a beloved maiden, stifle a son's love for his mother;
and Hamlet finds within himself the strength and the will to
fulfill all this. With great fortitude he overcomes all obstacles
for the sake of human justice and truth, and in the name of
retribution. Hamlet is not weak, nor does he lack the ability
to act. On the contrary, he overcomes everything within himself that might appear to be weakness, everything that keeps
him from fighting. The image of Hamlet, like all Shakespeare's images, is complex and contradictory. We find in
him a combination of purity, honesty, nobility, irony, humor,
and lyrical enthusiasm. He has kindliness, but at the same
time strictness, and a passionate hatred for his enemies. Hamlet says of his father, "He was a man." We should apply that
phrase to Hamlet. Historical parallels do not always bring
out the meaning of the analyzed theme at hand. But speaking
of Hamlet, in Russian life the character most kindred to
Hamlet is Pushkin: we think of the fate of that great poet
and humanist at the hands of the Tzar as Pushkin fought
fiercely the reactionary ideas of the Tzar.

Oh, how we deviated from Vakhtangov's conception, we,
his students, when ten years later we presented *Hamlet* on
our stage. Vakhtangov would surely have found a very special
form for *Hamlet*—a poetical form, full of restrained passion,
and in the spirit of classic tragedy.

The Vakhtangov Theater also made a serious creative failure in plays of the classic repertoire, such as Gogol's *A Wedding* and Schiller's *Love and Intrigue*. In *A Wedding* our theater was carried away by the desire to produce this comedy in the style of Gogol's fabulous tale *The Nose*. Kotchkorev (the leading character of *A Wedding*), in the process of action, was doubled—and sometimes even three Kotchkorevs acted on the stage simultaneously. The sets were ultra-stylized. Everything on the set was overemphasized, and the make-up of the actors turned the Russian Gogol into the German Hoffman and robbed Gogol of his national traits, of his distinctive Russian humor. It is interesting to note that when our theater gave up the stylized sets and the doubled and trebled Kotchkorevs and began to play *A Wedding* without all those contrivances, the spectacle, acquiring realistic character, became one of our best productions, with the finest acting ensemble of that time. The play *Love and Intrigue*, by Schiller, produced in 1933, was marred by the same incongruities of realistic acting and conditional sets.

In my opinion, the mistakes of Vakhtangov's students were no fault of their teacher. The deviations from realistic traditions were the result of our infatuation with pure aestheticism and, at times, our simply trying to be different. But those productions were not characteristic of the Vakhtangov Theater even during those difficult years of search for the future creative road. While continuing to develop Vakhtangov's traditions—and also keep in step with the times—the theater named for Vakhtangov, during the first ten years of its existence, created a number of productions reflecting the events of the Revolutionary days. Here I would like to dwell on two productions: one is *Break-Up*, by B. Lavrenev, and the other *Intervention*, by L. Slavin. *Break-Up* was directed on our stage by A. D. Popov, at the tenth anniversary of the Soviet Government. Popov was not a member of our theater, but he worked with our collective on a number of plays.

Knowing the group, he was able to accomplish as responsible and important a work as *Break-Up* in a month and a half. Popov's conception of the production sharply switched the center of attention from the family drama in the apartment of the captain, Bercenev, to the story of the Revolutionary-inspired seamen. This was a truly mass spectacle about the preparatory days of the Revolution. The incidental characters were played by the leading actors of the theater. The play was centered around the seamen from the warship Aurora; they represented people imbued with a sense of the righteousness of the Revolutionary ideas. It was a fiery, emotionally stimulating play for which Popov used a vivid scenic form. Working on a Soviet play, and striving to find the most picturesque expressions, our theater had bravely brought to life the creative legacy of Vakhtangov. The stormy events of the play, and the dynamics in the development of the action, demanded absolute preciseness. This was strongly emphasized in each episode and in the play in its entirety. The director, Popov, and the artist, Akimov, broke the play into episodes which gave purposefulness to the development of the action and made each episode eloquent in its intensity and color. The stage became a unique cinema on which "sequence-scenes" were created by theatrical means. Here an open place —that outwardly resembled deck armor—revealed a mess hall and a chart house, as though they were being photographed from above. By the same device the captain's (Bercenev's) dining room and Ksenia's room and a number of other episodes were shown. For the scenes in which large groups of people appeared, the scenic platform was used in its entirety: spacious upper decks were revealed and a vista of boundless sea was the landscape. The finale of the play was magnificent. On the deck stood ranks of seamen in parade formation. A red banner—emerging from beneath the stage floor—was hoisted higher and higher into the blue sky to the accompaniment of the "Internationale." *Break-Up* will remain in the history of the Soviet Theater as a "line of communications" production—optimistic, festive, truly theatrical; a production that was perfect in form, Revolutionary, and romantic. *Turandot* was the production-holiday for the celebration of the new theater; *Break-Up* was the production-holiday for the victory of the Revolution, the celebration of the new life in Soviet Russia.

Schukin's creation of the role of Bercenev contributed a great deal to the success of *Break-Up*. As he played the role we saw the character change subtly, throw off the burden of former days step by step and grow closer and closer to the Revolutionary ideas of the character Godunov, who succeeded in finding the correct and subtle approach to the irreproachably honest captain. A joyous comprehension of the new life, and a gradual self-inclusion in it, was the basic theme of the role. This interpretation was conveyed by Schukin with great inner strength, and at the same time, with great artistry: with barely perceptible smiles sliding across his lips, with gay eyes growing young again, with firm step and strong, resilient movements, Schukin's Bercenev, climbing the captain's bridge with ease, was accepting the responsibility of the ship's captain who rose to the defense of the Revolutionary achievements.

Kuza, the actor who played the role of Godunov, was an actor made for "hero" roles—to use the language of "emploi." He was tall and slender, with a handsome face, a well-trained body, great vitality, and a strong, pleasant voice. This important, responsible role in a contemporary play served as a serious test for Kuza, and he passed the examination, creating with great success the romantic image of the Bolshevik seaman. What helped the young actor? The training he had received in Vakhtangov's Studio, the training of the inner and outer technique.

The leader of the seamen, a skillful provocateur who bitingly ridiculed the enemies of the Revolution, was Puzir, played by Gorunov. On stage Gorunov breathed health and love of life. His wit and unyielding integrity blended with an innate kindness and gentleness: a rough curtness toward his enemies, a warmheartedness toward his comrades. The school Gorunov went through in *Turandot* undoubtedly helped him to find the right manner to handle jokes and comedy lines—which the audience received with bursts of laughter.

The ensemble of young actors trained by *Turandot* was an excellently trained collective, masters of rhythm and tempo, such an important element of theater art. The mastery of the director and actors who created and worked out the mob scenes deserves special notice. Among the actors who participated in the mob scenes of *Break-Up* were many who had performed in *Turandot,* and who had learned much from their work in that production: Mansurova, Rucinova, Mironov, and others. How often now our theater lacks that buoyancy that gives art cheerfulness, energy, courage, freshness; keeps it from being dull and humdrum.

*Egor Bulichev,* by Maxim Gorky, was produced in Moscow almost at the same time by two ideologically kindred theaters, the Moscow Art Theater and the Vakhtangov Theater. The two productions differed strongly in their treatment of the same play, in content as well as in formation, although both productions were in a realistic style. The interpretation of the central role, that of Egor Bulichev, by the magnificent actors D. Schukin and L. Leonidov, clearly revealed the difference in the two productions. Schukin—as I understand—created the image of Bulichev as the epitome of the class he represented in society; Leonidov, on the other hand, portrayed more deeply the human fate of Bulichev. Schukin played the social tragedy; Leonidov, the personal drama.

The outward appearance of those two productions were also dissimilar. In the Vakhtangov Theater the set consisted of a two-story house. Action moved from one room to another, which made the play dynamic and gave the production a rhythmic mobility which corresponded to the events taking place outside the windows of Bulichev's house in the days of the February Revolution and the inevitably approaching October. In the Moscow Art Theater the play had one set, thus taking on a psychological everyday character. Vakhtangov's direction for Chekhov's *A Wedding* unquestionably had a strong influence on Zakhava, who directed *Egor Bulichev*. That influence was most especially felt in the scenes between Bulichev and Pavel Trubashom and the Mother Superior— these were profoundly treated by the director and brilliantly, plastically expressed. Vakhtangov had showed us how to present Chekhov without imitating the mode of the Moscow Art Theater, and in a new way. Vakhtangov's students showed their organic understanding of Gorky's dramas when they directed the works of that great people's writer.

After *Bulichev*, we produced *Intervention*, by Slavin. During the period of work on this play important questions concerning Vakhtangov's creative heritage deeply agitated the acting collective of our theater and its directorial staff. How could we develop Vakhtangov's teachings further? Eugene Vakhtangov used to say: "Correctly discovered theatrical means give to the author a true life on the stage. One can learn the means, but it is necessary to create the form. It is essential to exercise one's fantasy to the nth degree."

The artist's fantasy does not work automatically. In order for fantasy to begin feeding the artist, the artist must have the same deep devotion to the theme which the writer or director had and carried within himself for a long time, lovingly nurturing it in his dreams and thoughts. I think the artist is always looking for an excuse—let us say "a motive"— to reveal to others his understanding of life. Such a motive was for me the play *Intervention*, the dramatization of the novel *The Heir*. The plot of the novel told of a rich young man who became accidentally involved in the Revolution and then sank into the criminal world, which was ruled by the anarchist Filka. The play is about the heroic Bolshevik underground movement in Odessa in 1918, at the time of the struggle of the young Soviet Republic for its freedom and independence, and about the remarkable group of communists who fulfilled the instructions of the party on the home front. Inspired by the lofty ideas of the Revolution, people sacrificed their lives in the name of victory for the working people. Their fiery words reached the hearts of sincere men dressed in French, English, or American uniforms. Ideas of an international friendship of the working people of the world brought together Russian communists with the communists and working people who served in the armies of the fourteen powers attacking Soviet Russia. It became a creative necessity for our theater to tell about this marvelous poetical page of the Russian Revolution, to find the scenic means to convey the grandeur of the events, to show the simple but courageous people who took part so selflessly in the heroic struggle.

How was the plan of this production, *Intervention*, discovered and developed? First, the director who undertook the presentation of the Soviet play had to arouse in himself a feeling of poetical excitement, to learn to think in images, tune his lyre to a tone of poetic compassion, in contrast to the cold, prosaic analysis of the text, which often dries up the director's and actor's fantasy by limiting and binding it. Fantasy gives birth to a particular kind of enthusiasm which arouses that creative state which in the language of art is called "inspiration." According to Pushkin, inspiration is the disposition of the soul to the keenest perception of impressions, to the understanding of ideas, and the realization of cause and effect. How is that keenest perception born?

The place of action in *Intervention* is Odessa. I visited that beautiful, romantic maritime city in 1925. I tried to visualize the Odessa of 1918, the Odessa of the time of *Intervention*. People are strolling on a seaside boulevard; they have come to Odessa from all corners of the country. There are generals from Petersburg, merchants from Moscow, representatives of various counter-Revolutionary parties who were escaping the Bolsheviks from a number of cities of old Russia. Here one may hear the French, English, Rumanian, or Greek speech of the officers of the Entente Army. Here one may see native Odessa men and women of the Madam Ksidias class, resurrected and blossoming luxuriantly on the dubious and vacillating soil of the counter-Revolution. Coffeehouses and restaurants are overcrowded; Rumanian orchestras resound, violins throb buoyantly, executing the old Russian romances: "You Are Sitting by a Fireplace," "Coachman, Don't Drive the Horses"—all that fashionable repertoire of Vera Cholodnoi, an actress who happened to be in Odessa then and was sauntering on its boulevards.

I tried to picture for myself another Odessa, the workers' section of the city: its port, the place of the Revolutionary movement, with its strikes and confrontations. Here, almost next to the pier, was a famous lodging, the night house of the stevedores, in which Maxim Gorky lived in his youth while he was in Odessa. I strolled through the outskirts where the factories and mills, surrounded by one-story houses, were located. In those houses had lived Revolutionary-inclined workers, who were fighting for the establishment of Soviet power in the south of Russia. I recalled the famous catacombs, later described so adroitly by Valentine Kataev in his novel about the year 1905, *The White Sail Is Lonely*. And, finally, I imagined how the center of Odessa looked, where communists—who were called by their underground name "a foreign committee"—lived in hiding while they carried out orders from the party among foreign soldiers and seamen. Their Revolutionary task was complex, entailed great danger, and demanded a special conspiracy—one both clever and subtle. While preparing myself for the production of *Intervention* I made the acquaintance of many former underground workers and "foreign committee." Their biographies, their tales about their work in the enemy rear, gave me remarkably authentic material which helped my understanding of events and their embodiment in the action, images, and characters of the play.

Here is Comrade C, former chairman and leader of the "foreign committee." He is a school teacher. Comrade C spoke fluent French and headed the work among the French soldiers and sailors. Here is Comrade T, chairman of the Odessa Regional Executive Committee. He remained in town, on orders from the party, to guide the work of organizing a militant advanced detachment of Revolutionary-inclined workers, peasants, and intelligentsia. Here is Comrade R, chairman of the Odessa Cheka (all-Russian extraordinary committee for fighting counter-Revolution activities, sabotage, and profiteering), who had been in the prison cell of the White Guards' counter secret service and who had miraculously escaped. Through meeting the workers of the Odessa underground, I understood the humbleness and the greatness of the heroism of the sons of the Communist party who so selflessly served the Revolution. The theater had to reveal the heroic fervor of the spirit of the Odessa communists, along with their modesty and simplicity. The place of action was of great significance to the play *Intervention*: the city, its singularities and its individuality. I, along with the artist E. M. Rabinovich, was striving to establish through the mounting of the play, the theme of the sea as its decorative leitmotif. It is visible in that first scene on the boulevard, behind the Tzar's tri-colored flags, and can be seen receding in the distance. The sea was also indicated in the night scene in the Ksidias shipyard by the far-away ship lights that stood on the roadstead. The sea, submerged in darkness, is felt behind the fence of flowers in the night café, where the officers of the counter-intelligence service are arresting Brodsky. And, finally, when we see the famous Odessa Staircase—which leads to the sea—it reminds us of it; that staircase which French soldiers and sailors who remained in Soviet Russia climbed. The sea was never shown pictorially on the stage as a set, but the audience always felt it, was always aware of it. The musical accompaniment contributed to the effect, too, and gave the magnificent feeling of sea breakers in a number of scenes. Such a device was prompted by the basic principle of the play's mounting. I like to call that principle "decorative-constructive." What does it consist of? I will tell you.

While talking about the mounting of *Turandot* I mentioned that Vakhtangov was not happy with the basic platform of the set. He felt that the set was not exactly what it should have been although, in principle, it was correct for a play with a folk character. In *Intervention,* planned as a production of Revolutionary-romantic character, we also intentionally took the line of folk theater for its mounting. That device helped us to handle the many-scened play—that demanded dynamic development of action—without the trying intermissions for the rearrangement of sets between scenes, a process which always dampens the ardor of the audience.

In Shakespeare's many-scened plays, in long-ago times, the most simple setting was used: in the famous Globe Theater planks were put up, on which was written where the action took place, and that was all. That great work of Pushkin's, *Boris Godunov,* has never yet been done convincingly. First of all, the right principle for the setting of this tragedy demands uninterrupted flow of its beautiful verse, which should resound like a symphony. The whole play should have only two entr' actes. To make frequent stops in Pushkin's work is just as nonsensical as it would be for the conductor to stop the orchestra in the middle of the final part of Tchaikovsky's Sixth Symphony. In general, the problem of intermissions, including so-called "sitting intermissions," requires careful attention on the director's part. The excessive striving by

225 |

many of our artists for lavishness and splendor seldom in-
creases the artistic quality of the setting, but it almost always
causes long intermissions and complicated changes. We carefully considered the plan of having no intermissions between
the scenes of *Intervention*. The large proscenium extended
far beyond the curtain of the stage and covered the orchestra
pit (the proscenium reached the first row of the auditorium),
and this afforded an opportunity to perform the interlude
pantomimes in front of the curtain. And on this "boulevard-
proscenium" the people of Odessa sauntered to the music—
brilliantly written for the play by composer B. Asafiev—
which came from the summer coffeehouse.

Along this boulevard walks the Tzar's general, strolling
past a young cadet who stands at attention. Here are nurses
with modestly lowered eyes—the red-cross bands on their
sleeves—followed by youngsters from the White Guard secret
intelligence, clinking their spurs. Here is a typical representative of the Odessa lower class in the *Intervention* time, the
anarchist Filka, with his secretary and his assistant, Tokar-
chuk, strutting slowly along, treading on the heels of his next
prey—a personage who, in the list of characters, was called
"Robbed Citizen." All that "fore-run pantomime" brought
the audience to the scene of the "night public house"—which
gave the illusion of being a floating restaurant far out on the
sea. In the finale of the play, on the proscenium-pier, a noisy,
hustling group of refugees were grasping at their only chance
to get on the last boat. This is the Russian bourgeoisie, flee-
ing in panic from the approaching Red Army. Beside the
proscenium, serving as part of the setting, a sloping platform
was used as a basic playing area. With the help of additional
riding wagons on the sides of the stage, the sloping platform
easily changed its form behind the curtain and turned into
either an interior—a French barracks or a linen workshop—
or an exterior—the Ksidias shipyard, an entrenchment of the
French army, or the tent of the commanding officer of the

Soviet army on the offensive. In the setting of the play the "principle of details" was widely utilized; this made it possible for the scenic artist to discard the unnecessary details of the action. A minimum of essential characteristic details convincingly led the audience into the atmosphere of the action. For example, in the cabinet of the French colonel, Fredembe, an enormous full-length portrait of President Poincaré hung on the wall, and parallel to the footlights was a large writing desk adorned by a gold desk-set. Three chairs with high golden backs completed the decoration of the rich cabinet office. The room occupied by Eugene, the heir to the wealthy house of Madam Ksidias, was delineated by a huge wardrobe with open doors, in which was an enormous number of suits, ties, hats, and other articles of elegance that would be used by a pampered mama's boy. On the wall was a map, long forgotten, which at some time Eugene had studied in school. On the table, to crystallize the picture already created of the owner of the room, there were playing cards thrown about in disorder.

All the scenes of the play were framed by cloth and curtains. This constituted a unique theatrical frame, and because of it we were able to dispense with the cumbersome ceilings and side walls of the rooms. The organic inclusion of music in a play is a very complicated problem and requires the finest taste and sensitivity on the part of the director and composer. The leitmotif of the musical score of *Intervention,* chosen by the composer B. Asafiev, was a song by the French composer Montegust: "Salute to the 17th Regiment Who Refused to Fire at Strikers." Vladimir Ilyich Lenin loved that song very much. Forceful, march-like, that music made one think of the fiery songs of the French Revolution. That leitmotif harmonized with the spirit of the play, which was a call to fight for freedom. In line with this heroic basic theme were various other musical numbers, called for by the specific mood of the scene: a potpourri from fashionable operettas played by the orchestras on the boulevard, and songs sung sadly or lyrically by French soldiers, or gay dance tunes. In the scene of the public house, the anarchist Filka sang a famous song of the Odessa bandits, "Thunder Thundered," and was joined by his followers to the accompaniment of the café orchestra. But music was used most interestingly in the "seamstress workshop" scene and during the episode of Brodsky's arrest in the public house. The seamstress's workshop served as the meeting place for the members of the "foreign committee"—Michael Brodsky, Joan Barbie, and other communists—with comrade Orlovskya, who was the leader of the underground organization. The outer room was a sewing room, where four charming young girls worked. The moment a customer entered the workshop the girls would start to sing a song, which served as a danger signal to the communists who were having a meeting in the next room. The melody sounded in the orchestra really before the beginning of the scene, and was picked up by the girls: "In beautiful Odessa, in the country of the White Guard, four seamstresses live most famously." The girls sang gaily and lightheartedly, fully aware they were risking their lives every minute. In the next room, in full view of the audience—the stage was divided into two rooms—the conference stopped and a complete silence fell, to be broken as soon as the girls stopped singing.

The contrast between the gay singing in one room and the dramatic event taking place in the next room gave the scenic and musical action added intensity. The music in the scene of the public house was included as a necessary part of the scene. I would particularly like to describe the finale of that scene—the arrest of Brodsky, who was to meet with French soldiers and seamen in the public house. On the stage of the public house (public houses had entertainment) a couple were executing a fashionable waltz in a very slow tempo, to the accompaniment of the orchestra. The waltz music, in a minor key, creates a sensation of emptiness and hopelessness.

Simultaneously with the beginning of the waltz, the members of the counter-espionage appeared in every entrance of the public house. Slowly they began to surround Brodsky, who was sitting downstage by a small table, hiding his face behind a newspaper. Abruptly the music shifted to a rapid, agitated part of the waltz, which coincided with the swift move of the counter-espionage men to Brodsky's table to examine his documents. Brodsky attempted to break through the cordon, but he was caught, beaten, and his hands finally bound behind him. The guests in the public house were paralyzed. The music was cut on the half-phrase; the dancing pair stopped short. The head of the counter-espionage group shouted: "Continue the music! Dance! Back in motion!"

The orchestra began to play slowly, the dancing couple whirled sensuously, and the customers in the public house, shocked by the unexpected arrest, walked slowly back to their tables, following with their eyes the group that were taking away the government criminal, Brodsky.

While talking about the production of *Intervention,* I want to remind my reader once more of Vakhtangov's great concern about music and the rhythm of words and movements as an active stimulus for the actor's recollection of his experiences, which bring him to true thoughts and feelings. Vakhtangov's expression "the form must be created . . . imagination must be utilized to the nth degree" tells us that he believed that an actor, or a regisseur, must not depend solely on an inspiration visiting him suddenly. Vakhtangov demanded of a regisseur the most thorough preparation for each rehearsal. How many hours are usually lost in idle "talking" with actors about their roles, sitting around a table; how much time is lost in trying the *mise en scène,* only because the regisseur did not take sufficient time to prepare properly for the rehearsal!

The *mise en scène* is born of the understanding of the very spirit of the play that is being produced. *Mise en scène* is life on the stage. The feeling of the *mise en scène* comes out of a thorough knowledge of sculpture, painting, music, rhythm, and understanding of scenic movement. When the regisseur finds the correct *mise en scène* it arouses the needed feeling in an actor with lightning speed; but the endless "let us try it this way" or "let us try it that way" is evidence of the regisseur's helplessness.

The most complicated and interesting work of contemporary Soviet and classic dramaturgy can not be realized according to one formula: "I, in given circumstances." We adhere to Vakhtangov's formula, which for us resounds today as follows: "I, the Soviet actor, having all the means of the actor's mastery—fantasy, inner and outer technique—conceive and embody my image, beginning from an inner—but also sometimes from an outer—perception of the role. The aim of my art is the scenic image, which is created for the purpose of relating to the audience my conception of contemporary people, of our life, of which I am an active builder."

Citizen—human being—master—actor—this we must affirm in the theater today, proceeding from the teachings of Vakhtangov. In the production of *Intervention* we were striving to utilize the knowledge which we had received from our teacher. In our hearts we will always guard Vakhtangov's precepts for our students: Never rest on what has been attained. Move ahead, examine your experience, be alert to the times in which you live, and always study your people's lives.

The response to these very thoughts of Vakhtangov was the play produced by our theater in 1937 on the twentieth anniversary of the Soviet regime—*The Man with the Gun,* by N. Pogodin. The theater at last had a play that had been Vakhtangov's dream. In 1918, in the days of the first anniversary of the October Revolution, Vakhtangov, being very upset by the deterioration of the First Studio of the Moscow Art Theater, wrote of his dreams: "It is necessary to flap the wings, but there are no wings. I want to direct *Cain,* by Byron. I have a daring plan for it—even though it might be an absurd one. There is a need to produce *Zori,* to dramatize the Bible, to portray the restless heart of the people. A thought just flashed through my mind: It would be good if someone wrote a play without individual characters. In each act, only the crowds would play. The crowd goes to a barrier and takes possession of it . . . rejoices . . . buries the fallen . . . sings the world's peace song. What a curse that I cannot do anything myself, and there is no one I can order to write for me. There are some who are talented, but their vision is limited; the ones who volunteer to write have no talent."

*The Man with the Gun* is a work close to Vakhtangov's dream, and when we produced it, the image of Vakhtangov, who dreamed "to flap his wings," was always with us. We cannot tell how he would have developed today; but we can determine the line which he dreamed of following on the basis of his productions, his discussions with the students, and, finally, on the basis of his diary. Confronting his dream "to portray the restless heart of the people" with his intention to produce *Hamlet,* we must suppose that a people's heroic spectacle of a tragic, noble character would have been a most alluring, creative task for Vakhtangov. And one can only think that he would have fulfilled that task magnificently, because the art of Vakhtangov comprised every element that a great artist could possess, a great artist who chose the complicated and challenging profession of a regisseur.

# Afterword

I STARTED writing this book in 1952. In the Soviet Union, actors and directors have time to write only during the summer while on vacation. The chapter on *Turandot* was written almost completely in Crimea during the summer and the beginning of the fall of 1952. Nineteen fifty-three and 1954 were spent on the chapter of *A Wedding;* 1955 and 1956 were spent on the preparation and writing of the chapter on *The Miracle of St. Anthony.*

During the last fifty years many important events have taken place in theater life that have changed the face of the Soviet theater. I was writing a book about my teacher, not thinking whether the book would ever be published or if it would see the light. I felt a great urge to tell what I knew of Vakhtangov. I thought in the beginning that years and years would have to go by before I could talk openly about that extraordinary regisseur and his work. But, luckily, it turned out that all the trends in the contemporary Soviet theater have moved to meet Vakhtangov. In recent years, the theater that bears the name of Vakhtangov has begun to return to the temporarily lost discipline of Vakhtangov's art. The "sickness" of conformity, experienced by all the theaters, has vanished from our theater at last; performances have appeared in a new light.

Strange as it might seem, a resurrection of Vakhtangov's tradition has taken place during the past years in our theater: his conception of the varieties of style, of unison between the inner feelings and the embodiment of the role, the constant search for new forms for each performance—forms that permit the most sharpness in order to express the idea and content of the dramatic work and greater contemporaneity. A

feeling of contemporaneity is significant in choosing the correct artistic means, with the help of which one creates one or
the other performances. That is what guides the aspiration of
a regisseur and an actor to give to the play and the role a
form corresponding to the psychological and spiritual demands of the contemporary theatergoer, and to emphasize
and bring out in the dramatic work the elements that would
excite and captivate the contemporary theatergoer. Aspiration for the new is always the reason for the growth of the
theater. That is why today when I see our youth absorbed in
searching for the new I feel sincerely joyful, because it is
natural, constructive, logical, and fruitful. The aspiration for
the new reveals itself when the artist is endowed with a feeling for the present.

Contemporary life does not merely flow; it races. In com-
parison with the past century, its rhythm and colors change
with immense speed. The feeling of the present is a profound
knowledge of life, science, and technique; it is the penetration into the psychology of the man of today who necessarily
takes an active part in the life of the people. Also the feeling
of contemporaneity is the feeling of rhythm: rhythm of the
time, rhythm of the country, rhythm of our way of living.

I am sure there will come a day when there will be a new
kind of actor, armed with perfect mastery, inspired with the
high ideals of the present. There will come a day when a
new dramatic style will be born—a great people's creation will
be born. The character of our life foretells the birth of new
forms for the theater which will embody the great and important events of this epoch. One way or another, the development of art in the sphere of content and form will undoubtedly be closer to the people. And if the Theater of
Vakhtangov will go in step with the life of our country—
answer the essential questions of contemporaneity—and if
each actor of the Vakhtangov Theater will carry in his heart
that dedicated, that inspired, relation to the theater which

was inherent in Vakhtangov, and will be aware of his responsibility to the people as Vakhtangov was, then we can say that we are true to the precepts of our great teacher—that we are WITH VAKHTANGOV.

# Chronology

1883, February 1     Born in Vladikavkaz (now Ordjonikid-ze).

1893, August     Entered the preparatory class of Tiflig gymnasium.

1894, August     Entered first class of Vladikavkaz gym-nasium.

1900, January 22     Participated in the school performance of N. B. Gogol's *Marriage,* in the role of Agafia Tikhovna.

1903, May     Graduated from Vladikavkaz gymnasi-um.

1903, August     Took competitive examination for Ri-ga Polytechnic school, but was not ac-cepted.

1903, August     Entered the the Moscow University Faculty of Natural Science.

1904, August 15     First regisseur work on the amateur stage of the Vladikavkaz Students' Workshop in Grozny on *Holiday of Peace,* by Hauptmann. Also played the role of Wilhelm. Started to attend the Juristical Faculty of Moscow Univer-sity.

1905, January     Worked as a regisseur in the Workshop of Smolensco-Vyazemskoe Association of Countrymen at Moscow University. The play was *Pedagogics,* by O. Erista. Vakhtangov played the role of the ped-agog Flashman.

1905, October 9     Married Nadejda Mikhailovna Baitzurova.

1906, June     Organized the Vladikavkaz Students Association.

1906, June 29     First performance of Musical-Drama Circle of the Vladikavkaz Student Society—*Strong and Weak,* by N. Timkovsky. Vakhtangov was the regisseur of this play and also performed the role of George Preturov.

1906, October     Organized the Drama Circle of the students of Moscow University.

1906, December 15     Performance by the Drama Circle of the students of Moscow University of *Datchniky,* by Gorky. Vakhtangov was the regisseur and also played the role of Vlas.

1907, January 1     His son Sergei was born.

1907, August     Wrote a number of articles for "Terek," the Vladikavkaz newspaper.

1908     Became chairman of the Smolensco-Vyazemskoe Association of Countrymen at Moscow University, regisseur of the student performances, and also acted in the small towns around Moscow.

1908, July 30     Regisseur of Gorky's play *The Lower Depths* for the Vladikavkaz Musical-Drama Circle—also played the role of the Baron.

1909, June 28     Regisseur of the play *Zinotchka,* by Nedoline. Also played the role of the student Magitsky at the Vladikavkaz Art-Drama Circle.

| | |
|---|---|
| 1909, July | Published two articles in the Vladikav-kaz newspaper "Terek." |
| 1909, July 19 | Regisseur of K. Hamsun's play *At the Czar's Gate,* performed at the Vladikav-kaz Art-Drama Circle. Vakhtangov also played the role of Ivan Kareno. |
| 1909, July 30 | Regisseur of A. P. Chekhov's play *Uncle Vanya* in the Vladikavkaz Art-Drama Circle, in which he played the role of Astrov. |
| 1909, August | Entered the School of Drama of A. I. Adashev, artist of the Moscow Art The-ater. |
| 1909-1910 December 27- January 29 | Trip to Paris with L. A. Sulerjitsky. |
| 1910, January 30- February 8 | Return to Moscow through Geneva, Berne, Zurich, Munich, Vienna. |
| 1911, March 1 | First interview with V. I. Nemirovitch-Dantchenko. |
| 1911, March 11 | First meeting with K. S. Stanislavsky in the Moscow Art Theater. |
| 1911, March 12 | Graduated from Adashev's School of Drama. |
| 1911, March 15 | Accepted by the Moscow Art Theater. |
| 1911, May 9- July 30 | Tour to Novgorod-Seversk as the head of the group of young actors. |
| 1911, May 30 | First performance in Novgorod-Seversk of the play by G. Suderman *Fires of Saint John.* Vakhtangov was the regis-seur and also played the role of Pletz. |

237 |

| | |
|---|---|
| 1911, August 1 | Started to conduct lessons with the group of young actors on the Stanislavsky Method at the Moscow Art Theater. |
| 1911, September 3 | Started to teach in the Drama School of C. V. Khalutinoi, where he taught until 1915. |
| 1911, September 23 | Cast for his first role in the Moscow Art Theater, that of Gipsy in *Living Corpse*, by L. N. Tolstoy. |
| 1912, March 26- May 31 | First tour with the Moscow Art Theater—Petersburg, Warsaw, Kiev. Took the part of Gipsy in *Living Corpse* and of the actress-queen in *Hamlet*, as well as other roles. |
| 1912, June 15- August 7 | Second trip to Europe. Summer vacation in Sweden. Returned to Moscow through Norway and Denmark. |
| 1912, December 19 | First presentation in Mikhailovsky Drama Circle of *The Strong and the Weak*, by N. Timkovsky. |
| 1913, January 15 | Opening of the First Studio of the Moscow Art Theater—the play *The Good Hope*, by Heijermans. The regisseur, P. V. Boleslavsky. |
| 1913, April 15- May 31 | Tour with Moscow Art Theater—Petersburg, Odessa. Vakhtangov took part in Molière's *Imaginary Invalid*—played the doctor and other roles. |
| 1913, June and July | Summer vacation on Knyagei Gore, near Kanev, Kiev province, with L. A. Sulerjitsky, the members of the Moscow Art Theater and the First Studio of the Moscow Art Theater. |

1913, November 15    Première of Hauptmann play *Holiday of Peace,* Vakhtangov's first regisseur's work in the First Studio of the Moscow Art Theater.

1913, December 23    The first meeting of the Drama-Studio with Vakhtangov's participation. Commencement of work on the play *Country Estate of Lanins,* by B. Zaitzev.

1914, March 17    Cast for the role of Kraft in Andreev's play *The Thought* in the Moscow Art Theater.

1914, March 26    Performance of Drama-Students Studio, *Country Estate of Lanins.*

1914, April-June 1    Tour with the Moscow Art Theater: Petersburg, Kiev. Vakhtangov appeared in the role of Kraft in Andreev's *The Thought,* the doctor in Molière's *Imaginary Invalid* and in Dostoevsky's *Nikolai Stavrogin* (a guest at the ball).

1914, June-July    Summer vacation on Knyagei Gore, with L. A. Sulerjitsky, the actors of the Moscow Art Theater, and the First Studio of the Moscow Art Theater.

1914, November 24    Première of *Cricket on the Hearth,* by Charles Dickens, in the First Studio of the Moscow Art Theater. Vakhtangov played the role of Tackleton.

1915, April 26    First public evening in the Students Drama Studio: *Eger,* by Chekhov; *Feminine Rubbish,* by I. Tcheglov; *A Page of Romance,* by M. Prevo; Vaudevilles —*A Match Between Two Fires* and *The Salt of Marriage.*

1915, May 4-June 2    First tour of the First Studio of the

Moscow Art Theater to Petersburg. Vakhtangov played Tackleton in *The Cricket on the Hearth*.

1915, July, August  Summer vacation in Evpatoria (Crimea) and on the Knyagai Gore with Sulerjitsky, members of the Moscow Art Theater, and the First Studio of the Moscow Art Theater.

1915, December 14  Première of *Deluge*, by Berger, in the First Studio of the Moscow Art Theater. Vakhtangov as the regisseur. In the following performances, he played the role of Frazier.

1916, December  Second public evening in the Students Dramatic Studio: *Fashionable Wedlock* and *Before the Open Doors*, by Sutro; *A Page of Romance*, by Prevo; *Eger*, by Chekhov; and *The Port*, by Maupassant.

1917, March  The Students Drama School takes the name of Moscow Drama Studio under the leadership of Vakhtangov. Third public evening in the Studio of Vakhtangov: Dramatization of the following Chekhov stories: *Eger, Story of Miss N. N., Enemies, Ivan Matveevich, Long Tongue, Verotchka, Malefactor*. Also *The Port*, by Maupassant.

1918, April 13  The dress rehearsal of Ibsen's play *Rosmersholm*, in the First Studio of the Moscow Art Theater. Vakhtangov, the regisseur, appeared in the role of Ulric Brendel.

1918, April 23  Première of Ibsen's *Rosmersholm* in

the First Studio of the Moscow Art Theater.

1918, September 15    The first presentation of Maeterlinck's *The Miracle of St. Anthony* in Vakhtangov's Studio.

1918, October 8    The opening of the Habimah Theater. Vakhtangov the regisseur of the evening of one-act plays: *The Older Sister,* by Ash, *The Fire,* by Peretz, *The Son,* by Katznelson, and *Misfortune,* by Berkovitch.

1918, December 17    Opening of the People's Theater. The plays presented by the Vakhtangov Studio: *The Port,* by Maupassant; *The Thief,* by O. Mirbo, and *When Will the Moon Rise?,* by Gregory.

1918    Leader of the A. O. Gunst Dramatic Studio.

1919    Joins the Board of the Second Studio of the Moscow Art Theater.

1919, March 23    Vakhtangov's article "To Those Who Write About the Stanislavsky Method" printed in the periodical "Vestnic of the Theater."

1919, June-July    Works with the group of actors of the Second Studio of the Moscow Art Theater on the play by Leo Tolstoy, *The Tale About Ivan the Fool and His Brothers,* in Shishkeevo, Penzenski province. Appears in *Deluge* in the role of Frazier, and in *The Lower Depths* in the role of Satin, in Shishkeevo and Ryazaevka.

1919, August    In Simbirsk, he appears in *Deluge* in

241

the role of Frazier, with the Second
Studio of the Moscow Art Theater.

1919,
September 6-
October 14

Touring with the First Studio of the
Moscow Art Theater to Leningrad. In
*Cricket on the Hearth* he played the
role of Tackleton; in *Deluge*, by Berger, he played the role of Frazier, and
also took a number of roles in *Twelfth
Night* by Shakespeare. He gave lessons
in a drama school named after Chaliapin, in an Armenian drama school, and
also in a cinema school named after
Tchaikovsky.

1920, June

Tour of the First Studio of the Moscow
Art Theater to Kcharkov. Vakhtangov
took part in *Cricket on the Hearth* and
*Deluge*.

1920, September

The first variant of *A Wedding*, by
Chekhov, presented in the Vakhtangov
Studio.

1921, September 13

The Vakhtangov Studio was included
in the Moscow Art Theater and given
the name of the Third Studio of the
Moscow Art Theater.

1921, January 29

Première of the second variant of *The
Miracle of St. Anthony* in the Third
Studio of the Moscow Art Theater.

1921, March 29

Première of *Aerick,* by Strindberg, in
the First Studio of the Moscow Art
Theater. Vakhtangov, the regisseur.

1921, April 7

The celebration of the tenth anniversary of Vakhtangov's work in the Moscow Art Theater and in the First Studio of the Moscow Art Theater.

| | |
|---|---|
| 1921, September | Second variant of Chekhov's *A Wedding* is shown at the Third Studio of the Moscow Art Theater. |
| 1921, November 13 | The opening of the Third Studio of the Moscow Art Theater on Arbat 26. The presentation of *The Miracle of St. Anthony*, also a recital with the participation of Stanislavsky, A. I. Eugine, Vakhtangov, Michael Chekhov, and others on the occasion of the opening. |
| 1922, January 31 | Première of *The Dybbuk*, by Ansky, in the Habimah Theater; Vakhtangov, the regisseur. |
| 1922, February 27 | A dress rehearsal of *Princess Turandot*, by Carlo Gozzi, in the Third Studio of the Moscow Art Theater. Vakhtangov, the regisseur. |
| 1922, February 28 | Première of *Princess Turandot*, by Carlo Gozzi, in the Third Studio of the Moscow Art Theater. |
| 1922, May 29 | Vakhtangov died at 9:55 in the evening. |
| 1922, May 31 | Vakhtangov's funeral. |